NEW WAYS IN SCHOOL MENTAL HEALTH

Early Detection and Prevention of School Maladaptation

Emory L. Cowen
Mary Anne Trost
Raymond P. Lorion
Darwin Dorr
Louis D. Izzo
Ruth V. Isaacson

Human Sciences Press

A Division of Behavioral Publications, Inc.

72 Fifth Avenue

New York

New York 10011

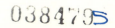

Library of Congress Catalog Number 74-11815

ISBN: 0–87705–214–X

Copyright © 1975 by Human Sciences Press, a division of Behavioral Publications, Inc., 72 Fifth Avenue, New York, New York 10011

Printed in the United States of America
56789   987654321

Library of Congress Cataloging in Publication Data
Main entry under title:

New ways in school mental health.

   Bibliography: p.
   1. Student adjustment. 2. Personnel service in education. I. Cowen, Emory L. [DNLM: 1.   Mental health services—In infancy and childhood.   2. School health.   WA352 N532]
LB1027.5.N65   1975   372.1'4'6   74-11815

NEW WAYS IN SCHOOL MENTAL HEALTH

Contents

LIST OF ILLUSTRATIONS

Preface

Schools are a powerful socializing force in human development. For better or worse, virtually all members of modern society carry important imprints of their school experience throughout life. The school places two broad sets of adaptive demands on the child. He must learn to master and assimilate increasingly complex bodies of knowledge, and he must learn to meet the school environment's behavioral and interpersonal requirements. These two sets of demands often interlock. Thus adaptive failings restrict the child's ability to learn, just as deficits in educational mastery generate psychological or adaptive problems.

It is precisely around the intercept of these two sets of requirements that school mental health services first came into being and still find their prime justification. But because the school adjustment problems of young children, whether educational or behavioral, are so rampant and the school mental health services available for dealing with them are spread so thin, past services have necessarily been limited to a tiny fraction of school children—those with evident, profound, nonpostponable problems. This has left many others in desperate but less obvious need of help to find their own way as best they can or flounder.

These facts raise several obvious questions. How can the school experience be optimized for all children? How can effective helping services be brought to the great masses of maladapting young children who urgently need such help? How can school children be served so that they do not end up as society's casualties? These critical questions underlie both this book and the innovative approach to delivering school mental health services—the Primary Mental Health Project (PMHP), which is the book's core.

Those of us who have been closely involved in PMHP's 17-year history are persuaded that this approach, emphasizing as it does widespread early detection and prevention of school maladaptation, has much to recommend it in today's real world of limited mental health resources. Although this conviction may reflect only the pride of parenthood or, even more simply, the isolation of our own "tight little island," it nevertheless remains firm.

Our prime goal then is the remarkably uncomplicated one of telling the story of our efforts as it has unfolded. In that story and in the issues it addresses, we hope to provide important clues to new utilitarian ways of approaching the stubborn, but socially critical challenge of maximizing the educational experience of young children.

The most important decision we had to make before starting this book was not *what* we wanted to say, but *how* we wanted to say it. Essentially the choice was between a technical-scientific versus a narrative report paradigm. We opted for the latter because we believed it would yield a crisper, more readable, less cluttered document that would be of greater value to a wider audience. Our decision implies no disrespect for research or even for the turgidity and exclusivity of technical-scientific reporting. Indeed, the work to be described has flourished because of its relatively sound research base, among other reasons. The decision to write a primarily narrative account also does not imply that our research heritage and discoveries will be ignored.

Rather, our findings, distilled and purged of technical detail, will become part of the narrative, with appropriate cross-references to the professional literature. Only one chapter (Chapter 8) is reserved for a panoramic overview of PMHP's research efforts and findings. A project of this scope, with its venerable 17-year history, has been touched and bettered by many individuals. To reflect the significance of their contributions adequately could well add 20 pages to the final product. At the time of this writing, for example, PMHP is an entity that involves four school districts (Rochester, Fairport, Rush-Henrietta, and West Irondequoit, New York) and 17 elementary schools. Each district has administrative personnel—including superintendents, assistant-superintendents, pupil personnel, or clinical service directors—who are active in project governance and contribute importantly to its functions. Among the latter we wish particularly to thank Morris Sandgrund and Alfred Gelerinter of the Rochester City School District and Mitchell Salim, Neil Mutschler, and Alan Stewart, who represent the West Irondequoit, Rush-Henrietta, and Fairport school districts, respectively. Although the profile of participation and contribution is understandably different in different schools, principals, teachers, mental health workers, and, not infrequently, reading teachers, speech teachers, counselors, supervising teachers, nurses, lunchroom monitors, crossing monitors, and custodians have been important cogs in the project wheel.

We are deeply indebted, of course, to the venturesome band of school mental health professionals who have "quarterbacked" the project in individual schools. Our current roster includes the following social workers: Wayne Brigman, Eleanor Eksten, Ann Farie, Alice Hebing, Mary Lowery, Lillian Mooney, Doris Morgan, Douglas Randall, and Helen Tuttle. Also included are the following psychologists: Philip F. Cassara, Joseph A. Harte, Warren Kneppcr, Martin Krupnick, Gene McCabe, Allan Mendler, Steven Prisco, Carmen J. Scalea, Andrew Steinbrecher, and Robert Stewart. Earlier, Patti Fidele, William Haffey, David Law, Horace Lethbridge, Gordon Palmer, Alice Rubenstein, Genevieve Russo, and David Worl served as project professionals. Although we cannot cite each of our nearly 100 devoted nonprofessional child aides individually, we can at least cite our senior aides, who can "field" well-deserved bouquets for the group they represent and in which they have their origins: Frieda Behrmann, Norma Finzer, Nina Kalen, Claire Lewis, the late Sanni Linkins, Sue Meyer, and Dina Zwick.

Our colleague, Dr. Melvin Zax, was an important contributor during the early phase of the project and has remained an interested friend and constructive resource person throughout. Similar important contributions were made by Drs. Earl Telschow and Harold Miles and Miss Helen Palmeter, Mrs. Mildred Potter, and Mr. Louis Goldberg. An array of doctoral and postdoctoral trainees has passed through the PMHP portal, especially in recent years. Each in his way has enriched the product, and we hope that the project has in some ways contributed to their development. Among those who have served as predoctoral trainees are Drs. James Laird, David Beach, Julian Rappaport, Gerald Specter, Irwin Sandler, David Terrell, Spencer McWilliams, Steven Clarfield, and, more currently, Messrs. Michael Pratt and Ellis Gesten and Mrs. Cheryl Kimbrough. At the post doctoral level we cite Drs. Jerry Saffer, Philip Edwardson, Eugene Evans, James Schuh, Joseph Kluger, Lee Marcus, and Ruth Bolton. Drs. Joseph Messineo and James Ashbrook remain as consultants with the project.

Angelo J. Madonia, M.D., our chief psychiatric consultant, whose clinical sensitivity and skills have reverberated positively both at the staff level and in all participating schools, has been a backbone force in the program from its inception.

The project's flowering and on occasion very survival are due directly to the unstinting devotion of a group of citizens comprising a supporting, nonprofit community group (PMHP Inc.). Three people in particular—Mrs. Jane Goldman, Mr. Nelson Millard, and Mrs. Marie Hanson—have been towers of strength, encouragement, and moral and practical support in the last critical five-year period of project growth and expansion. Their efforts have been nobly supported by Mr. Gardner Burt, Mr. Samuel Hall, Mr. Irving Norry, Mr. Richard Fischer, Mrs. Ann Camilio, and others.

We also wish to express appreciation to several persons who have had long-term, significant involvement in the mammoth research operation: Mrs. Alice B. Wilson, Mrs. Barbara Kreling, and Messrs. Ron Kraus and Robert Caldwell. Overlooked in the process are some 30 individuals who participated in more circumscribed ad hoc ways in research studies.

Those who are banded together as authors of this book thus are a group as the result of accidents of geography and time. Had this volume been written five years ago or five years hence, a somewhat different accidental array of authors would have emerged. The sense of the project is one of continuous evolution and change, an extraordinarily broad base of participation, and important contributions coming from many people. Trost, Izzo, and Cowen have been associated with the project since it began. Dorr was its research director during the critical expansion period (1969–1972); Lorion is his successor. Isaacson, technically dubbed our community liaison representative, was first an aide, later a senior aide, and for the last four years has been the "girl Friday" who has kept our rattling parts glued together.

We have not yet mentioned the mundane matter of fiscal support. To tell that story as it is could well consume many additional pages. In oversimplified terms, our support base may be considered to have two major strands: (A) research and training, and (B) service. Our initial support (1959–62) came from the Community Mental Health Services Division of the New York State Department of Mental Hygiene. The bulk of our research and training support over the subsequent ten-year period has come from the National Institute of Mental Health, first from the Community Services and Research Branch (MH-01500) and later from the Experimental and Special Training Branch (MH-11820). Indeed this volume also serves as a final report for the 1969–73 NIMH grant period. Support for the service aspects of our program comes from sources so diverse that they put the most complicated patchwork quilt to shame. Four such backbone sources have been (1) the participating school districts themselves, (2) the Rochester Monroe County Youth Board and the New York State Division for Youth, (3) the New York State Urban Education Program, and (4) the Board of Cooperative Education Services (BOCES), No. 1. Beyond that, at least 25 different individuals, organizations, foundations, and trusts have generously contributed to the ongoing service aspects of the project. Many of them, by their own choice, shall remain nameless. We can, however, cite the following and do so with gratitude: Max A. Adler Foundation; Ruth C. Applebaum; Davenport-Hatch Foundation; Emmet Blakeney Gleason Memorial; Natalie L. Goldberg; Rochester Jobs, Inc.; Teen League (Hike for Hope); John F. Wegman Foundation, Inc.; Mrs. Andrew Wolfe; and the Margaret Woodbury Strong Fund.

Our sincerest gratitude also goes to Patti Sullivan, Virginia Youtzy, and especially Yetta Cross, who labored valiantly and successfully in transforming the scrawls and hieroglyphics of several tortured drafts into a clear, readable final copy, and to Alice B. Wilson, who took time off from her Anovas and computers to bring her editorial eagle-eye and know-how to the product.

Our debt to individuals, groups, and organizations is enormous—as can be seen, even from this highly condensed resumé. This brief citation hardly begins to do them justice. Equally grievous, it omits many other individuals who have been an intimate part of the fabric of the project's growth. No one-man show, no 50-man show has this been! The authors merely act as spokesmen for the many who have collectively put their shoulders to a massive, but intriguing and highly challenging wheel.

1

Some Problems
of the
Mental Health Fields

Seventeen years ago in Rochester, New York, a small group of us became absorbed with several serious concerns about the purpose, scope, and efficiency of existing school mental health services. Our absorption was not triggered by the absence or mismanagement of local services. On the contrary, Rochester was among the first communities in America to introduce school mental health services (1906), and over the years its programs have been sufficiently enlightened, imaginative, and pioneering to serve as models for mental health innovation in school districts across the country. Moreover, the per-student ratio of mental health professionals in the Rochester school system was then and is today among the most favorable in the country. Our thinking thus began in a context of a relatively strong rather than a weak delivery system. Figuratively, our reactions germinated in the shadow of what was more like a "Taj Mahal" than a "Tobacco Road." Indeed, it was the system's very strength and willingness to explore openly that provided the fertile climate needed for further self-scrutiny.

Our thinking, which fluctuated initially from muddled to diffuse, began with the vague but gnawing feeling that despite favorable local conditions, school mental health services were not operating with optimal efficiency. No matter how impressive the professional-to-student ratio was in relation to other less favored or forward-looking communities, absolute shortages in professional time were evident. Future extrapolations indicated that because of local, and more critically, national limitations with regard to manpower and funding, resources were likely to diminish rather than increase. Furthermore, available resources were targeted for children in crisis and for those with entrenched dysfunction. Thus limited resources were being directed toward the relatively few children whose problems were most firmly rooted and refractory. In practice this meant that many referred children could not be seen at all and that even when dysfunction was identified as early as kindergarten or first grade, it often remained unattended for many years.

It seemed clear to us from the start that resources would not increase significantly in the future. Thus our prime challenge was to develop alternative uses of scarce resources that would have greater impact and a more socially utilitarian payoff for the many. Our conviction was that any practical solution would have to include mass, early detection of dysfunction, backed by a functional system for bringing effective help to young children before their dysfunctions became rooted and led to more debilitating general consequences. We did not then, nor do we today believe that this was an ideal conceptual approach. A preferable goal, at least conceptually, would have been to engineer school environments that encouraged adaptation in the first place. However, we lacked the skills, leverage, and sociopolitical clout needed to bring about such change. Moreover, putting the issue in abstract, futuristic terms, such as creating health-producing school environments, made it difficult, if not impossible for school districts responsible to children in immediate need to see the relation of the proposed solution to all-too-apparent pressing current problems. In other words, the route of early detection and prevention, while conceptually less desirable as a first choice, seemed to be the best pragmatic meeting ground for innovation among existing crisis, pathology-oriented delivery systems and the theoretical ideal of creating health-producing school environments. At least early detection and prevention were things that we as well as school districts could view as relevant, useful, and potentially more effective than traditional delivery systems as well as promising good short-term payoff.

Our story, still unfinished, has by now achieved a certain wholeness, although in truth there have been many moments when it seemed that this would never happen. Only the passage of time has leveled the peaks and valleys into something resembling a trend. On balance, however, we believe that we have gained sufficient experience and new knowledge to say things that may be helpful to others in school mental health. At its core, that's what this book is all about: a report of our thinking, our history, our actual programs, and our findings, which together offer an alternative to dominant, present-day school mental health practices. The book's sequential approach is designed to convey a sense of the project's unfolding and development between 1957 and 1974. Moreover, the book progresses from broad issues to specific program details. Thus we begin by considering some current unresolved mental health problems that gave rise to our efforts and then narrow our focus increasingly to more concrete descriptions of the program that hopefully will permit the reader to grasp enough of the project's concrete approach to be able to implement relevant aspects of it in other communities and settings.

New ways of doing things begin with ideas—some concrete, others vague. But practice often precedes and helps to formulate such ideas explicitly. Indeed, ideas may crystallize only after the methods that evolve from them are found to be pragmatic. In our own case, it is difficult, after the fact, to unravel the classic chicken-egg dilemma of which came first, ideas or practice. Although we can identify germinal ideas that oriented us in particular directions, we can also say that much of our early impetus derived from concrete knowledge about schools and school mental health programs. Important strands from both these sources somehow began to blend, more than 15 years ago, in ways that made it sensible for us to move in certain directions. Yet if the reader is to have a clear framework in which to view our work, he must have some understanding of its ideological wellspring and the issues it was designed to address. By providing such a smoothed-over, retrospective account, we do not, however, intend to suggest that the program sprang crisply and logically from that rationale.

This first chapter thus presents a view of some pressing mental health problems of modern society. Although it is important to keep the school's special qualities in mind, in terms of the challenges and opportunities it affords, neither the rationale nor modus operandi of the Primary Mental Health Project (PMHP) can be isolated from the broader matrix of social problems that the project addresses. One of PMHP's key assumptions is that both school adaptation problems and school mental health delivery systems mirror, in microcosm, the larger concerns and failings that plague the mental health fields today. Thus it is appropriate first to consider some of these pressing problems and alternative pathways to their resolution.

UNRESOLVED MENTAL HEALTH PROBLEMS

The house of mental health is, and has been for some time, far from orderly. This statement is not intended to be accusatory or "holier-than thou." It is a descriptive fact, reflecting the hard-boiled serious judgment that those of us in mental health currently face a nasty conglomeration of unresolved problems. Moreover, there is reason to suppose (Cowen, 1973; Zax & Cowen, 1972) that if we continue to follow the established ideological guidelines and practices of the mental health fields, good solutions to these problems will not be found.

Changing Views of Mental Health

Society's views of psychological dysfunction and attempts to cope with it have hardly remained static over time (Zax & Cowen, 1972). Although no simple summary statement captures the full complexity of the evolutionary changes in mental health approaches that have occurred over many hundreds of years, two critical patterns of change can be discerned: (1) an ever widening range of human conditions is viewed as having major psychological determinants and (2) increasingly subtle conditions are considered to be psychologically rooted.

Man's earliest concerns about behavioral peculiarity were restricted to flagrant, profound, poorly understood, frightening departures from prevailing norms. His views of causation were equally simplistic. Possession by the devil or demoniac spirits was a handy way of explaining whatever could not be comprehended rationally (Golann & Eisdorfer, 1972). Such views of causation shifted over time as new knowledge was accumulated. Possession by spirits yielded to religious explanations. These in turn were displaced by biological and physicalistic interpretations of psychic dysfunction that followed the important scientific and medical discoveries of the eighteenth and nineteenth centuries (Bloom, 1965).

Changing conceptions of causality were paralleled by comparable changes in society's views of what was and was not disordered behavior. Initially, only the grossest, most extreme behavioral abnormalities attracted attention or concern; at the present time, far more subtle entities are considered abnormal. This progression has been sequential. Initially, the concept of abnormality only included indisputable cases of psychosis. It was later broadened to include the evident but less extreme symptom neuroses; later still, the less blatant character neuroses; and then the intricate psychosomatic states, with their complex mind-body interactions. Today's concepts of abnormality include highly abstract contemplative states, such as the philosophical-existential neuroses, featuring man's preoccupation with the nature and meaning of life and his relation to the universe. No longer do we look for the obvious ravings of the lunatic to judge dysfunction. We now readily accept the view that unhappiness, loneliness, or the failure to live up to one's potential also properly fall within the province of the mental health specialist.

These changes have had their effects. For example, the number of individuals who fall within the "proper scope" of the helping professions has vastly increased. The demand for direct helping services is greater than ever before. The search for determinants of dysfunction has broadened to include both the interpersonal and environmental influences that shape human development. Exploration of new treatment modalities, especially for the less obvious dysfunctions, has also increased dramatically in recent years. Society's mounting concern about social problems such as addiction, racism, and urban riots as well as the issues raised by such problems, places new demands on mental health professionals to find solutions. Overall, the burdens and pressures on the fields of mental health have surely grown. Simultaneously, their failings and need to account have become more obvious than ever before. Such an atmosphere demands critical self-scrutiny. Efforts must be made to separate effective and ineffective approaches and to identify new approaches that deal meaningfully with major unresolved problems.

Supply and Demand

Mental health professionals have known for some time that they lack the resources necessary to bring adequate help to those who need it. (Albee, 1959; 1967; Arnhoff, Rubenstein & Speisman, 1969; Gartner, 1971; Joint Commission Report, 1961; Sobey, 1970). However, the matter is even more serious and complex! Many observers have pointed out a sharp distinction between the demand and need for mental health services. Indeed, Schofield (1964) uses the term "the countable thousands" in speaking of demand for services and the term "the hidden millions" to identify the underlying need for such help. These terms, like the classic iceberg analogy, emphasize that only a small proportion of those who need services actually get them. This of course is a rough guess since it is much easier to determine demand than need. One can get a reasonably clear picture of demand by counting the number of client contacts, professional activities of mental health personnel, and settings. Examples of such data include the number of people who seek help annually from mental health clinics, community mental health centers, various kinds of social agencies, and private practitioners and the number of beds occupied in mental hospitals. Thus the demand for mental health services can be operationally defined and is approximately knowable.

Defining the need for mental health services, however, is an extraordinarily complex task. Demand underestimates need for several reasons. Many people take their psychological problems to social "caregivers" other than mental health professionals and are thus not included in the demand statistics. For example, Gurin, Veroff, and Feld (1960) report that about 70 per cent of those with psychological problems turn to clergymen or family physicians. Thus large numbers of individuals cannot or do not define their problems in psychological terms. Others, who do define them in such terms and want help find that mental health facilities are either geographically inaccessible or financially unfeasible.

As often happens when supply and demand are out of balance, available resources are inequitably distributed. This is certainly so for mental health services—a subject that will be discussed more fully later. The critical point to be made here is that the mental health fields have not succeeded in developing the resources necessary to solve pressing individual and social problems. This basic failing underscores the need for conceptual alternatives.

The Graver Conditions

As noted previously, the earliest conditions defined as aberrant were those involving flagrant, profoundly disturbed, bizarre behaviors. Ironically, mental health professionals have been least successful in treating these dysfunctions. No better illustration of this point can be found than schizophrenia, long considered to be among the most baffling of the profound psychic disorders. Mental health professionals have certainly not been disinterested in studying or trying to find cures for this condition. On the contrary, schizophrenia has attracted the interest and energies of the mental health fields, however defined, for many centuries, and countless concerted clinical and research efforts have been mounted in an attempt to unravel its mysteries. The results of these efforts, however, have been disappointing. Scheff (1966) concludes that despite the more than 5,000 studies conducted over the past five decades, the mental health fields have recorded virtually no advance in understanding the causes or cures of this debilitating disorder. He believes that this is so because we have asked the wrong questions and used the wrong approaches.

In other words, once schizophrenia becomes rooted in an individual, the prognosis for genuine improvement is guarded. Indeed, Zax and Cowen (1972) have drawn a structural analogy between schizophrenia and terminal cancer. Our lack of progress in this field points once again to the need for bonafide conceptual alternatives that go beyond past efforts, speaking symbolically, to lock the barn door after the horse has escaped.

Although schizophrenia is the first and most striking example that can be cited in identifying substantive failures of the mental health fields, it is by no means the only one. Much the same can be said for the other functional psychoses as well as for other dysfunctions that mental health professionals have failed to understand or overcome, for many centuries: for example, psychopathy and sociopathy, addictive states, and delinquency. Although sincere, indeed valiant efforts to overcome these problems continue in a number of clinically significant spheres, the mental health fields' overall track record has been poor. If we continue to focus on such end-states and begin interventions only after the fact, we may have lost the battle before it is joined. For that reason, the original recommendation of the Joint Commission on Mental Illness and Health (1961)—that major mental illness is the most important unfinished business of the mental health professions and that the lion's share of mental health personnel and resources should be given over to finding solutions for such problems—seems particularly unpromising. The mental health fields' failure with profound disorders points logically to the need for prevention, an orientation that undergirds our work in the schools.

Some Limits of Psychotherapy

When, through the pioneering efforts of Sigmund Freud, psychotherapeutic methods first began to evolve, an important new breakthrough for mental health took place. The

very concept was a liberating vista-expanding one. For the first time in man's history, systematized, controlled verbal discourse between two people was codified as a promising method for dealing with major psychological disorder. To be sure, psychoanalysis met with significant early resistance, both because it was such a radical departure from already established ways of doing things and because specific aspects of its theoretical underpinnings were offensive to many people. Its early struggles notwithstanding, dynamically oriented psychotherapy eventually became the method of choice for dealing with many human psychological dysfunctions. In the process, what was initially a liberating development became rigid and institutionalized (Eisenberg, 1962) and, as such, limited the development of new mental health approaches.

During psychotherapy's long period of growth and solidification, many mental health professionals staked out their turf and came, more and more, to protect their vested interests. Such circumstances did not favor objective evaluation or critical self-scrutiny. Accordingly, during psychotherapy's rapid growth period, insufficient attention was paid to critical issues concerning its clinical and social effectiveness. Only in the 1950s and 1960s did such issues begin to surface and to be examined carefully.

Among the first to raise serious questions about psychotherapy's clinical effectiveness was Eysenck, who published a series of critiques on this topic over a 20-year period (1952, 1961, 1966). His by now well-known two-pronged assault was that (1) psychotherapy has been generally ineffective in alleviating neurotic conditions and (2) the more intensive forms of psychotherapy were relatively least effective. Levitt (1957, 1963, 1971) developed similar arguments about the ineffectiveness of psychotherapy with children. Because these reviews touched on firmly held views and deeply vested interests, they understandably generated controversy and rejoinder. Indeed, the debate continues right up to the present moment! Several recent scholarly reviews by persons deeply involved in the study of psychotherapy (Bergin, 1971; Garfield, 1971; Rotter, 1973; Strupp & Bergin, 1969), although less pessimistic than Eysenck's critiques in outlook, nevertheless conclude that psychotherapy is at best only a moderately effective procedure. The current inclination is not to try to evaluate psychotherapy as a global entity, but rather to look at more discrete evaluative questions such as: What is the most effective technique for a particular individual who is experiencing a particular set of problems? The most sober current appraisal of psychotherapy is that its clinical effectiveness is limited. Furthermore, although psychotherapy is an important method of expanding the mental health professional's armamentarium, it is neither a total nor near-total answer to today's mental health problems.

No matter how real and significant the concerns about psychotherapy's limited clinical effectiveness, they are less grave than concerns about its social effectiveness. The latter problem, long recognized, has been a focus of serious concern in a continuous series of contributions (e.g., Hollingshead & Redlich, 1958; Lorion, 1973, 1974; Myers & Bean, 1968; Myers & Roberts, 1959; Riessman, Cohen & Pearl, 1964; Sanua, 1966). Because the "supply" of psychotherapy has always been less than the demand expressed for it, psychotherapy's limited resources have been distributed inequitably. Indeed, it was once remarked that a person's chances of seeing a therapist improve dramatically if he is well educated, relatively affluent, personable, articulate, lives in a major urban center in the northeastern quadrant of the United States, and suffers from a relatively interesting, exotic dysfunction such as an anxiety neurosis.

Moreover, the typical methods of psychotherapy are not equally well suited to all segments of the population. Certainly psychotherapy is an approach that has evolved and flourished primarily in an upper middle-class mental health milieu. Some trappings of that approach have not generalized well to other groups—e.g., the poor, who often perceive and define problems more pragmatically in terms of jobs, financial concerns, poor housing, and restricted life opportunities (Lorion, 1974; Miller & Riessman, 1968; Reiff, 1967). In addition, the typical amenities of middle-class styles of intervention, involving variables such as when, where, how, by whom, and for how long people are seen, do not suit the life-styles and mores of all social groups equally well.

Thus, because of the scarcities in available services and because of the way they are packaged and delivered, psychotherapy is available only to a small fraction of the population. The rest must fend for themselves as best they can; find alternative, sometimes less appropriate services; or go without help. If the mental health professional can fill his weekly calendar with $50-an-hour clientele, it is all too easy for him to ignore or even repress the woes of the many who cannot afford such a luxury.

The thrust of this section is that the bedrock technique of the mental health professions, i.e., psychotherapy, is an inexact approach of limited clinical and social effectiveness. If that is so, there are further grounds for seeking out socially utilitarian alternatives.

Allocation Problems

Sociological reports going back more than three decades (Faris & Dunham, 1939) show that the incidence of mental disorders and emotional problems increases steadily as one moves from the outskirts to the center of the city. This distributional pattern is similar to those reported for other key sociological variables such as general population mortality, infant mortality, crime and delinquency, unemployment, and poverty. Related issues pertaining to mental health have been studied specifically over the last 20 years.

Thus, for example, Hollingshead and Redlich (1958) found higher rates of mental illness among the poor. Furthermore, they found that the problems people brought to mental health specialists and the treatments they received varied strikingly according to their socioeconomic status. These findings have been confirmed by later investigators. Reviews of the literature indicate that low-income individuals are less likely to seek therapy than other groups or to be accepted for treatment if they do apply (Sanua, 1966). Even if they break through these initial barriers, they are more likely to be seen by relatively inexperienced therapists, terminate early, be given supportive or somatic rather than intensive treatment, and have less successful outcomes (Lorion, 1973).

Ironically, these findings betray an implicit distributional law that governs the allocation of mental health services: i.e., where help is most needed it is least available! Thus the mental health delivery system bypasses major segments of the population. In addition, the fact that the services offered to such groups are often inappropriate to their life-styles, experience, and perceptions of need (Lorion, 1974) betrays yet another major failing of today's mental health establishment.

ALTERNATIVE CONCEPTUALIZATIONS

Althouth different observers would doubtless attach different weights to the problems considered in the preceding section, there is little question that they add up to a considerable sum. What they suggest, in the aggregate, is that to continue mindlessly the practices that the mental health establishment has used in the past and with which it is now comfortable and secure will only compound these already serious problems. Recurrent themes in the analysis include the following: (1) mental health resources are insufficient to meet obvious need, (2) limited resources are distributed inequitably, and (3) we have, for too long, been under the influence of an end-state mentality, which predisposes the mental health professional to begin his interventions only when entrenched dysfunction is first identified. This means that too few people are being reached, the wrong people are being reached, and the limited number who *are* being reached are reached at the wrong time. In effect, then, present delivery systems limit or defeat professional intervention before it starts.

If we have defined these problems correctly, conceptual alternatives to established mental health practices are desperately needed. One of the most attractive alternatives, in principle, is prevention, i.e., cutting down the flow of disorder. In the past, the term prevention has been used many different ways. Classically, a distinction has been made among primary, secondary, and tertiary prevention. Primary prevention seeks to prevent the occurrence of disorder in the first place. It emphasizes reducing, over long periods of time, the occurrence of various kinds of disorders by dealing with the environmental factors that adversely affect human development before they cause damage. In other words, primary prevention seeks impersonally to promote emotional and psychological well-being in groups and communities. Thus as soon as individual distress or dysfunction is identified, the procedure used, by definition, is other than one of primary prevention.

Secondary prevention, by contrast, seeks primarily to shorten the duration, impact, and negative effects of disorder. At its core are the methods of early identification and treatment of dysfunction. It is important to distinguish between ontogenetically early and late secondary prevention (Cowen, 1967); the more usual applications of secondary prevention have been late. For example, the community mental health center that reaches into the community to diagnose and treat difficulties early exemplifies ontogenetically late secondary prevention. Thus trying to reduce the toll of an unfolding schizophrenic reaction in a 35-year-old adult by intervening in the first week rather than in the first three months would illustrate an ontogenetically late secondary prevention. By contrast, ontogenetically early secondary prevention focuses on dysfunction early in the individual's life. Early intervention with maladapting preschool or kindergarten children in an effort to avert later, more serious disorder exemplifies ontogenetically early secondary prevention. There are important differences between the tactics and strategies of these two approaches to secondary prevention. Early secondary prevention focuses on the young child and underscores the value of studying his environment and the social systems and institutions that influence his development. Conceptually, then, ontogenetically early secondary prevention is closer to primary prevention than is ontogenetically late secondary prevention.

The term tertiary prevention is a misnomer. Tertiary prevention seeks to reduce the consequences of severe dysfunction and to minimize its residual effects. It focuses exclusively on individuals who are already experiencing profound difficulty. It attempts to restore, to a minimal degree at least, the ability of such individuals to carry out effective interpersonal relationships and essential life roles.

Much of mental health's past thrust has been toward ontogenetically late secondary prevention and tertiary prevention. The argument has been made (Cowen, 1967; Cowen, 1973; Zax & Cowen, 1972) that it would be helpful to drop the term tertiary prevention from the mental health vocabulary since it does not mean prevention. Only primary and ontogenetically early secondary prevention are genuine alternatives to the mental health fields' past emphasis on restoration and rehabilitation.

The need for the mental health professions to shift their conceptual stance implies several important, more specific focuses. The first of these is to reverse the classic question, How can damage be repaired? to its 180-degree opposite: How can mental health or resources be built into individuals in the first place? The answer to the latter question will ultimately involve fine-grained analysis and modification of existing social systems. This in turn requires that we first develop methodologies to describe the basic impact of various social systems and then determine how such attributes affect positive or negative development. The traditional background, training, and expertise of the mental health professional make him ill-prepared to engage such issues. New skills and knowledge, not heretofore included in mental health training, must be developed. And new alliances must be formed with specialists such as urban planners, architects, and political scientists, who formerly were not considered to have legitimate input into the special arena of the mental health fields. A truly preventive focus must also serve many more people much sooner than ever before. This necessarily implies new professional roles and activities that collectively expand the reach of mental health services geometrically. Approaches such as crisis intervention, mental health consultation, early detection of dysfunction, and the training and use of nonprofessionals would support this new thrust.

The argument being developed here emphasizes the need for new, quite different roles for the future mental health professional. The first role is that of the social system analyst or modifier, who strives to create social environments that produce mental health. The second role, that of mental health "quarterback" (Cowen, 1967), aims to extend the effective wallop of the mental health professions to reach many more people in need earlier in their lives. Most basically, the mental health fields must replace their past, almost exclusive emphasis on disruptive end-states and focus instead on the settings and life conditions that shape early adaptation. Hopefully, it will be as legitimate in the future for a mental health professional to ask "How can a first grade classroom be structured to promote health?" as it has been for him to ask "What can I do to cure schizophrenia?" Such a shift in focus demands that the mental health fields turn increasingly to the social networks, institutions, and settings that affect human development. It was this conviction that first made us turn many years ago to the schools—particularly to the primary grades.

SCHOOLS AND MENTAL HEALTH

The Challenge of the Schools

If one asked sophisticated observers the question, "Which social institutions most profoundly affect early human development?" most would name the family and school first. At birth the human infant is utterly helpless and dependent. His care is vested in a family, which over many years provides the necessary physical and psychological supplies, close interactions, and rich affective experiences that are important in shaping his development. The family necessarily is a factor that potentiates or limits the child's development.

Although there is no question about the family's importance, it is for many reasons difficult to work preventively within the family structure. Families are separated geographically from each other, and access to them is difficult. Accordingly, a second major social institution, the school, is extremely attractive to those interested in prevention. Schools are relatively large, communal, geographically bound settings under a consolidated administrative organization. Although the child is already somewhat preformed when he arrives in school, the school is nevertheless a vital ongoing shaping force. No matter how difficult it may be to modify a school environment to optimize children's mental health or reduce their dysfunction, it is nevertheless easier than trying to do the same thing in 1,000 families. The school is indeed the only communal institution in modern society that affects all people during their formative years (Bardon, 1968). The child spends six to seven hours a day, five days a week in school for 12 or more years. There he acquires knowledge, develops cognitive skills, and learns ways of interacting with people. Moreover, he encounters important adults with whom he identifies and who therefore profoundly influence his development. Thus schools and especially the primary grades are among the most attractive of all settings for developing preventive programs to shape more effective, meaningful, life experiences for children.

Education versus Mental Health Orientations

At some level, however vague, we were aware of the potential of the school many years ago. Trying to restructure the school as a social system then would have been impossible because we lacked the knowledge and skills to do so and because it was then, as it is today, very difficult for schools to define problems in terms of the social system. Schools more readily perceive and respond to concrete problems, such as helping Billy learn to read or helping Johnny get along with his classmates, than to abstract questions, such as: How can the school environment promote adjustment for all children? Like the emergency room of a hospital, the school must deal with the here-and-now injury or dysfunction. But schools are very much concerned with the failure of young children. Teachers and parents react at that level daily. And, increasingly, parents and community organizations are calling on school authorities to account for school failures.

A child is seen as a school adjustment problem if he does not meet minimal standards of educational progress or if he seriously violates the environment's prevailing behavioral norms and tolerances. Glidewell and Swallow, in their Task-Force report to the Joint Commission on Mental Health of Children (1969), point out that there are many different types of school maladaptation, which in the aggregate affect about three out of ten American school children. But educators and mental health professionals often view school maladjustment from different perspectives. Whereas educators emphasize signposts of educational progress, mental health professionals stress behavioral and adaptive factors. Although these two orientations are different, they are not, as some have suggested, incompatible. In fact there is often a reciprocity between the young child's educational and psychological problems. For example, some children with good early histories and sound family relationships fail to acquire a rudimentary skill (e.g., reading), which blocks their further educational progress. As a result, the child is subjected to psychological pressures such as shame and ridicule by peers or adults, a sense of anxiety, and feelings of inadequacy as well as damage to his self-concept—all of which predispose him to later, more serious adjustment problems. Thus chronic educational failure can precipitate psychological problems that further undermine the child's ability to learn.

As noted previously, the term school maladjustment covers a wide range of phenomena that vary in intensity as well as content. Such problems are handled differently as a result of differences in administrative views, educational philosophies, and individual teachers' styles, skills, and tolerance levels. Unfortunately, we still know relatively little about the remedial effects of various sanctions typically applied to children's school maladaptive behavior. For example, the so-called corrective of nonpromotion has been shown to be remarkably ineffective in modifying or improving children's school adjustment (Levine & Graziano, 1973).

How Teachers See and Deal with Children's Problems

There is little question that the teacher is a vital determinant of whether a child's school behavior is viewed as maladaptive. Although some extreme deviations are almost universally regarded as maladaptive by teachers, in most cases how serious a problem is considered to be depends on the teachers' personal views. It is they who formulate and revise judgments about a child's school adaptation. Teachers, like anyone else, have idiosyncratic views about child behavior. They differ in their tolerance for deviation in general, for particular behaviors, or for certain personality characteristics, and they use different interaction styles, management techniques, and disciplinary approaches. Some teachers, for instance, can accept virtually any behavioral deviation as long as the child shows good educational progress. Others fail to appreciate even remarkable educational progress if the child evidences a significant behavior problem—especially a disruptive one. Some teachers view restlessness as normal in six-year-olds; others cannot tolerate such behavior because it interferes with their beliefs about the need for tight class management and invites similar behavior from other children.

There are many reasons why children should behave differently when they first arrive at school. They have highly individualized socialization histories, different abilities and life-styles, and different success and failure experiences in their limit-testing behaviors. Many first grade teachers, sensitive to children's individual differences, see the initial school year as a honeymoon period. Thus they allow wide behavioral latitudes, operating on the assumption that transgressions will dissipate with time as part of the normal school socialization process. If a child continues to violate norms—if his misbehavior becomes more exaggerated, disrupts class activities, or interferes significantly with his educational progress—the teacher eventually begins to view him as a school adjustment problem. At that time, she may feel a need to seek outside help.

Teachers vary as much in dealing with school maladaptation as they do in defining it. Fortunately, many instances of maladjustment in class are minor, and teachers can handle them well with a standard repertoire of classroom management skills. Gentle admonitions such as "Here, we don't hit other children!" or "The Robins are quiet when they read!" help teachers to meet simple norm-challenging behaviors. Part of the very fabric of being a teacher is knowing that minor behavioral transgressions will occur and having the skills to deal with them. During the early school years, these norm-challenging behaviors are expected, and an important part of the child's school socialization is to learn appropriate responses to new situational demands.

After a while, however, teachers may sense that their management techniques, although effective for most children, are not sufficient to stop or even slow down the chronic misbehavior or educational failings of some children. By that time, the situation may involve not only one particular child but also the well-being and educational development of other children—perhaps even the manageability of the entire class. When a teacher will sense that different management approaches are needed depends on her individual experience, style, personal threshold, and personality as well as the school's resources for dealing with such problems.

Even when the teacher has made a firm decision that the child's problems of adaptation are beyond her, she can still choose among several nondrastic options. If, for example, she believes that the difficulties are related to inadequate discipline, lack of interest, or poor management at home, she can speak to the child's parents in hopes that somehow they will be able to bring about positive behavioral change. This is a particularly likely option if the teacher knows or suspects that there is a connection between the child's home situation and his disconcerting behavior or performance in class. If no such connection exists or if the family is disinterested or inaccessible, the teacher may turn to sources within the school for help. Her specific request will depend on the system's resources and how she relates to the individuals who make up the resource system. For example, she may contact, formally or informally, a respected peer, a supervising teacher, or the principal for help on some variant of the question, How can we get Jimmy to shape up? This overture may elicit friendly counsel designed to broaden the teacher's perspective and help her devise new ways of handling the child's classroom problem by herself. If the school has the resources available, a second, more drastic possibility is to call on a specialist, such as the school psychologist or social worker, to energize a process of assessment and intervention designed to overcome the difficulty.

If such efforts do not solve the problem, further administrative steps can be taken. The assumption may be made that since the child's problems have not yielded to the remedial efforts of individuals, perhaps they can be solved by environmental manipulation. For example, the child may be transferred to another classroom in the same building in hopes that he will get along better in a modified environment with a new teacher. Occasionally this step helps, and the combination of an especially settled classroom and a skilled resourceful teacher can arrest the difficulties. More likely, however, the child, already identified as a problem, is introduced into a new class and continues his maladaptive ways. This may lead to transferring the child to a different school—sometimes as a swap for a comparably maladapted child. By this time, however, many people have been alerted to the child's difficulties, a number have given up on him, and the shift is largely a matter of grasping at straws, with little hope that the change will solve the problem.

When all these procedures fail, the next drastic step involves any one of a cluster of administrative actions, described variously by different school districts as suspension, expulsion, or exemption. The child subjected to such actions is literally and functionally separated from the educational arena and is vulnerable to unfortunate, longer lasting interpersonal and educational consequences. He is identified and labeled as a failure. Where he goes and what happens to him from then on depends largely on the community's resources and the skills and interests of key people with whom he will have contact during the separation process. A substantial proportion of children who reach this unhappy point are by then already prime candidates for adverse personal and social outcomes, such as a sense of being alone and adrift; antisocial, delinquent, or acting-out behavior; or referral to a clinic or agency for long-term, more complex interventions to overcome the problems.

The hypothetical sequence of steps depicted in the preceding paragraphs is an obvious oversimplification. It does not represent an inevitable course of events for all children. Problems can indeed be short-circuited at any point in the sequence. Some children, whose difficulties are less obvious and do not intrude on the lives of others, tend to remain unidentified by the system and are simply accepted as they are, performing ineffectively, and never approach their full potential.

If the preceding account is at all realistic in its portrayal of the range of ways in which school maladaptation is handled, it suggests several interesting dimensions of analysis. One is the extent to which the various procedures label the child, formally or informally, as a misfit. Effective, on-the-spot handling of a child's problems in the classroom is likely to be less rutting than transferring the child to another school or suspending him. If the teacher can handle the problem effectively in the classroom, the situation remains less obvious to the child, his peers, and the teacher herself. When problems are labeled, particularly chronically so, they tend to become self-fulfilling prophesies.

Another important dimension of analysis is the extent to which various actions interfere with the child's normal living circumstances and/or separate him from his natural environment. Effective classroom or school management is less disruptive than sending the child to a residential treatment center or a mental hospital. The more drastic the action, the more likely it will be perceived as drastic by others, be labeled as such, and interpose severe barriers to the child's ability to resume normal school activities. Thus strategies for dealing with children's school maladaptation can be dimensioned according to their parsimony. More immediate, more natural, less drastic, less disruptive and less labeling alternatives are preferable to their opposites. The challenge thus posed is to develop efficient strategies for dealing with school maladaptation that will increase the likelihood of effective outcomes.

As we have already suggested, a preferred theoretical approach is to design school environments that promote adjustment in the first place. But this option was not available to us in 1957 when PMHP started. Indeed, at that time, although we sensed that school maladjustment problems were extensive and serious, we lacked a good framework for categorizing them. Accordingly, our first focus was to develop techniques for systematic early identification of school maladaptation. This step was not taken in isolation. Rather, as a result of it, we hoped to reach a clearer understanding of the magnitude of school adjustment problems as the basis for exploring interventions to help youngsters who were already identified as problems.

SUMMARY

This chapter has presented a conceptual matrix from which the PMHP experiment evolved. The full matrix did not exist before the project; rather, it evolved slowly as the latter itself developed. Viewed retrospectively, PMHP can be divided into three major historical periods. The first five years (1958–1963) were devoted primarily to developing procedures for early identification and to exploring a primitive program of early secondary prevention. During the second period (1964–1969), nonprofessional child aides (i.e., housewives) were trained for roles as human service helping agents with identified, early-maladapting primary graders. In the third period (1969–1973), the model developed over the preceding ten years was polished, refined, and extended on a system-wide basis to a number of schools in several school districts in Rochester, New York, and the surrounding county. The final period also witnessed the dissemination of the model to school districts in other geographic areas of the country.

Chapter 2 presents a cross-sectional overview of the current PMHP—i.e., a global summary of the project as it now exists. The rest of the book is devoted to a more detailed consideration of the history and evolution of the project as well as its specific procedures. Throughout the book, but especially in Chapter 8, PMHP's research findings are woven into the main narrative. Hopefully, this approach will provide readers with sufficient concrete, practical information about the program to start similar projects of their own and at the same time enable mental health professionals and students to form searching, data-based impressions about PMHP's procedures and effectiveness.

2

An
Overview
of PMHP

In its early days, PMHP was relatively easy to describe because it was located in only one school. Currently, the project is located in 17 schools in four school districts in the greater Rochester area: the Rochester City School District (RSCD) and the three nearby county districts of Fairport, West Irondequoit, and Rush-Henrietta, New York. It is thus far from a homogeneous entity, and program specifics differ considerably from school to school. The project's common elements are its shared goals and philosophical objectives and new, structurally similar ways of using school mental health personnel. PMHP's detailed implementation varies appreciably across settings because different schools face different problems and have different orientations and resources. Thus today's PMHP can best be described as a federation of like-minded programs, each with its own personality and profile.

For this reason, no simple descriptive account can fully portray PMHP. This chapter describes a composite PMHP —in one sense, it is an illusory account because the pro-

gram does not exist in that precise form in any single school. Nevertheless, it will help to provide the reader with an approximate cognitive map of the entire program from the start. Later in the book, some exceptions to this composite will be noted.

Since its inception, PMHP has included two interdependent components—service and research. The service component in turn has had two basic elements: (1) screening for and early detection of school adjustment problems among primary grade children and (2) helping interventions in which nonprofessional child aides, supervised by school mental health professionals, work with children identified through screening as being at risk. The research unit has developed screening procedures and has evaluated the effectiveness of various project interventions; the latter function has included critical assessment of the program to identify and reinforce effective procedures and to modify or discontinue ineffective ones. Service and research components have thus contributed in mutually supportive ways to PMHP's aims of identifying and alleviating school maladjustment.

The two main program components are reflected in PMHP's organizational and personnel structure. The central PMHP staff includes five people: a director (ELC), who is also a professor of clinical psychology at the University of Rochester; a chief psychologist (LDI) and a chief social worker (MAT), both initially school district employees who are now primarily employed by the project and share responsibility for supervision of personnel and service operations in the field; a research coordinator (RPL), also a clinical psychologist at the University of Rochester; and a community liaison representative (RVI), a "girl Friday" who is charged with public relations, budgetary, and administrative planning responsibilities. Others who extend this core group include professional school mental health consultants, doctoral and postdoctoral trainees in the helping professions, research associates and technicians, and secretarial and clerical help. The central project staff is housed in the University of Rochester Center for Community Study—a converted mansion located about one and one-half miles from the university's main campus. This building is the center for PMHP's training and research operations. A private nonprofit citizens' group, incorporated in the State of New York as PMHP Inc., serves as the project's fiscal coordinating board and contributes to its long-range planning. The community liaison representative is the main link between staff and corporation, although the latter two meet together regularly.

Close working relationships have been developed between project staff and representatives of participating school districts. At the school level, the project's basic staffing pattern is as follows: two schools share the services of a school psychologist and school social worker. The amount of professional services available in a particular school depends upon the resources of the parent district. On the average, about ten hours a week per professional is available to each school, with considerable variability. Typically, professionals who staff PMHP are experienced school psychologists and social workers who receive additional specialized training from PMHP staff to enable them to function in the project. The central project staff and school professionals are jointly responsible for the selection and training of nonprofessionals, who receive focused, time-limited training before they start to work as child aides. Each pair of schools has the half-time services of about ten carefully selected and trained nonprofessional child aides (mostly housewives). Depending on the school's style and profile, other school personnel who are actively involved in PMHP may include principals, teachers, lunchroom monitors, custodians, crossing monitors, reading and other special teachers, nurses, and attendance personnel.

When arrangements have been made with appropriate school district administrators and school personnel to locate PMHP in a school, the program begins with the assignment of the mental health professionals. Professionals then become actively involved in a series of steps that collectively can be thought of as "greasing the skids." This includes briefing school personnel (especially teachers) and parents about PMHP's objectives and procedures. As much information as possible is communicated during this early period to give prospective participants the clearest possible picture of PMHP's operations and to encourage their early interest and involvement.

Early detection, a critical element of PMHP, includes several basic components. Shortly after the start of the school year, the school psychologist administers a test battery consisting of intellectual and personality screening instruments to small groups of first grade children. In the initial PMHP prototype, a full-time school social worker interviewed parents of all first grade children. But current shortages of social work staff make it necessary to restrict such interviews to children at risk (i.e., those being considered for referral into the program). In addition, data are collected systematically from teachers about specific children in the primary grades who have early school adaptation problems. Two screening devices are now widely used for this purpose; both are brief, objective, behaviorally oriented, and can be related by the teacher to day-to-day problems that she sees in children in the classroom. These two devices are the AML (the letters refer to aggressiveness, moodiness, and learning problems), an 11-item quick-screening instrument that requires only about 20 to 30 seconds per child to complete, and the Teacher Referral Form (TRF), a 41-item behavioral screening measure that depicts, in greater detail, aspects of the child's everyday classroom functioning and problems. These measures provide information concerning the frequency and severity of three major clusters of classroom maladaptation: aggressive–acting-out behaviors; shy, timid, withdrawn behaviors; and learning problems.

Thus relatively early in the school year, typically within the first three months, a body of information is available to school mental health professionals pertaining to the family background, school adjustment, and test performance of first grade children. Similar information concerning school adjustment is also available about other primary grade children considered appropriate for PMHP's services. Specific referrals to the program are then generated. Although the teacher is the prime referral agent and perhaps 85 to 90 per cent of all referrals come from her, other people are also actively involved in this process. For example, school principals, reading teachers, nurses, and, in some instances, parents have referred children. At times, school mental health professionals are invited into the classroom to observe the child's behavior directly as part of the referral process.

When all background data have been gathered and a referral has been made, relevant personnel come together to review the available data and make specific plans for the child. The sources of information available at such an assignment conference typically include the child's first grade screening battery; the social worker's report of the interview with the parent; the teacher's screening instruments, with additional relevant comments she has made; and summaries of interactions with parents, teachers, principals, and other school personnel associated with the child. The purpose of the assignment conference is to put together as complete a picture of the child's difficulties as possible in order to work out the most appropriate intervention plan. In some instances, all that is called for is discussion between school mental health professionals and teachers or parents to clarify the child's situation and to make recommendations about how best to handle it. This usually happens when some lack of understanding on the part of a teacher or parent seems to be the key factor in the child's difficulties and when, by correcting this source of difficulty, a more effective school situation can be developed for him. In most cases, however, the decision is for the child to begin a series of contacts with a child aide to overcome his school adjustment problems.

Before reviewing what child aides actually do with children, we should describe briefly who the aides are, how they have been trained, and what they are prepared to do. Most child aides are housewives, selected primarily because they are warm giving women who are interested in and able to work with children. They started to work in PMHP about ten years ago, after our initial early identification studies demonstrated that children who experienced moderate to severe maladaptive problems needed help to survive in school. This fact challenged us to develop an approach that geometrically increased the reach of helping services. Since there was no possibility of doing this with professionals alone because such personnel were in short supply, we chose to train nonprofessionals as help-agents. Considerations involved in that decision are described more fully later. At this point, we only need to emphasize that the aide program rested heavily on selection rather than training inputs. Thus we selected women with good helping reflexes and provided them with focused, time-limited training designed to meet two objectives: (1) catalyze a way of thinking about children and their psychological and educational needs and (2) cut the keen edge of the anxiety that many of these women felt about the prospect of entering a heretofore sacrosanct professional domain. In other words, aides were not trained to be junior psychiatrists, psychologists, or social workers; rather, they were women whose life-styles, experiences, personalities, and interests already qualified them for helping roles with young children having trouble in school.

After screening information has been collected and assignment conferences have been held, aides begin to see the children. This is done in a variety of ways. Modally, children are seen twice weekly outside of class for 30-to-40-minute sessions during the school day. Some youngsters are seen once a week or less frequently; others are seen as often as three or four times a week. Most aide-child contacts are individual, although some children, especially shy, timid, undersocialized ones, are seen in groups. A common element that characterizes aide-child interactions is the presence of a committed human relationship. That concept, however, is misleading because it masks the considerable diversity of aides' activities with children. Aides use those modalities with which they feel most comfortable. Thus some describe themselves as "arts-and-craftsy" types; others, as "puppety" or "expressive-media" types; and still others, as "fun-and-games" types. With aides, children have an opportunity to be themselves, unfettered by the constraints of the classroom situation; to express their concerns openly; and to work through the educational, personal, and family problems that relate to their school adjustment difficulties.

What the above description really says is that the women selected as aides are chosen for their good "helping reflexes." They are given relatively little formal pretraining and much of their growth and development comes from on-the-job experience and both formal and informal supervision. School mental health professionals supervise the aides regularly, although the frequency and format of supervisory contacts vary as a function of professional styles and available time. Throughout the school year, the central project staff provides multipurpose school consultation for professionals, aides, and other school personnel. Some visits feature clinical case consultation in which children with especially difficult or interesting problems are considered in detail. Other visits deal with concerns that school personnel have about their roles, relationships with staff, or program effectiveness. Often the consultant visits with other school personnel, such as principals and teachers, to get their perspectives on the program and the problems they are having.

Thus PMHP rests on an ongoing educational process for all school personnel. It does not simply focus on a few maladapting children; it provides an opportunity for all school personnel to learn more about children's problems of adaptation and about approaches that will optimize the adaptation of the many. Schools that house PMHP for a period of time report that they reap broad benefits. For example, principals have commented that the school atmosphere improves. They cite data indicating that disciplinary actions such as suspension and expulsion have decreased or stopped altogether. Several principals perceive as PMHP's greatest benefit the enrichment of the classroom teacher through her contacts with professionals, aides, and consultants. Through such in-depth exposure, teachers learn what makes children tick and how best to intervene with them. Such learning translates meaningfully back to the classroom in terms of more effective teacher management of children's day-to-day problems as they occur in the natural situation. To the extent that this happens, it is indeed a desirable outcome because, by its parsimony and naturalness, it is an important step toward the ideal of primary prevention.

After the child has been seen by an aide for a while, typically around midyear, progress evaluation conferences are arranged to review what has been happening. Such conferences generally include the aide, mental health professionals, the teacher, and other school personnel who have information about the child's original problems and the progress he has made with respect to them. The main aim of the progress conference is to review the child's interactions with his aide to determine the extent to which these contacts have helped to reduce his problems. It is important for teachers to be at the progress conference to provide needed input about the child's class adaptation. Although a child may progress well in the relatively sheltered interaction with an aide, such progress must be measured against the harsher criterion of whether generalized gains also show up in class.

The progress conference, for children who are doing well, can be quite brief. Its main message may be either to terminate aide contacts shortly or to continue on the same course a little longer. However, if the child is not making good progress, either with the aide or in class, several critical questions must be posed, including whether the child needs services other than those PMHP can offer and whether such services are available. Also, when appropriate, revisions in tactics and strategy may be considered to increase the likelihood that the original objective of reducing the child's difficulties will be met. Although progress conferences are very useful, their scope and depth are limited by the resources the school has at its disposal.

At the end of the school year, termination conferences are held to review children's progress in PMHP and to make recommendations for the future. These meetings, like referral and progress conferences, are attended by those who have meaningful input into the child's situation. Thus mental health professionals, aides, teachers, and other school personnel are involved in such conferences. Various alternatives are considered during the termination meeting: termination, continuation in the program for another school year, or a "wait and-see" decision that allows for additional contacts with the aide, perhaps only for a limited period, if the child's future behavior suggests that such contacts are needed.

Although the foregoing skeletally describes PMHP's direct-service components, it does not fully describe the project. To those direct-service activities, several program-maintaining functions can be added. The central PMHP staff, for example, monitors a network of contacts with school and district administrators. Thus staff consultants often spend time with principals to review the program's progress and to consider its operational problems. Periodic progress meetings with groups of principals are held to encourage discussion about their impressions of the program. Project staff also meet regularly with district administrators to discuss the program's staffing and operation and to plan concretely for its future. Recently such planning has focused on the steps needed to permit school districts to be more autonomous in conducting the program.

PMHP staff has also conducted some half- or full-day teacher workshops to provide an in-depth view of the project and its mechanisms. One approach we have used calls for each school to select its own teacher-participant for the workshop. As a result, each school ends up with one staff person, i.e., a teacher who is sufficiently familiar with program details to serve as a resource person for others in her school.

PMHP staff participates in the initial rooting of programs in schools. Informational presentations are provided for school personnel who know little about the project. In addition, PMHP staff conduct parent meetings, often through PTAs, during which information about the project and its objectives is presented and parents' questions about the program are discussed. These activities are part of an effort to get PMHP off on the right foot from the start. PMHP staff and corporation members have often participated in school budgetary hearings, not only to protect the project's vested interests, but also to provide citizens and taxpayers with an idea of its scope and effectiveness. This is an important step since PMHP must compete with many other worthy projects for the limited funds available to school districts. It must, therefore, account for and represent its activities so that informed decisions can be made about allocating moneys.

The latter point highlights one of PMHP's most important realities. The project exists in a world of shrinking educational resources and thus has a tenuous fiscal footing. Its survival depends not only on obvious considerations such as its effectiveness but also on its ability to compete with other programs for scarce resources. PMHP Inc., a nonprofit citizens' support group, has been a vital force in this survival process. It has spearheaded the public relations and fund-raising activities needed to assure the project's continuity and expansion. Without such a broad, active base of support, the project could not have continued, no matter how useful its research findings showed it to be.

PMHP significantly modifies the role of the school mental health professional. Much less of his time is spent in direct clinical services with children, and much more of it goes into educational, consultative, supervisory, and re-source functions. For example, the PMHP school mental health professional has frequent contacts—some formal, some informal—with principals, teachers, aides, and other school personnel about children and their development. This way of operating is part of PMHP's basic approach, and much of the learning that results from the project derives from a network of informal contacts. Although re-moving the professional from many of his direct service contacts with children could easily be misinterpreted by some as heralding professional obsolescence, it would be incorrect to do so. The professional's role is not bypassed in PMHP, it is changed. Hopefully, this change leads to more socially utilitarian long-range outcomes such as being able to reach far greater numbers of children effectively much earlier in their school careers before their difficulties are compounded and become overwhelming.

Thus a core PMHP aim from the start has been to expand geometrically the reach of helping services. A re-cent review of our four-year record (1969–1973, a period of expansion) provides an index of our success in this effort. On the average, PMHP brings intensive helping ser-vices to about 11 per cent of the primary graders in the schools in which it is located. This is about a 1,000 per cent increase in services rendered, in comparison with tradi-tional school mental health delivery systems. Recalling the data cited by Glidewell and Swallow (1969) that roughly 30 per cent of American school children today experience moderate to severe school adjustment problems, PMHP brings service to a substantial proportion of that group, even though more needs to be done. Moreover, the project provides extensive services, averaging 30 to 35 contacts per child per school year. Data to be considered later describe the effectiveness of these services and point to options for modifying and expanding them. The combination of in-creased reach and effectiveness of services is appealing.

Viewed in pragmatic, cost accounting terms, it suggests that for an approximate 40 per cent increase in program costs, a 1,000 per cent increase in effective services can be purchased. If, as a result, society can cut back on later social problems such as delinquency, addiction, and confinement to mental hospitals, which are extremely costly in both human and economic terms, the cost of prevention is truly a bargain.

Research is a second integral component of PMHP. Early empirical findings documented the extent and potentially negative consequences of untreated school maladjustment. These studies clarified the need for expanded services and the potential value of using supervised nonprofessionals to meet that need. Equally clear, however, was the realization that program services had to meet the needs of referred children effectively. Among the prime causes of the failures of traditional mental health delivery systems cited in Chapter 1 has been the erroneous assumption that providing treatment automatically alleviates a problem. As PMHP began its intervention, it relied heavily on the clinical experience and best guesses of its founders for evaluation. The project's earliest strategies for identifying problem children and for intervention by aides were based largely on their face validity—i.e., on what seemed to make good sense. One major goal of PMHP's research has been to determine systematically what does and does not work so that the former can be reinforced and the latter modified or eliminated.

Because PMHP's initial interventions were at best only first approximations of a maximally efficient, responsive, child aide program, a multipronged research effort was needed. Various aspects of screening, referral, consultation, and direct service were considered legitimate focuses for research because we expected major research findings in these areas to translate into constructive program modifications. Thus a symbiotic relationship has existed in PMHP between service and research. Service points to research needs, and research findings are fed back into modified, improved service.

PMHP's many facets have been researched extensively. Although the findings are discussed in detail later in this book, especially in Chapter 8, we can briefly summarize them here. Much time and effort have been invested in developing brief, objective, mass-screening instruments for detecting early school maladaptation. Factor analysis of such measures has yielded a clear picture of principal referral clusters and has made possible the systematic study of the different project experiences and outcomes of children with different referral problems. Process analysis studies have clarified the overall nature of the interaction process and differences across various referral and outcome groups. We have studied in detail the personal and attitudinal characteristics of aides, their interests, criteria for their selection, variables related to the effectiveness of their performance, and changes in aides as a function of their participation in PMHP. There have also been a number of practical PMHP studies: for example, the effects on outcome of seeing children few versus many times per week or for long versus short periods of time.

The central question, Does the PMHP approach work? has been extensively researched from many perspectives. We have not only examined the broad question of PMHP's differential effectiveness for children with different problems, but we have done such studies more specifically on the basis of sex, socioeconomic status, and city or county residence. We have, when appropriate, replicated and directly compared such data to those reported for non-PMHP children with similar initial adjustment problems. Our focus on outcome has included both short-term global studies and long-term follow-up evaluations of project and nonproject children. Such studies have had major methodological and interpretive problems; these too are considered in a later chapter.

The points to be emphasized in this preliminary overview are that research has indeed been very basic to PMHP and that the project's solid underpinning of research is an important aspect that differentiates it from many other worthy school mental health projects. Through research we have gained important information about the program's strengths and weaknesses. This in turn has enabled us to modify and improve the program. Although much research is still needed in many areas, at least sufficient data are available to permit others who are interested to make informed judgments about the project's value.

The main objective of Chapter 2 has been to provide an overview, however fuzzy and tentative, of what PMHP is about and how it operates. At this point the reader will hopefully have a broad cognitive map of the program, even though he will still have many specific questions about details. The remaining chapters are designed to flesh out these bare bones.

The emphases to be kept in mind in reading further are PMHP's overriding commitments to early detection and early secondary prevention. The project is predicated on the view that identifying school adjustment problems as soon as possible and responding immediately and constructively to such problems will greatly maximize the likelihood of positive gain. Mass screening is the key to early identification, and the use of nonprofessional child aides is the key to early geometric expansion of helping services. PMHP assumes that early resolution of problems simultaneously increases the likelihood of effective school adaptation later and reduces the probability of adverse personal and social outcomes in the future. If this is so, the project meets several crucial individual and social objectives. In living the philosophy that "an ounce of prevention is worth a pound of cure," PMHP thus offers a genuine alternative to traditional school mental health delivery systems.

3

PMHP's
Early
History

Chapter 1 considered some broad strategies for approaching present-day unresolved mental health problems. Although PMHP evolved in part from a felt need to explore such new approaches, the project's rationale was not yet clearly developed when it started. In truth, PMHP began primarily as a result of two recurrent clinical observations. First, teachers often reported, on the basis of their personal, everyday classroom experiences, that children's difficulties did not seem to be equally distributed. A small number of children (perhaps two, three, or four out of a class of 28 or 30) required from 40 to 60 per cent of the teacher's attention and extra help. This observation is similar to data on industrial accidents, which suggest that about 75 to 80 per cent of such accidents occur to about 20 per cent of the industrial work force. The fact that a relatively small number of children usurped disproportionately large amounts of the teacher's time had three negative effects. First, the children in question were not profiting from school; they were mired in an educational rut. Two, their disruptiveness and the heavy demands they placed on the teacher's time also prevented the rest of the children in the class from getting the most out of their educational experience. And, third, for teachers, the extra demands for time and attention and the distractions from other classroom duties were exasperating. Thus one crucial early challenge was: What can be done to help the two, three, or four significantly maladapted children that one can expect to find in almost any primary grade classroom?

Another observation that encouraged PMHP's initial development was the report by many school mental health professionals that numerous youngsters with serious behavior and personality problems were being referred from the upper grades, particularly at the transition point between elementary and high school. Sufficient services were rarely available to meet these late but sometimes urgent calls for help. After-the-fact examination of the school records of these youngsters suggested that their current difficulties, far from springing up suddenly, often merely capped earlier school problems that had been unattended or ignored. This clinical observation led to a more formal survey of the cumulative school records of preadolescents referred for services in the period preceding entry to junior high school. The survey, in many cases, turned up evidence from prior school records of histories of adaptive difficulties or failure in school that went back as far as third, second, first grade, or even kindergarten. Either helping resources for these youngsters were not available earlier or people had hoped that the problems would eventually vanish. Instead, however, the difficulties often fanned out and became more entrenched, only to surface in more serious forms later.

These two sets of problems converged. On the one hand, many youngsters had been spotted who already seemed headed for disaster very early in their school careers. And beyond that, because school adjustment problems tended, like lead poisoning, to cumulate over time, there was a pile up in the demand for intervention at the transition point between elementary and junior high school. An obvious reaction when one grasps these realities is to say: "We need more help!" Although this need is understandable, rarely if ever can it be met. Society in general and schools in particular lack sufficient resources, using traditional delivery systems, to bring effective help to the many who need it. Given the finite nature of society's pool of resources, hiring 100 more psychologists and social workers might have solved Rochester's problems, but it would only have created 100 vacancies for professionals in other communities. Moreover, the likelihood of financing a solution that depends upon the massive addition of professionals to one's staff does not differ appreciably from zero. A more promising alternative was to concentrate the limited but available manpower at the primary grade level in an effort to identify and alleviate children's early adaptive problems. Hopefully, by so doing, later, more drastic, time-consuming troubles might be short-circuited. We recognized, given the finite nature of our resources, that to locate all services in the primary grades would require a reduction in service for the upper grades. This was a calculated but, we believed, worthwhile risk.

After this formulation had evolved, a grant application for a pilot program of prevention in the primary grades of a single elementary school was submitted. The key structural element of the plan was to use a full-time mental health team (consisting of a school psychologist and social worker) in the primary grades of one school. Although we recognized that this was an atypically rich professional saturation, it nevertheless seemed desirable in a pilot exploration to have the richest possible program, including research. We received a small grant from the New York State Department of Mental Hygiene, and with additional outside support, the first PMHP prototype got under way in 1958. Its major objectives were to develop methodologies for the early detection of school dysfunction and to test the efficacy of a prevention prototype.

During its initial five years, PMHP was located in the primary grades of a single elementary school. All developments reviewed in this chapter took place in that school. The neighborhood was very much like Rochester at large, ethnically and racially, except for some underrepresentation of black and Jewish children. The school was neither a middle-class school nor a disadvantaged inner-city school; its socioeconomic makeup was predominately upper-lower class. It was selected primarily because the project psychologist and social worker were assigned there and because there was enough space for the project.

As noted previously, the grant provided for the full-time services of a psychologist and social worker for the primary grades of the program school. A small amount of traditional school mental health services for the upper grade levels was provided by a second professional team, starting in 1960. Two geographically contiguous and demographically comparable schools were selected as controls to provide a framework for evaluating the program's effectiveness during its first three years.

EARLY DETECTION PROCEDURES

Psychological Testing

At the time PMHP got under way, RCSD children were not formally evaluated until the third grade, except for a first grade reading readiness test. Unless a child was referred for detailed individual study, the only estimate of his ability or psychological status during the first three school years came from the teacher. We believed that earlier and more systematic information was essential for a prevention program. Accordingly, a test battery was developed, including the California Test of Mental Maturity (Short Form) to estimate ability and the Goodenough Draw-A-Man Test to assess adjustment status. These tests were administered by the PMHP psychologist to small groups of ten to fifteen first grade children, usually during October. The testing was done directly in the classroom with teachers serving as proctors. While the psychologist administered the battery, he also recorded his observations of individual children's behavior. The purpose of this evaluation was to provide a preliminary gross assessment of the child's academic potential and emotional status as a guide for further programming. The psychological test data were routinely discussed with the school social worker before her interviews with parents and, when appropriate, with other school personnel including the teacher.

Social Work Interview with Parents

Another important aspect of the early detection project was to establish meaningful contacts with parents, promptly. Accordingly, the school social worker made arrangements to interview mothers of all first grade children soon after the start of the school year. Such contacts were designed to bring the project to the parents' attention and to elicit information about the child's background and family that might help in dealing with evident or incipient problems before they became more aggravated. With these objectives in mind, the PMHP social worker sent all parents an appointment letter signed by her, the psychologist, and the principal. The letter briefly indicated the purposes of both the project and the interview. Every attempt was made to find a mutually convenient time for the interview. If mothers failed to respond to the letter or could not come to an interview because they were working or for another valid reason, a sincere effort was made to reschedule the appointment at a more suitable time.

Before starting the interview, the social worker familiarized herself with the child's project folder, which by then included identifying information, a description of the family structure, comments made by kindergarten teachers, results of reading readiness tests, health and attendance data, and the psychologist's test findings and behavioral observations. Thus diagnostically meaningful data were available to the social worker, permitting her to follow up and to seek clarification as appropriate during the interview.

Interviews were structured for mothers as part of a standard get-acquainted procedure and as a reflection of the team's interest in learning more about the child. If the social worker knew about or suspected that the child had problems, she did not typically bring them up unless they were first introduced by the mother. The major purposes of the initial social work contact included: (1) establishing an early relationship with mothers of first grade children, (2) gathering background information about the child and his family, (3) giving mothers a chance to express attitudes about the school and the child's education, (4) explaining to mothers the school's educational goals and the role of the team and the project, (5) encouraging mothers to feel free to contact the school or the team at any time about their concerns with respect to the child's educational, emotional, or social well-being, and (6) formulating tentative casework impressions about the child.

Beyond those broad objectives, the social worker also sought to obtain the following information during the interview: the child's health and developmental history; his attitudes toward eating, sleeping, and toilet training as well as family practices concerning these matters; interaction patterns among family members, particularly those involving the child; the child's relations with siblings, playmates, and others in the community; the parents' perception of the child's school functioning and adjustment; the parents' own education, background, work history, and attitudes; and the parents' goals for themselves and their children. At the end of the interview, the social worker wrote a summary for the child's confidential PMHP folder that included specific notations about unusual or foreboding indicators if present. If a mother spontaneously expressed concern about the child's or family's problems, the social worker discussed possibilities for longer term helping arrangements and, if asked, cooperated in working out a referral to an appropriate treatment facility. An effort was made during the PMHP's first three years to interview all mothers of first graders, and this goal was largely achieved.

Red Tagging

Available screening information (test data, social work impressions, teacher reports, and classroom observations) was then reviewed and evaluated by the team, and a diagnostic-prognostic judgment was formulated for each child. Initially, this was an arbitrary, binary judgment to place the child in one of two mutually exclusive categories: "Red Tag" or "Non-Red Tag." The term Red Tag designated children who already showed moderate to severe problems of school maladaptation or seemed likely to show such problems in the near future. About one-third of the total sample for three consecutive-year groups was so classified. All other children were classified as Non-Red Tag, meaning that they were progressing normally or there was no specific indication of maladaptive behavior (e.g., if a child was not well known, if his family had not been seen, or if he had only recently entered the school). No matter how arbitrary and fallible the Red Tag judgment was, it provided a crude framework for focusing preventive efforts and tracking children's progress in the primary grades.

EARLY PREVENTION PROCEDURES

Consultation

PMHP's initial preventive approaches were the precursors of current, more elaborate formats. School mental health consultation was a key element in the original prevention program. After all test data had been collected and the parent interview had been completed, consultative conferences between the school psychologist and social worker and teachers, particularly first grade teachers, were set up. The main purpose of such meetings was to permit teachers to consider, in depth, children with serious adaptive problems about whom they were most concerned. Typically, children were discussed in the order of apparent need. During a single school year, the team thus discussed as many as one-third to one-half of all first grade children with teachers in depth. During these meetings the team shared pertinent information with teachers and helped to clarify objectives and concrete plans for the children. When appropriate, recommendations about specific ways of working with these children in class were offered. The consultative sessions gave teachers a chance to raise problems of classroom management and to consider aspects of the role demands of being a teacher. An effort was made to create an atmosphere that encouraged teachers to contact the team at any time for needed feedback or information. Open lines of communication between team and teachers thus developed in a climate of a shared interest in children. There was a strong orientation toward the importance of early identification of children's problems and toward doing something constructive to resolve them as soon as possible.

Consultative contacts were not limited to teachers. As circumstances dictated, other school personnel, ranging from principals, attendance teachers, and teachers of special subjects to lunchroom monitors and school nurses, also participated in such sessions. Among the main benefits of this early consultation were that it helped teachers to recognize and understand young children's classroom behavior problems better, and it enabled them to apply this new information in the service of more effective classroom management in general.

Another aspect of early consultation deserves mention. At the teacher's invitation, the team and the consulting psychiatrist often observed children directly in the classroom. These observations served two purposes. They permitted the consultant to "see for himself" specific children about whom teachers had serious concerns (often the teacher had already submitted some objective information about the behavior of these youngsters). They also enabled him to overview the total classroom situation and the teacher's classroom style. The consultant then met with the teacher to discuss his observations; suggest more effective management techniques; and provide feedback that might make for a more satisfying and effective classroom situation. The consultative role, so basic to PMHP's early preventive thrust, remains a central focus of the current expanded project.

After-School Activity Groups

Even in PMHP's earliest days, it was already apparent that many children had serious behavioral or educational problems. Additional services were not available for those youngsters, even though they clearly needed immediate help if they were to profit from school. Accordingly, the decision was made to establish several after-school activity groups to provide a relationally based corrective experience for children with early detected dysfunction. The judgment that a particular child might profit from such an experience was made jointly by the mental health team and the teacher, based on currently available data and impressions.

Several teachers were chosen as activity group leaders. The group selected was characterized by such qualities as genuineness, a sincere interest in children and their problems, a demonstrated ability to work effectively with emotionally or socially deprived children, and being a good mother or father figure. Before the activity program began, group leaders were given resumés of the children's backgrounds and a description of their current problems, as viewed by teacher and team. On this basis, preliminary goals were established for each child. During the course of the activity group sessions, leaders met regularly with the team to discuss their observations and impressions of children, to assess progress, and to make suggestions and recommendations for the future. These conferences provided the team with additional information that helped them work out optimal class placements for the children for the next school year.

The group program included in-school activities, such as woodworking, soap carving, arts and crafts, cookie baking, and games as well as occasional outside trips. The groups met for an hour a week after school for 20 weeks. Group membership was confined primarily to second and third grade children, known by the team, through screening, early identification, and consultation, to have significant class adaptation problems. This early activity-group program has historical significance as the precursor of the later child aide program, which began in 1964.

Teachers' and Parents' Meetings

There were two separate discussion series in the early PMHP: one for teachers and one for parents. Both series were designed to increase understanding, not only of the project, but also of topics such as mental health, personality development and functioning, and children's emotional and psychological problems. Topics for the teacher meetings were selected jointly by the team and a teacher committee. A year's schedule included about 12 sessions on matters such as the socioeconomic and ethnic structure of the neighborhood, problems created by differing standards in the school and community, applications of mental hygiene principles in the classroom, the consequences of emotional deprivation, the mental health of the teacher, children's attitudes in school, classroom management, and indicators of anxiety in children. This forum gave teachers a chance to upgrade their background and knowledge in several key substantive areas and to discuss, in a group format, issues relevant to understanding children and classroom management.

Parallel with the teachers series, meetings were also held for parents, who were invited by letter to attend a series of six prescheduled coffee hours. The purposes of these meetings were to provide parents with a better understanding of children's emotional and psychological development and an opportunity to discuss these areas more fully. The meetings were held once every two weeks for three months, using a "buzz session" (small discussion groups of ten or twelve, with one member as the recorder and, later, full-group interchange) plus discussion. The meetings were led by project staff and consultants with expertise in particular areas of parent education. Meetings lasted about two and one-half hours. Discussion topics included discipline, social relationships, the changing role of parents, attitudes toward responsibility and authority, and sex education. The meetings were targeted for parents of first to third graders. Attendance at these sessions ranged from a low of about 25 on the evening of a particularly heavy snowstorm to a high of about 70.

Research Evaluation

The first PMHP evaluations centered around two questions: (1) What are the effects of the early detection and prevention programs? This involved comparing children who participated in the program for three years to youngsters from demographically comparable, geographically contiguous control schools with traditional school mental health services. (2) What differences, if any, are there after three school years between Red Tag children (i.e., those with early detected dysfunction) and their Non-Red Tag (normally adapting) peers? Whereas the first question involved comparison of experimental and control children, the second focused on two groups of children within the project school.

To answer either of the above questions, a set of assessment procedures by which comparisons could be made had to be developed. Since these criteria changed somewhat during the initial evaluation period, only the final battery that evolved is described here. We wanted this to be a broad-based battery reflecting a variety of measures for assessing different areas of functioning. School records were used to estimate the child's actual performance. This cluster of measures included the number of times he had been referred to the school nurse during his third year and cumulative nurse referrals for his first three school years; attendance data, measured as total days absent; report card grades, consisting of the average of the child's grades in major subjects; a series of five achievement test scores, including reading comprehension and vocabulary, arithmetic reasoning, concepts, and computation; verbal, quantitative, and total IQ test scores; and an achievement-aptitude discrepancy score based on the difference between the child's potential, as defined by his IQ, and his achievement, as defined by report card grades.

Rater's judgments comprised a second group of evaluative criteria. These included a 17-item Teacher Behavior Rating Scale, reflecting such characteristics as dependency, immaturity, disruptiveness, worrisomeness, and moodiness, which yielded both a total behavioral maladjustment rating and a single overall maladjustment score. In addition, the project psychologist and social worker submitted adjustment ratings for all third grade children—a judgment of the child's current and/or expected level of difficulty.

Several measures were used to evaluate children's behavior, including the Children's Manifest Anxiety Scale (CMAS) (Castaneda, McCandless & Palermo, 1956), a self-report measure in which the child responds yes or no to a series of questions such as: "I get nervous when someone watches over me" or "It is hard for me to keep my mind on anything." The CMAS includes Lie-Scale items that indicate how trustworthy the child's responses are. Another self-report measure was Bower's Thinking About Yourself (TAY) test (Bower, 1960). This measure contains a series of descriptions concerning specific attributes of young children. The child indicates the extent to which each of these actually describes him (self-concept) and how he would like to be with regard to each (ideal self). The discrepancies between these ratings is taken as an index of self-dissatisfaction.

The last evaluative measure was a sociometric device, Bower's Class Play (CP) Test (Bower, 1960). Children are asked to imagine that a hypothetical class play is being produced. A series of roles, half positive and half negative, are identified. The child's task in Part I is to make a free sociometric choice listing all the children in the class whom he would nominate for each role, good or bad. Several scores are derived from the class's cumulative patterns of nomination. For example, the total number of times a child is designated for any role is a "visibility" estimate. Since total nominations include both positive choices (liking) and negative choices (disliking) of peers, the test yields an estimate of the child's sociometric popularity. Part II of the CP test includes 30 sets of four multiple-choice role options, each with two positive and two negative roles. In ten of the 30 items, the child selects the role for which he considers himself to be best qualified; in another ten, the role for which he believes the teacher would nominate him; and in the last ten, the role for which he thinks peers would nominate him. Once again, both positive and negative estimates are derived from the child's perception of how others view him.

This array of school record, observer rating, self-report, and sociometric measures comprised the total evaluative battery used, both to assess the effects of the experimental prevention program and to contrast early school careers of Red Tag as opposed to Non-Red Tag children. Two such comprehensive evaluations, based on consecutive independent yearly samples, were carried out (Cowen, Izzo, Miles, Telschow, Trost & Zax, 1963; Cowen, Zax, Izzo & Trost, 1966a). Although the initial study (Cowen et al., 1963) yielded several fragmentary findings that suggested direct or indirect program benefits, its data were basically equivocal. The second investigation (Cowen et al., 1966a), however, had internally consistent, significant, interpretable findings. Thus direct comparison of the experimental children, who had been in the prevention program for three years, and their controls identified a cluster of differentiating measures, each significantly favoring the experimental group. Program children had fewer referrals to the school nurse, higher report card grades and achievement test scores, superior achievement in relation to their aptitudes, lower self-rated anxiety, and teachers' behavioral ratings that indicated better adjustment. This set of differences straddles diverse measures and covers a broad spectrum of the child's functioning. Moreover, sev-

eral other directional but nonsignificant differences between groups supported the preceding findings. Overall,
this evaluation strongly suggested that the prevention program had successfully met several important educational
and behavioral objectives.

Data from this same study, comparing the early school
careers of Red Tag versus Non-Red Tag children, were
even more compelling. At the end of the third school year,
Red Tag children were functioning significantly more
poorly than Non-Red Tag children on many school record
measures (including attendance and nurses' referrals) and
performance measures (including report card grades,
achievement test scores, and achievement-aptitude discrepancy scores). Moreover, behavioral and adjustment indexes—including behavior ratings made by teachers and
mental health professionals and peer sociometric ratings—
yielded similar findings, which supported the firm conclusion that Red Tag children had gotten off to an extremely
poor start in all areas of school functioning.

Although the initial prevention program was gross and
ill formed, two important conclusions emerged from the
second study: (1) the prevention program had significant
positive effects on several critical dimensions and (2) early,
ineffective functioning in school was widespread, affecting
roughly one out of three primary graders. Moreover, without intervention, the dysfunctions of these children had
visible, miring consequences by the third grade, and the
likelihood of chronic school failure among such children
was considerable.

We did not consider these findings to be definitive.
They did, however, suggest that we were on the right track
and thus established a hunting license for further, more
intensive inquiry. We understood relatively little, then,
about which program elements contributed actively to children's positive development or how this happened. What
emerged more clearly from the early research was the real-

ization that school maladaptation was a massive problem and that early correctives were needed for many children if they were to profit from future school experiences. Although there was thus some satisfaction about what had been accomplished, there was no smugness about it. Indeed, the experience served mostly to whet our appetites and to put our future challenge into sharper focus. Now that school maladapting youngsters could be accurately and rapidly located and the serious early consequences of early school maladaptation had been better documented, what could be done to reduce school casualties and to increase the likelihood of an effective school experience for the many?

4

Enter
the
Aide

FACTORS LEADING TO AN AIDE PROGRAM

Much was accomplished during the initial phase of the project. A method for systematic early identification of school maladaptation was developed which showed that roughly one out of three primary graders was experiencing moderate to severe school adaptation problems. Moreover, a prototypic program for early secondary prevention was evolved, with demonstrably positive effects.

If the finding that one out of three school children was maladapting was accurate, then in an intermediate-size district, such as the Rochester City School District with 40,000 children, an estimated 13,000 might need help to profit maximally from their school experience. This awareness underscored the need to expand helping services in the schools geometrically. The inevitable downward spiral that resulted when help was unavailable had to be stopped. No matter how promising the original work in early detection, Caplan's (1964) warning remained: even the most effective of such procedures is limited in value unless backed by resources to repair the dysfunction.

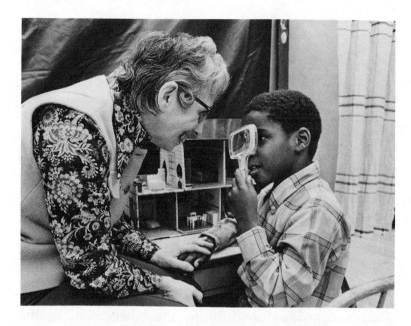

The further PMHP developments described in this chapter can best be understood in the context of the climate of exploration that existed in the early 1960s. In 1961 the Joint Commission on Mental Illness and Health issued its report, *Action for Mental Health,* establishing a blueprint for mental health programming for the next 20 years. Two aspects of that report particularly influenced PMHP developments. First, there was George Albee's (1959) documentation of the professional manpower situation in mental health, which identified widespread and serious shortages in all fields. Albee estimated that such shortages ranged from 25 to 75 per cent, depending on whether minimal or ideal standards of care were used. Second, growing demand for services from institutions and settings that had not previously used them was increasing the strain on already limited resources. These stark facts led to the Commission's recommendations that the mental health professions should adopt and practice, a broad liberal philosophy of what constitutes, and who can do, treatment within the framework of their hospitals, clinics or other professional service agencies. . . . [and] that non-medical mental health workers with aptitude, sound training, practical experience, and demonstrable competence should be permitted to do general, short term psychotherapy. . . . Such therapy, combining some elements of psychiatric treatment, client counseling, someone to tell one's troubles to, and love for one's fellow man, obviously can be carried out in a variety of settings by institutions, groups and individuals . . . [pp. ix–x].

In short, the joint commission paved the way for the use of other than traditionally trained professional mental health workers as help-agents.

The joint commission's recommendations simultaneously reflected and encouraged a variety of innovative explorations of the use of nonprofessionals in human service. Among the earliest of these projects was the pioneering work of Umbarger, Dalsimer, Morrison & Breggin (1962) in which college students were used as help- and socializing-agents with chronic hospitalized schizophrenics. Similarly, Holzberg and his associates (Holzberg 1962, 1963; Holzberg, Knapp & Turner, 1967) carried out a related project using college undergraduates as help-agents with chronic schizophrenics. Holzberg et al. sought to identify the discriminating characteristics of student volunteers and how these changed as a result of participating in the program (Knapp & Holzberg, 1964; Holzberg, Gewirtz & Ebner, 1964). At the Philadelphia State Hospital, subprofessionals (usually college graduates) received brief training to function effectively in a state hospital milieu-therapy program (Sanders, 1967; Sanders, Smith & Weinman, 1967). In a substantively different but conceptually related program (Reiff & Riessman, 1965; Reiff, 1967;

Riessman, 1967; Riessman, Cohen & Pearl, 1964), the use of indigenous nonprofessionals as help-agents in neighborhood store fronts proved to be an effective means of providing services to many needy inner-city people who would not otherwise get help.

Another intriguing development, highly relevant to our situation, was an exploration at the National Institute of Mental Health (Rioch, Elkes, Flint, Usdansky, Newman & Silber, 1963; Rioch, Elkes & Flint, 1965; Rioch, 1967), where a group of housewives was trained to provide psychological services, particularly psychotherapy. In Rioch's program, a small group of well-educated women from the Washington, D.C., area received part-time training (about 32 hours per week) for two years to prepare them as therapists. These women acquired considerable knowledge and skill, as demonstrated by the fact that they scored higher than psychiatry residents on the Psychiatric Board Examination. After training, they were successfully placed in settings ranging from mental hospitals to outpatient clinics to schools and functioned effectively. A follow-up study of Rioch's original group of housewives (Magoon, Golann and Freeman, 1969) presented data demonstrating that these women continued to work effectively and productively in mental health positions three years later.

A related program (Donahue and Nichtern, 1965; Donahue, 1967) recruited and trained housewives in a suburban school district to work individually and in small groups with severely disturbed (e.g., schizophrenic and brain injured) children within the school system. These women worked effectively as volunteer teacher-therapists of children who could not profit from the regular school experience—a major accomplishment, in that these severely handicapped youngsters would otherwise almost certainly have failed. Thus a program manned by part-time nonprofessionals enabled severely disturbed young children to return to and function reasonably well in a regular class.

Project Re-Ed (Hobbs, 1966, 1967, 1969; Lewis, 1967), conceptually related to Donahue and Nichtern's work, was also targeted for young children with severe emotional problems and significant school maladaptation. In Re-Ed the help-agent was a specially trained teacher-therapist, and the intervention was based on a short-term residential stay. Once again, research data (Hobbs, 1966; Weinstein, 1969) indicated that a program manned by other than traditional mental health specialists brought significant help to maladapting children.

One final project bears specific mention because of its rigorous experimental evaluation. Poser (1966) compared the effectiveness of naïve, 18-year-old college undergraduates versus trained mental health professionals as group workers with chronic hospitalized schizophrenics. Based on an elaborate test battery, including perceptual, verbal, and motor-coordination measures classically used to assess schizophrenics, Poser showed that the students were *more* effective than the professionals with these patients.

From our vantage point, there was much to be learned from this innovative and intriguing set of developments. For one thing the range of potential uses of nonprofessional help-agents seemed almost limitless. It had already been shown that college students, housewives, and relatively uneducated, indigenous neighborhood residents could work effectively in this capacity. Furthermore, programs staffed with nonprofessionals had apparently been helpful for a variety of target groups, including chronic hospitalized patients, elementary school children, and inner-city ghetto residents. These programs involved groups that had had little prior access to or effective help from mental health professionals. Thus it seemed that mental health services *could* be expanded geometrically by using nonprofessionals as help-agents, with parallel changes in professional roles.

Faced with the challenge that one out of three primary graders had moderate to severe school maladaptation problems and that few professional helping resources were available to deal with them, the prospect of using non-professional help-agents was appealing. Thus the results of innovative experiments in the use of nonprofessionals prompted us to reexamine traditional assumptions about what is required for one person genuinely to help another. Such requirements had typically been defined in terms of IQ, educational background, specific course work, particular types of supervised clinical experience, and advanced degrees. The mental health fields had long been wedded to a guild view of help-agents, which required that necessary "rites de passage" be negotiated. A modest amount of reflection on the dire need gave us reason to question this traditional view. One obvious point of challenge came from the base of human experience that all people share. Everyone at some time finds relief or help through the words, actions, or understanding of persons other than mental health professionals. Certainly many personal problems, including serious ones, are resolved that way. Furthermore, although all mental health professionals are highly intelligent and have extensive training and experience, they are not equally effective as help-agents. And even the most sophisticated, well-executed interventions of mental health professionals are less than 100 per cent effective.

But overriding all our other concerns was the gut realization that even if the collective efforts of the mental health fields were 100 per cent effective clinically, they were still highly restricted in the critical social sense. In other words, it could be said in 1963, as it can be said in 1975, that society's mental health problems are far more attributable to what has *not* been done than to what *has* been done and how. This point bears strong emphasis, given the vocal argument of some professionals that it is dangerous or irresponsible to entrust people's well-being to nonprofessionals because they may do things that seriously or irrevocably harm others.

As we groped with these concerns in the early sixties, it became more and more admissible that variables such as personality characteristics, interest patterns, life-styles and prior experience could be as or more important than traditionally defined professional credentials in determining whether one person could genuinely help another. Although we were less than 100 per cent certain of this view, the extent of school maladjustment, the lack of resources for dealing with it, and the encouraging findings of the programs cited previously moved us to explore the use of nonprofessionals as help-agents with maladapting primary graders.

Since our targets were to be young children with school adjustment problems, the first "species" of help-agent we decided to use was the housewife. We assumed that many housewives had relevant, prior experience with children that could meaningfully translate to helping interventions with maladapting primary graders. In selecting an initial group of six child aides in 1963–1964, a process described in greater detail later, we exercised all conceivable biases consistent with the thinking summarized above. Thus we looked for characteristics such as warmth, empathy, seeming effectiveness in interpersonal relationships with adults and children, psychological-mindedness, strong interest in children, and evidence that the women selected had been effective mothers with their own children. However, in selecting our initial group of trainees, we deliberately snubbed the traditional criteria of education and advanced degrees.

Our first training program was also consistent with the views thus far expressed. Since we were prepared to go with the life-styles and natural reflexes of these women, we made no attempt to transmit a talmudically sacred body of knowledge or to develop a concentrated mini-Ph.D. program! Thus the program differed from Rioch's earlier project involving housewives in several important ways.

First, by selecting women on the basis of their personal qualities rather than extensive prior education, we hoped to expand the help-agent population. Second, the projected training experience was much more compact than Rioch's, again reflecting our willingness to bank on lifestyle and experiential variables. Third, training did not prepare the women for roles as psychotherapists; it prepared them to act as help-agents with young maladapting primary graders.

The training program for the first group of child aides consisted of six weeks at less than half time. Some major substantive areas touched on during training included principles of child-development, behavior and adjustment problems in children, early blocks to learning, and parent-child relationships. Material was not, however, presented in an academic lecture format. Rather, topics such as those just listed, following limited initial input, became the focus of searching discussions. Classroom observations and film-viewing sessions were also an integral part of the first curriculum. Each session was followed by discussion of the events that the trainees had witnessed. Two critical goals of the compact training sequence were less than obvious. One was to sharpen or catalyze a way of defining, thinking about, and approaching children's problems. The second, even more important one was to blunt the keen edge of the anxiety that these women understandably were experiencing because they were about to tread on sacred terrain previously reserved for mental health professionals.

THE AIDE PROGRAM

With the preceding abstract as a basis, more detail about the program's pivotal features can be presented. In the fall of 1963, PMHP moved from its original location to a new school, which housed the project for its next five years: i.e., stage two, during which the child aide concept was piloted and developed. The new school was set in a large gerrymandered district that contained students from a broad range of racial, ethnic, and socioeconomic backgrounds.

Selection of Aides

Although it was possible to visualize the broad profile of an aide program, its precise details could not be specified before the fact. Typical of the general statements that could be made beforehand was that the aide would use her interpersonal skills in the classroom to help children profit from their educational experience. But that platitude reflected little more than our initial vague ideas that, 1) aides should be stationed right in the classroom, and, 2) when children were not doing well, aides could interact with them either individually or in small groups. We also considered it likely that aides would have to take a child out of the classroom if he couldn't profit from what was going on or was disrupting others. But whatever the mechanism of interaction, our hope was that aides would work with children in ways that would ultimately help them to adapt effectively in the class.

This vague "job concept" left many unanswered questions for aides, for teachers, and those running the program, both before the program started and indeed throughout its entire first year. For the moment, however, it was sufficient for all concerned that the globally defined purposes of the program were accepted and applauded. All agreed that the program was desirable, at least in principle, as a way of helping children to find a more effective school experience.

Aide recruitment was the first problem. Our conviction, based on knowledge of the local community and current experiments in the use of nonprofessionals elsewhere, was that effective part-time aides *could* potentially be found among the vast pool of mothers who, because their children were now independent, were looking for a socially contributory activity of their own outside the home. Although many of these women had previously worked as volunteers in diverse settings, during the early 1960s (and even today) professionals tended to use them in routine, menial, "less important" activities rather than as central help-agents in mental health programs.

Because we lacked experience in programs using nonprofessionals and because we intended to work closely and intensively with the new aides, we decided to limit the program to a small pilot group of six women. To avoid a massive screening procedure that would involve much work, result in turning away many good applicants, and possibly create public relations problems because many women would have to be rejected, we decided to prescreen by circulating a "Help Wanted" flyer to a small number of mental health professionals at the University of Rochester and the RCSD. The announcement described briefly the attributes and characteristics of the type of woman we thought would make an ideal child aide. Such an announcement would enable professionals to call the program to the attention of a small number of suitable candidates from among their friends, neighbors, and acquaintances, and in the process enable them to do some informal prescreening that would bring us well-qualified applicants.

The announcement said only that a small group of women would be trained for a new program in early detection and prevention of school adjustment problems in primary grades. Duties were described sketchily, emphasizing that aides would serve as "an extra pair of hands" to help teachers provide hyperactive, withdrawn, periodically upset, or underachieving children with the extra attention they needed to adjust better in school. We said that aides would work half of each school day, five days a week, and that we would pay the modest sum of $25 per week for these services. The attributes of the women being sought were described as follows:

> The woman we would like to recruit should possess a personal warmth and liking for children, in connection with which the experience of having successfully reared children of her own would seem to be an important prerequisite. In addition, flexibility, genuine commitment to the type of work we describe, a life situation which would permit her to devote the necessary time to the project, and an interest in the school situation would also be important. Hopefully, the person would herself be relatively free of major personal problems. These attributes would be valued above formal education.

This procedure attracted some excellent candidates, 11 of whom were interviewed. During the screening period, an instructive incident occurred. Unintentionally, the "Help Wanted" announcement fell into the hands of a local minister, who published it in his weekly church newsletter. Within two days we received about 75 phone calls from potential applicants. This suggested that the pool of women who were interested in such work was indeed large.

The women interviewed were seen first by a team including one of two University-based, program-connected clinical psychologists and an advanced clinical psychology trainee. These loosely structured one-hour interviews sought information and impressions that permitted the interviewers to rate applicants on a series of 21 seven-point scales reflecting personal, social, intellectual, and attitudinal qualities. Ratings included judgments about how much the interviewer liked the applicant and the estimated likelihood of her success as a child aide. Interviewers also listed what they considered to be the applicant's major assets and limitations.

Applicants filled out a form, describing themselves, their husbands, and their children with respect to factors such as age, education, employment history, interests, hobbies, skills, group affiliations, health, and personal goals. Applicants were asked to state their reasons for applying for the position, what they hoped to get out of participating in the program, and what they considered their assets and liabilities for such work to be. The rating scales and application form helped to orient the interview and, later, to familiarize the staff with the women's backgrounds and interests. After the initial screening interview, the most promising candidates were interviewed again, this time by the chief psychologist in the project school. If he concurred with the initial interviewer's judgment, the applicant was accepted for the program.

The six women who were finally selected ranged in age from 26 to 58. Although three had some college training, none had a college degree. All were mothers who were judged to have reared their own children successfully, and none of them appeared to have a need to compete with or supplant the teacher in her role as an imparter of knowledge. On the contrary, their interest in the program seemingly stemmed from a genuine desire to work directly with and to help young children in need.

Preparation of Aides and Teachers

A six-week, part-time training program was developed to provide child aides with (1) some background in relevant psychological areas; (2) an appreciation of several basic concepts, such as psychic determinism and the importance of early experience in personality development; and (3) an opportunity to ease gradually into the classroom situation and the actual role of aide. Fundamentally, however, we were banking heavily on the aides' personal and experiential qualities as the program's most potent resource. Thus the training was primarily designed to provide emotional and intellectual support and to help assuage the feeling that aides were being thrown into an arena without weapons or tools.

The first week of training included a presentation of material on the mental hygiene movement, manpower shortages, and the need to augment society's helping resources. In the second week the earlier history of PMHP was described. Six two-and-one-half-hour sessions, spread over the first four weeks of the program, were devoted to material on personality development, behavior disorders, and parent-child relationships. The only other didactic sessions involved two later meetings that oriented the women to the schools and the elements of teaching. These sessions, conducted by the team, the teachers, and the principal, gave aides a clearer understanding of classroom routine, the teacher's role, and also some rudimentary teaching skills. In all training sessions, materials were presented informally in a discussion-oriented, issue-centered manner. The approach encouraged aide participation and discussion to sharpen ways of thinking about children's adjustment problems in the schools.

A second major component of the training program involved the use of clinical materials and case discussion. This started in the second week of training with a film called *Unconscious Motivation*. During the third week another film, *The Quiet One*, was used in one session, and aides spent another morning observing children directly in several classrooms. The films and observation sessions were followed by discussion of what had been seen, what it might mean psychologically, and what actions and interventions aides might use to help the children in question. During the last two weeks of training, there were more classroom observations and discussions as well as meetings in which the team presented actual case reports of children's school adjustment problems for discussion. A child psychiatrist, who served initially as consultant to the project and later as a resource person for the aides, participated in these sessions. During the last week, aides were assigned to classes and were encouraged to participate in classroom activities. Each classroom contact was followed by a meeting with the team, during which the aides' observations and impressions were aired in detail and possible actions and interventions were considered.

While the aides were being selected and trained, PMHP staff met several times with the school principal and the six primary grade teachers to orient them to the program. The principal was most receptive, and all six teachers expressed a willingness, at least in principle, to be in the program. Indeed, this was the reason for deciding to recruit six aides. Though understandably a bit anxious about how things would actually work out, the teachers seemed genuinely accepting of the program's concept. Subsequent events, however, suggested that some of their acceptance and initial enthusiasm may have been attributable to social pressures implicit in the situation. All six teachers were under 30 years of age, two had tenure, one was a third-year probationer, and three were in their first year of teaching. Thus, for four teachers, there were real situational pressures, both because they were still evolving their own roles and because they had attendant concerns about being observed and evaluated. This was so despite numerous attempts to assure them that teacher evaluation was not our function.

Just before the program actually started, a meeting was held with the teachers to consider role conflicts that might arise between them and the aides. The teachers were encouraged to maintain their role as the person in charge of the class and to define clearly the limits within which the aide should function. It was emphasized that these limits might vary from teacher to teacher and that there would undoubtedly have to be some arbitrariness in making such decisions. This point was grasped better intellectually than emotionally, as will soon become clear when the teachers' impressions about the effectiveness of the initial program are reviewed.

During the aides' two-week school orientation period, the principal, teachers, team, and consultants met with them frequently at lunch to discuss the morning's classroom observations. A recurrent theme during these "brown-bag" sessions was that since we were all entering uncharted territory together, suggestions from all participants were not only welcome, they were essential. At these meetings the principal spoke of his philosophy of education, his goals for the school, and some of his approaches to teaching. Teachers described and further explained classroom activities about which aides still had questions. In addition, they provided more information about children whom aides had singled out because of their behavior or group interactions. We thus sought to involve teachers from the start by including them as sources of essential information concerning the children's educational adjustment status.

The program that was about to start was clearly "iffy" for the aide, since it simultaneously depicted her as "another pair of hands" for the teacher and as someone whose personal makeup and/or training provided her with unique skills for working with maladapting children. Our first attempt to resolve this ambiguity emphasized that the teacher would continue to be involved with the maladaptive child, but the aide's presence would free the teacher to teach the entire class while the aide worked more intensively with children experiencing special problems. We hoped that teachers would thereby see the program as a joint mental health and educational effort and would recognize their own important role in it.

Initial Program

As we look back, the fact that aides' contacts with children did not begin in the project school until March 1, 1964, seems fortuitous. Some of us—not the aides—had serious reservations about starting the program so late in the year because the summer recess was nearly upon us. Nevertheless, this trial run was important because it served a critical "shakedown" function. With relatively little explanation as to why aides were suddenly in the class, children responded almost intuitively to their presence. Even so, many problems—some anticipated, others not—arose for aides, teachers, principals, and the mental health team. All these problems had to be resolved. Roles and relationships had to be defined, worked through, and redefined before the future of the aide program was assured.

Aides were assigned to each primary grade teacher for a half-day, five days a week. Teachers were to use aides in ways that were most helpful to them. Aides were free to interact with children in ways that made them most comfortable—keeping in mind the program's goal of helping children educationally and interpersonally. The children quickly accepted the new format. Those who needed help as well as those who were just curious flocked to the aide in the back of the room to bid for her attention. One aide reported feeling overwhelmed by so many children coming to her and surrounding her at her table. (One or two children occasionally followed her to the powder room!)

Aides worked quite independently, comforted by the knowledge that they could turn at any time to the team for support, advice, or discussion of any aspect of their work. The team, sometimes with the consulting psychiatrist, also conducted regular weekly supervisory and discussion meetings for aides. Supervisory sessions were built around review of specific interactions between aides and children and, inevitably, between aides and teachers. Aides thus had ample opportunities to discuss issues concerning interaction and intervention with children and to clarify their own roles, options, and problems. Similar, though less regular meetings were held with classroom teachers. The teachers' first reactions to the program, although no less vehement than the children's, were less positive. Although some found the program's lack of structure to be challenging, the sentiment of most is captured by the following comment made by one teacher: "We've learned a lot by allowing the program to be free-wheeling and vague. We've found out what *not* to do very quickly."

As the program evolved, teachers began to impose more structure on their classes. Although all continued, in the abstract, to laud the program's lofty objective of helping children, a majority of the teachers began to complain that the aides' presence in the class was, at the least, somewhat disruptive. They argued that an aide, if stationed in the class, should not simply be a loving-mother surrogate; she had to be part of the educational process by helping children to learn to read, for example. Several teachers established a class rule that the children must finish their work before they could talk to an aide. One teacher insisted that children must first come to her with their problems and that she would then decide with the aide what should be done. Clearly, several of the teachers were threatened by the new program, and in those situations restrictions were imposed on the children's spontaneous interaction with aides. Because the teacher was responsible for maintaining order and aides were not primarily involved in classroom limit-setting, some children began to see the aide as the "good mama" and the teacher as the "bad mama." As one aide sagely observed: "We have taken something that belonged to the teacher from her—the part of her that is warm and maternal."

As a result of these early "returns," the team initiated a series of teachers' meetings as a forum for airing concerns about the program's progress. These sessions provided an opportunity for ventilating, expressing dissatisfaction, and offering suggestions for changes in the program. Teachers spoke of the problems of maintaining discipline and of competition with aides for the children's attention and affection. They talked about the polarization of the two adults in the room. One teacher reminded us that primary grade teachers, too, had maternal needs, and indeed that was why many chose to teach at the primary grade level. Several likened the aides' continuous presence in the room to having a "constant visitor observing you in the home, from whom you cannot escape." One teacher confessed to having the uneasy feeling that the aides might know more about child development than she did. She was sorry that teachers hadn't had similar training in this area—one that is largely overlooked in teacher preparation.

One consultant speculated that several of the younger teachers found it difficult to have a "mother" sitting in the back of their rooms. To someone recently out of college, the term mother could connote both experience and "sitting in judgment." At the very least, it was clear that some teachers felt that the aides either did not understand or did not support the teachers' disciplinary or limit-setting responsibilities. Overall, the teachers felt strongly that the program should be restructured so that the aides would be working with children outside the classroom.

Separate meetings with the aides indicated that they too had role confusions and concerns. Were they tutors, baby-sitters, or mental health aides? Aides felt that the children had responded well but that teachers were at best lukewarm to them. One aide said that the children had accepted her overwhelmingly, but although the teacher genuinely tried to accept her, she basically resented the aide's presence and found that it interfered with her teaching. This made the aide feel guilty about her close ties with the children. In practice, the teacher only allowed acting-out children to approach the aide and reprimanded others who tried to do so. What the aide sensed, in some measure, was that certain children were being "punished" for having contact with her. More generally, most aides were concerned that the teachers wanted them to relate to children primarily about school work. They felt that this inhibited their contacts with children at the "feeling" level. A specific example of this was the report by some aides that teachers saw the aide's role primarily as one of providing enriching academic experiences for children by bringing in magazines and other materials not provided by the school.

Thus, although aides found their new job challenging and in many ways rewarding, it was also frustrating, and it gave them the feeling of "being in the way." Occasionally, an aide was asked to take over the class to give the teacher a "break." Not only did they feel ill-prepared to do so, but they also felt that this role further blurred their image by forcing them to assume group disciplinary responsibilities. When asked directly how sensible they considered it for them to be class based, they agreed unanimously that this was not sensible because it promoted both role confusion and rivalry between teacher and aide. Thus, like the teachers, but for different reasons, aides also recommended that the project's mode of operation be changed. They felt that teachers should first identify children who needed help, that the aides should then observe the children briefly in class, and that ultimately the aide-child contacts should take place outside the classroom. It also seemed essential in everyone's eyes that ways be devised to improve communication, the exchange of ideas, and discussion of mutual problems between aides and teachers.

Aides indicated that their biweekly meetings with the team, which gave them a chance to speak freely and to share their frustrations, had been critical in helping them to weather the first year. Such meetings had also offered them practical on-the-job training and had served as an important vehicle for personal growth and development. Aides found that their vocabularies were expanding. Although case review and supervisory sessions were initially perplexing to some aides—especially when there was no prearranged topic and the discussion lagged, by the end of the year they agreed that they had learned much about children and themselves, that they had "grown" considerably, and that they had come far in learning to "listen with the third ear."

A check of the aides' activities several months after the program started showed that although aides were theoretically charged with promoting the well-being of all children, they were, after the novelty of their presence in class had worn off, spending most of their time with relatively few children. In most cases, these were the children previously identified by teachers and the team as having the most serious adaptive problems. Although aides occasionally did help children at their desks with school work, they spent most of their time in the back of the room with individual or small groups of children, chatting, reading to them, playing games, or working on classroom materials. Similar activities took place when an aide occasionally took a child out of the class to a vacant room or for a walk.

As we assimilated this first round of feedback, it became clear that we had taken some false turns. Both teachers and aides had independently come to the conclusion that the aides' prime base of operation and the focus of their ongoing contacts with children should not be in the classroom. Another point that became apparent was that we had brought the aides into the school with considerable ballyhoo and fanfare. Thus they had received intensive specialized training about the emotional well-being of children and, in the teachers' view, had been given expertise and know-how that the teachers themselves would have liked to acquire. Eventually, it registered that what we had failed to do was to create an atmosphere in which teachers and aides could feel they were working toward the achievement of common shared goals concerning children's well-being, sound development, and educational progress. To put it bluntly, the way we had engineered the program had encouraged justifiable "paranoia" on the part of the teachers. This awareness led to an important restructuring of the aide program; one that governed its operation for the subsequent decade.

Revised Program

Discussions with the principal indicated that he agreed with the converging suggestion of teachers and aides that the latter could better work with children outside of class. Although this would necessitate finding space—a precious commodity—he thought this could be done by judicious use of various nooks and crannies in the building. Up to that point, the team and secretary had been sharing a large drafty classroom, which had a small anteroom used for interviewing. The aides had no "home base" in the building—only a dark cloak room where they hung their coats.

As part of the proposed change in program format, the principal offered to convert an unused classroom into PMHP's headquarters in the building, with offices for the team and a secretary, a conference room, and a waiting area. The waiting area was also to serve as a center where aides could congregate. Things were indeed looking up! Further discussions involving teachers and aides led to a new set of project procedures. Teachers would first select the children about whom they were most concerned. They would then discuss them with the team to determine their suitability for referral. After that the teacher and team would meet with the aides to discuss educational and mental health goals and formulate an intervention plan. Following this newly initiated "assignment conference," aides would observe the children in the classroom before initiating individual contacts with them.

It was evident from their constructive suggestions that teachers wished to be part of the helping process with referred children. Our hope was that by having the teacher and aide meet together with the team to discuss and plan for a child, everyone would be on the same team instead of in separate polarized camps. Teachers also suggested that periodic evaluation conferences should be held to review the child's progress or lack thereof. All parties agreed that termination of aide-child contacts should be neither unilateral nor precipitous but based instead on a joint decision of teacher, team, and aide. It was also considered essential that termination decisions allow aides enough time to "work through" problems children might have about separation. Assignment, progress, and termination conferences with aides and teachers were to be scheduled as needed and could be initiated by any member of the group. The team would continue its biweekly group meetings with aides and would provide two hours of individual supervision per month per aide, both to optimize the aides' on-the-job learning and growth and to keep themselves *au courant* of developments with the child.

It was also agreed that aides would help children to cope with the realities of the classroom and would support teachers' disciplinary efforts. Since educational materials are the currency of the school situation, it was considered important that children be given direct educational assistance in the context of a meaningful aide-child relationship. Although school work was not to be the only or even prime medium through which aides would engage children, it was to be considered realistically as an important aspect of some children's problems. Finally, teachers also suggested that aides not begin to see children until October. This would allow them time to organize their rooms and become acquainted with their students. September was to be used for program planning and preparation by members of the expanded team, including teachers.

Earlier, we had considered having children seen on an as-needed basis. This would have meant they would have been seen by the aide that was free at the moment. In practice, however, such a procedure would have given "acting out" children priority over other less disruptive children whose long-term need for attention was equally great and would have structured the program in crisis-reactive ways. This plan was rejected; instead, the team assumed the responsibility of assigning children to specific aides, who would see them regularly for 30 to 45 minutes once, twice, or three times a week. This schedule gave aides the option of working two and one-half days a week rather than five half-days. Staggering the aides' working hours was also necessary for efficient use of the limited space available in the school.

Last but not least, we changed the aides' title from Teacher Aide to Child Aide. Since our intent had never been that aides would assist teachers directly, the title Teacher Aide was inappropriate. Mental Health Aide, another title we considered briefly, was one that we thought might frighten parents of referred children unnecessarily or might imply too close an identification with the team. Since the aides' time was primarily to be spent with the children to whom they were giving direct service, we decided to call them Child Aides—a title that "took" well initially and has worn well over the years.

The earliest version of the aide program had thus encountered many unexpected hazards and obstacles, which eventually led to major modification or discard of some of the original preconceived elements of the program. Practice and experience had won out over armchair theorizing! On the positive side, viable staff relationships had been established, the project concept had been accepted, teachers had suggested constructive modifications for improving program operation, and the principal had provided an attractive suite of rooms for the project, indicating his commitment, and had also located new working space for the aides. And notwithstanding evident conflict, some mutual temporary unhappiness, and real limitations of the trial period, the children had nevertheless been helped. Perhaps most important of all, the program's revised structure gave promise that teachers and aides would have a mutually rewarding way of working together and of better serving children's needs.

The second (or first full) year of the aide program began with a new principal, two new teachers, and only four of the original aides. One aide was not invited back; the other, who by sheer coincidence was the wife of the school's incoming principal, had to resign in accordance with the school system's policies. Although lack of adequate work space for aides was still a problem, the aides liked their new schedules and found that working individually with children outside the classroom was very challenging and rewarding. Since the project was the legacy of a former administration, its concept had to be "sold" again to a new principal. His involvement developed slowly because he was new, both to the school and to his job.

We also had to orient new teachers and strengthen our contacts with the entire teacher group. Notwithstanding their strong recommendations about program modifications the previous year, some teachers were still less than 100 per cent enthusiastic about aides taking children from the classroom. A few still had mixed feelings about children being seen regularly by aides; thus scheduling appointments with children was sometimes difficult. Two experienced teachers still wanted children to be seen primarily for academic purposes. On the other hand, several teachers were by now very cooperative and even began to seek out aides between sessions to discuss children's progress with them. The project's attractive new quarters, with their comfortable chairs, became a quiet sanctuary to which teachers could retreat during a "break," at the noon hour, or after school. (We conveniently repress the fact that ours was one of the few areas in the building where smoking was permitted and that this was probably as important to the teachers as the need to talk with us.) Hot water and instant coffee were always available and, not infrequently, aides brought in cookies or pastry. During that second year and later ones, we had a Christmas "open house" and occasional luncheons to which the entire school staff was invited. The teachers came to the project's suite to have coffee, to eat, to smoke a cigarette, to talk about a child, or whatever. The really important fact was that we were developing much more extensive and meaningful contacts with them.

Although the gap between teachers and aides did not disappear completely, communication between the two groups improved noticeably with each step to bring these units of an extended team together. During the second year, we began to consider with primary grade teachers the possibility of having in-service training seminars to help offset their feeling of being left out of the initial aide training. Teachers expressed strong interest in such training, and a committee consisting of one peer-selected teacher from each grade level was set up to explore the matter. In response to a questionnaire distributed by this committee, teachers expressed an overwhelming preference for discussion of case material and films dealing with topics such as discipline, aggression, and the withdrawn child. Noon meetings were proposed and attendance was voluntary. Everyone brought brown-bag lunches and the team supplied the coffee. Attendance was consistently 100 per cent, unless a teacher was absent from school. More than once, the principal had to remind the group that the bell had rung and that teachers had better hurry back to their rooms.

In the third year of the program, we first used substitute teachers to allow regular teachers to meet individually with the team and the aides to discuss children during the school day. No longer were teachers required to squeeze time from their lunch hour or come after school. This procedural change greatly enhanced the project's image as a service that was genuinely a part of the school program. No longer was the program seen as an "extra," a "bother," or something to "take or leave." Teachers looked forward to these meetings, often requested additional time to discuss problems, and became increasingly more involved. They now felt that they truly belonged on the team.

During this same period, the aides were developing rapidly. They benefited considerably, both from the twice-a-month staff meetings and seminars and their regular, biweekly, individual supervisory sessions with team members. The project office was always "manned" by either the psychologist or social worker so that someone was available if the going got rough. We also obtained a small budget to provide aides with activity materials and equipment that was not needed when the program was class based. Aides, thanks in part to these changes and to the increased space made available by the principal during the third year, felt that they too had "arrived." Not only did they feel accepted in the school milieu, but their caseloads had increased to the extent that most were seeing ten or eleven children in a full day. Sometimes this crunch meant that there was insufficient time for note taking, that children were picked up late, and that aides felt less than relaxed. In our eagerness to serve teachers, win their good will, and bring help to as many children as possible, we lost sight of some of the pressures created for aides.

Thanks to better communication between teachers and aides, however, teachers were now initiating contacts with aides and trying to coordinate activities with them, for example, by reinforcing in the classroom the things aides were doing effectively with the children. Although perfect coordination between aide and teacher activities was not always possible, the growing effort to achieve it was reflected in the teachers' more positive attitudes about the program. By then a few children were referring themselves or their friends to the program with their teacher's consent. The project concept had caught fire and became an important part of the school.

During these years, we had many visitors from far-off parts of the country. Teachers were most supportive during such visits, making themselves available for classroom observations, meetings, questions, and discussions. In fact, several times teachers even met with visitors during the summer vacation. In 1967 the Rochester Mental Health Chapter sponsored a workshop dealing with the project at a local suburban school. Invitations were sent to teachers, principals, pupil personnel staffs, nurses, and mental health workers throughout the metropolitan and suburban areas. We expected about 75 participants. Instead there were nearly 300. The program was scheduled from 4:00 to 9:00 P.M. and included dinner at the school. The school principal and several teachers participated with program staff in describing their roles, the use of aides, how school personnel related to the team, and how children were helped. The program was a huge success and served to augment awareness of and interest in PMHP in the area.

The preceding section is essentially an insider's clinical account of some of the vexing moment-to-moment problems and rooting difficulties associated with implementing a new program in new settings. How true it is, to quote Robbie Burns, that "The best laid schemes o' mice and men gang aft a-gley." Establishing a program is not just a matter of developing a good idea or a sound plan. The program's conception and ways of operation must also be sold to consumers, who must see it as relevant to their needs and nonthreatening. And effective, harmonious working relationships must be established between program personnel and other agency staff—in this case, the principal, teachers, and other school personnel. The principal is the host, with all that word implies, in terms of providing space, good working conditions, concern, mediation, and project promotion. But the teacher is the key! If for any reason she lacks confidence in the psychologist or social worker, it matters little how competent the aides are. She can refuse to cooperate, block referrals, or stymie the program in other ways. In fact she can prevent it from ever getting off the ground, particularly if she happens to be a power figure among peers. A first grade teacher in that position could seriously thwart the project's goals. High on the list of teachers' priorities for mental health workers are the ability to understand and deal with issues perceived by teachers as important, prompt service, and good communication. Once credibility is established and effective service is demonstrated, a good relationship between teachers and project staff is likely to develop. Most teachers want to be part of the program, to be included or at least consulted in planning, and to have the professional respect they merit. They want to be treated as colleagues. Being human, they appreciate an interest in them as persons with ideas, problems, concerns, and burdens. They look to the team to be supportive. Given a sound alliance between teachers and the program and well-screened, well-trained, and well-supervised aides, a program of this type should flourish.

Evaluation of the Demonstration Project

The child aide program served as a pilot-demonstration "probe" for four years. Further revisions and modifications of the program took place later when the project changed from a pilot-demonstration program in a single school to a broader system-wide approach in many schools in several school districts. The latter changes will be considered in greater detail later. For the moment we shall report two specific evaluation studies of the original child aide program, done between 1964 and 1969. In the first (Cowen, 1968a), 51 maladapting primary grade children were assigned randomly to experimental groups seen by either child aides or college undergraduates, or to a control group. These three groups were comparable in demographic characteristics and referral problems. The "treatment" groups were seen by either aides or college students for about four months. Teachers' judgments of behavioral change were the prime criteria for evaluating program effects. Thus teachers submitted behavioral ratings for all three groups, tapping both educational and developmental dimensions. The results of the study were clear. Although both experimental groups improved more than the control group, only the group seen by child aides improved significantly. As such it was the most effective of the interventions. The significant improvement in the behavior of children seen by aides, as suggested by the teachers' ratings, was strongly confirmed by the aides' ratings. Indeed the two sets of ratings correlated well. That aides did significantly better than college students was not surprising since they had been working in the school for several years, were well known to school personnel, and had been carefully screened beforehand for their helping qualities. In any case, the study's most important finding was that aides were effective in bringing short-term interpersonal and educational help to young maladapting school children.

The study, however, left open the question of the stability of these positive short-term improvements. Accordingly, a later follow-up study of the adjustment of these same children was undertaken (Cowen, Dorr, Trost & Izzo, 1972a). An interview format was used in this second study, with the mothers of children seen two to five years earlier in PMHP being interviewed by aides. Special care was taken to see that an aide who had worked with a particular child did not interview that child's mother. Thus the interviewers were not known to the interviewees. Generally, the interviews followed an open-ended format. Interviewers narrowed their focus progressively as the interview proceeded to elicit reactions about the following topics, if these reactions did not come up spontaneously: (1) the mother's feelings about the child's need for the project, (2) the project's helpfulness to the child, (3) descriptions of the child's current behavioral and physical status, (4) the child's subsequent educational performance, (5) the child's interpersonal relations with teachers and peers, (6) the child's family and neighborhood relationships, and (7) the child's current happiness or unhappiness.

On the average, the interviews took about one to one and one-half hours. And at the end of the interview, mothers were asked to complete a series of nine seven-point rating scales, each describing an important aspect of the child's functioning. The nine ratings concerned the following: (1) the child's educational performance, (2) how well he was getting along with teachers, (3) how well he was getting along with schoolmates, (4) how well he was getting along with his parents, (5) how well he was getting along with siblings, (6) how well he was getting along with neighborhood children, (7) how happy or unhappy he was, (8) his attitude toward school, and (9) PMHP's inferred role in bringing about any changes observed. The rating "set" for these judgments called for the respondent to report any changes between the time of the child's initial referral to PMHP and the present. While mothers completed the scale ratings, interviewers did the same ratings independently in a separate room. Significant positive change was judged to have taken place in the children seen by PMHP by *both* sets of raters on all but one of the nine rating scales, sibling relationships. Perhaps no method of intervention is sufficiently powerful to improve that culturally hallowed area of conflict.

We were concerned in this study that aide interviewers might be biased in their ratings because of their association with and positive closeness to PMHP. This possibility was examined by comparing the mothers' and aides' ratings in terms of degree of positiveness. In fact, mothers judged that *more* positive improvement had taken place than did the interviewers. This directional difference assuaged concerns about interviewer bias.

The most striking result of this study was its demonstration that the aide program, previously shown to have immediate positive effects for young maladapting school children, had long-term enduring value in several key educational and interpersonal spheres. This finding suggests that aide intervention is more than a momentary palliative; it contributes to the child's long-range school adaptation as well. The significance of this finding is enhanced by the fact that the sample included the most seriously maladapted children in the school. This demonstration of the lasting positive effects of an early intervention program, often lacking in the evaluation of more traditional interventions (e.g., psychotherapy), lends support to the argument that nonprofessionals, if carefully recruited, trained, and supervised, have much to offer in human service helping activities.

The studies cited above write a conclusion to PMHP's second phase. Methods for early identification of school dysfunction and a primitive program in early secondary prevention were developed in the first phase. In the second, the child aide program was initiated and yielded data testifying to the aide's effectiveness. During both phases, PMHP was located in only one school. Thus the project, for 11 years, emphasized the exploration, piloting, and understanding of the attributes and consequences of this new innovative program. By the end of phase two, with the development of sharpened early identification procedures and data on the effectiveness of aides in hand, we concluded that the model was indeed a viable, service-expanding approach. The most important issue to be faced next was how to involve more schools and school districts in it and thus expand geometrically the helping services available to many young children in need. That challenge was the impetus for PMHP's third stage (1969–1973), which is the prime focus of the next several chapters.

5

Preparing
for
Expansion

The project's first ten years built the base of the knowledge and experience needed for its future expansion. During that period, techniques for early detection of school dysfunction were developed, honed, and validated. The child aide role was articulated and piloted and the findings were encouraging. Functions of school mental health professionals were redefined to broaden their helping potential significantly. In effect, the necessary components for expansion had been assembled. The nucleus of a delivery system that offered a clear alternative to past traditional school mental health approaches had been identified. The next step was to move from an isolated pilot-demonstration project to a systemwide approach in multiple settings. Such a step required that we give up the shelter and security of pilot programs and face the real hazards typically associated with introducing new programs into school systems already burdened with tight budgets, competing educational philosophies, and vested interests in other approaches. We learned much during this period about "selling" programs to school districts and personnel and certainly about the fiscal realities of program expansion.

KEY TRANSITION STEPS

An important event relating to PMHP's expansion occurred near the end of the program's second stage. In 1967 the Children's Services Committee of the Rochester Mental Health Council, a local agency charged with mental health planning for this geographic region, appointed a Subcommittee on School Mental Health Services. This group was asked to review existing school mental health services and to develop recommendations for future programming in this area. The subcommittee met with nearly 50 city and county pupil personnel directors, school principals, psychologists, social workers, guidance counselors, teachers, and community mental health professionals. In addition, it gathered information from school systems in other communities and drew upon related data from earlier surveys by the local Mental Health Council. The PMHP pilot program was thus one of many included in the committee's review process, and through a series of meetings with PMHP staff, the committee learned about the project's history, objectives, and ways of operating. The committee was favorably impressed with PMHP's emphasis on the concepts of early detection and prevention, and it perceived the project as a sensible, effective, practical model that reflected those values. Accordingly, the committee's final report strongly endorsed "a broad range of school mental health services to include new and expanded programs for early detection and prevention." Specifically, it recommended immediate expansion of the PMHP pilot project in the local geographic region. The committee's final report was delivered to the Mental Health Council and to representatives of city and county school districts in April 1968.

Thus, at a critical moment in our development, impetus for project expansion came not only from the project itself but, more important, from an impartial community review body.

Unlike many committees whose work ends with their final reports, the Subcommittee on School Mental Health Services was sufficiently attracted to PMHP's approach to remain in existence as an implementing body. Indeed, to jump ahead of the story, as a result of PMHP's perennially complex problems of fiscal management, the committee eventually incorporated in New York State as PMHP Inc., as a way of dealing with such problems. In this role, it has continued over the years its active leadership in the fund raising and public education required for the project's survival and has served as a necessary fiscal intermediary in our negotiations with school districts. The activities of this citizen's group have been vital to PMHP's survival and expansion.

In their newly assumed role, following submission and approval of their final report, committee members met frequently with project staff to develop concrete implementation plans. They were involved actively in decisions about where the programs were to be located in the various school districts and in resolving even more basic questions about how the program would be financed. The broad fiscal plan called for seeking federal grant monies to finance the training of professionals and nonprofessionals, the development of new programs and research, and to obtain school district and local voluntary contributions to support program services.

During the exploration period in late 1968 and early 1969, many school districts in the area expressed strong preliminary interest in starting PMHP-type projects. This task-oriented but idyllic planning period came to an abrupt halt in the spring of 1969, following an announcement by the New York State Department of Education of drastic

cuts in state support for education—a crisis that has re-
curred annually since. The toll that such cutbacks have
extracted from educational programs has been enormous.
As a result, in the spring of 1969 many school districts in
the area were obliged to scrap all new programs and reduce
or eliminate many ongoing ones. Thus school districts,
which had earlier committed themselves in good faith to
starting PMHPs, were obliged to back off from these commitments. There followed a chaotic period during which
both PMHP staff and committee members spent countless
hours in meetings with principals, school boards, superintendents, school mental health personnel, and others trying to "save the pieces." Illustratively, in one 24-hour
period, project staff and committee members spent more
than 15 hours at seven different meetings. An additional
indication of the temper of those troubled times is the fact
that in the spring of 1969, the proposed budgets of 11 local
school districts were consecutively voted down by taxpayers. Indeed, several districts opened their schools in September 1969 without an approved budget and operated
day-to-day on contingency funds provided by the state.
The entire experience was a fundamental lesson in community psychology, underscoring the absolute necessity for a
firm base of community support if a project of this type is
to root meaningfully and survive. Without such support,
PMHP could not have weathered the stormy spring of
1969, during which its major expansion was finally established.

At the risk of departing somewhat from the main
theme, several vignettes can be cited that reflect the tribula-
tions of that period. For example, when project staff and
committee members met in what was to be a final implementation session with one school superintendent and a
school board that had all along expressed strong interest
in having a PMHP program, we were told that they had
been forced to sell three school buses and fire six bus

drivers to help balance the district budget for the coming year. On another occasion, we revisited a school superintendent who had expressed strong interest in the project. When we arrived at his office, it was clear that he was harried and psychologically "beaten." He invited us to sit down and recounted the following apocryphal story:

> There once was a superintendent of schools, a man in his early 50s, who had lived a lewd, lascivious, evil existence. Alas, one day this superintendent was suddenly smitten by a grievous heart attack and died within a matter of seconds. Because of his prior transgressions, there was no question but that he should be sent automatically and directly to Hell! There, he needed only a few seconds to look around before mustering his first response: "Beats being a school superintendent anytime!"

Part of the process of initiating and implementing PMHP in the various school districts involved direct participation by staff and corporation members in school board meetings designed to review district programs and budgets. Several informative incidents, humorous only in retrospect, evolved from participation in such meetings. We well recall, for example, one school board meeting in a county district on a sweltering, muggy July night. We were impressed and pleasantly surprised to find nearly 400 people in the audience for this occasion; indeed, we were flattered that so many knew about and were concerned with PMHP. What we had failed to note, however, was that there was another item on the agenda: a vote on whether hot lunches should be provided for fourth grade students. Apparently, during the earlier spring budgetary review process and voting actions, taxpayers had unwittingly voted hot lunches for fourth graders out of the budget. As soon as this became apparent to them, a ground swell developed to have the item reinstated. The meeting, which began at about 7:30 P.M., was as hot as the weather and far more acrimonious. Threats, veiled and open, were directed to board members who gave any hint of opposing the small, extra budgetary allocation for the fourth grade lunch program. The debate raged furiously for more than three hours. In the end, around 11:30 P.M., the decision was made to put the matter to a new voters' referendum. Once that decision was made, roughly 393 of the 400 people in the room got up and left. Seven diehards, plus a delegation from staff and corporation, were the only people left in the huge steamy auditorium to consider implementing PMHP in the district. As it happened, one of those seven taxpayers was a person whose 12-year-old child had had a tragic personal-emotional history, including school failure. This woman knew about PMHP and was able to relate its purposes to her own child's needs and unhappy history. She argued touchingly that such a project might have "saved" her child. The vote carried, and PMHP was thus installed in a new school district. Perhaps the most important message coming from this experience is the fact that no matter how "precious" (Sarason, Levine, Goldenberg, Cherlin & Bennett, 1966) we believe ourselves to be, mental health problems and services are a long way from the top on the list of priorities of parents, voters, or taxpayers.

A similar experience in another county school district reinforces the point. Not having learned enough from the preceding one, we were once again heartened to walk into a second board meeting, at which PMHP's adoption was a prime agenda item. Again we found several hundred people in the audience. On this occasion, hot lunches were not the competing item. Instead, the issue that had attracted the throng was how the floors of the new high school were to be carpeted. Thus PMHP representatives waited for several hours while broadloom salesmen individually presented their swatches for examination by board members and other interested fellow travelers. After two hours of such fanfare, critical decisions about how to carpet the high school were made. Only after that had happened was it possible to consider briefly the second and clearly less important question of whether PMHP should become part of the school district's mental health delivery system. Once again, concrete evidence of the lack of widespread concern with mental health was made clear to PMHP staff and committee members when scores of people left the room after the carpeting decision had been made.

Thus, during the spring of 1969 and the long hot summer that followed, much of the staff's and the committee's efforts were necessarily directed to budgetary survival. By then it was clear to us that no matter how favorably school personnel viewed the program as an abstraction, money for its widespread implementation simply did not, as had originally been assumed, exist. The committee had carried on a diligent public relations campaign in many districts, which strengthened the climate of "receptivity in principle" to the project. But "brownie points" for approval in principle were less meritorious than the money needed to run the project. Ultimately, through the combined efforts of project staff, the citizen's committee, and school district representatives, a concerted local fund-raising campaign was mounted and turned out to be successful. A base for conducting PMHP in four school districts in the area had been established for the coming school year. Although the project staff was indeed pleased that funds were available to support PMHP's expansion, we were concerned that such a high proportion of the project's service dollars was obtained from non-school district moneys—a consideration that portended ominous future difficulties.

The issue at stake far transcends our project. It is the general problem of the future of educational support and the extent to which federal subsidies are necessary for quality education to survive. Without being unduly speculative, we can cite from our experience some practical considerations bearing on this issue. A project such as PMHP, financed through a variety of tenuous sources, depends for its survival on the temper of key bodies such as school boards, city councils, and county legislatures. When budget is involved, as it always is, it must compete with other projects—be they proposals for driver education, hot lunches, or Astroturf for the high school football field. All such projects have identities, ranging from clear to murky, and more or less vocal constituencies. Programs that lack a clear identity and those without a "following" that will stand up and be counted at critical moments are especially vulnerable. Fund-allocation decisions by local bodies that disburse public moneys are typically determined, not by a project's abstract, theoretical, or scientific merits, but rather by the effectiveness and clout of its lobbying constituency. Distasteful as this fact is to the idealist or the scientist-scholar, it is part of the fabric of reality. Illustratively, of the many logical or empirical "selling points" used by committee members in discussing PMHP with school districts, the most effective was the simple fiscal fact that a special education program for one child for a single school year cost about $3,600, a sum slightly in excess of PMHP's average annual cost per school (Dorr, 1972). Thus we could say to school district policy-makers that if the project succeeded in "saving" one child per year per school from assignment to special education classes for the emotionally disturbed, the project would pay for itself. Of all the arguments mustered in support of PMHP, the fiscal was the most appealing to school district representatives and to board members.

In the end, the expanded PMHP model that evolved served two masters. The first was the committee (soon to become the corporation), which was responsible for the major fund-raising activities needed to float the program's services. The second was the participating school districts, responsible for the school programs, assignment of personnel, and allocation of time and resources. Thus, by the fall of 1969, an expanded PMHP was in operation that structurally bore little resemblance to the earlier pilot demonstration project. Although PMHP staff was now affiliated with four school districts in the area, its relation to them was largely consultative. Figure 1 presents PMHP's new (1969) organizational structure schematically. The project director was now simultaneously responsible both to the administrators of the participating school districts and to the citizens' committee. Three project subgroups were in turn responsible to him: (1) a clinical group headed by the chief project psychologist and social worker and including the chief psychiatric consultant, other project consultants, trainees, and service volunteers, (2) a research group, headed by the research coordinator and including research technicians, graduate, and undergraduate research assistants, and research volunteers, and (3) the community liaison representative, who acted as a bridge between the corporation and the staff in administrative planning, budgetary matters, and public relations.

All these people were centrally located at project headquarters. All others in the organizational chart were school based. The project's organizational structure was more complex in the county than in the city, if only because there were three separate county districts as opposed to a single unified city district. School mental health professionals from the city and county school districts reported directly, within the project, to the chief psychologist and social worker. In addition, they remained directly accountable to their immediate supervisors in their home districts. Although professionals spent different amounts of time in PMHP schools, the practice of pairing schools and of using professional teams was continued in the project's expansion. Thus psychologists and social workers were typically assigned to two schools, each having the services of a senior aide about one day a week and approximately five child

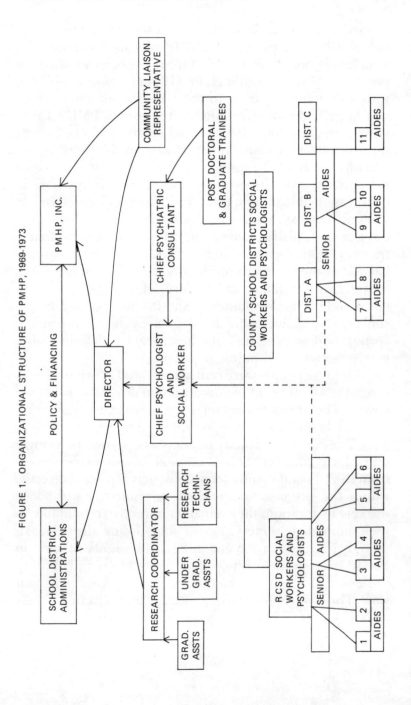

FIGURE 1. ORGANIZATIONAL STRUCTURE OF PMHP, 1969-1973

aides who worked half-time. The organizational chart at the school level thus reflects portions of the school psychologist's and social worker's time, depending on the district's resources, and ten half-time aides for each pair of schools. As things worked out in practice, this meant that psychologists and social workers spent anywhere from one-fifth to one-half of their time in any one school, or twice that amount in each pair of schools.

PMHP's fiscal structure, as implied by the organizational chart (Figure 1), was extraordinarily complex. Roughly 25 per cent of its total budget—targeted primarily for training and research—came through a grant from the Experimental and Special Training Branch of the National Institute of Mental Health. The remaining 75 per cent, targeted for service functions, came from a variety of sources, including (1) the participating school districts, which paid for professional salaries, psychometrists, and substitute teachers, (2) the Board of Cooperative Educational Services, a state agency charged with providing services for pupils in suburban schools, (3) specific grants of some magnitude to support specific PMHP service components (e.g., child aides' salaries) from agencies such as the Monroe City-County Youth Board and the New York State Urban Education Program, and (4) a patchwork of additional support from local voluntary sources in the Rochester area. Although this latter source of support was welcome, indeed vital in assuring the project's immediate survival in the transition and expansion period, most such moneys were short term, tenuous, and nonrenewable. Accordingly, our situation presented a major, ongoing fundraising challenge to corporation members.

As indicated earlier, PMHP expansion happened to coincide with a period variously described in educational circles as the "taxpayer revolt" or the "budget crunch." In such a climate, the citizens committee, later the corporation, was crucial in making the expansion possible financially. As a committee, they were heavily involved in program negotiations and fund raising. Since the moneys they attracted came directly to them rather than to the individual school districts, a "body" was needed to receive and disburse such funds. Initially, such budgeting was handled by the Health Council of Monroe County, which acted as a fiscal conduit. It quickly became clear on several counts, mostly practical, that a separate body would have to be formed to continue receiving contributions and disbursing project-related payments. Thus formation of a nonprofit, tax-exempt corporation became a necessity. Through a series of luncheons and meetings with local community and industrial leaders, committee members explained the rationale and goals of PMHP and gradually formed a ten-member corporation. After the necessary legal steps were taken, PMHP Inc. became a reality and held its first meeting on October 21, 1970.

Since then, the corporation has worked tirelessly to keep the program solvent and to buttress PMHP's efforts to provide needed services to school children in the area. As nonstaff, corporation members have been in an especially good position to present a citizen's view of PMHP and to approach school district, state, and local funding agencies for support. They have also been able to use their personal contacts and influence in the community to attract voluntary financial contributions from businesses and individuals in the area. Without question, the corporation was a major source of support to staff during the trying period of early expansion.

EXPANDING THE BASE

Staff and corporation agreed that the expanded project should have a broad base with respect to the types of schools included, their educational philosophies, and the socioeconomic background of the neighborhood on the assumption that this would make the program more generalizable. In particular, staff and corporation members felt that inner-city schools, where need was presumably greatest and where we had not had prior experience, should be included. Such issues were considered in program-planning discussions with the school districts in 1969.

The expanded project included 11 schools with about 6,500 children—4,000 of whom were primary graders. The schools were indeed quite different in terms of several basic dimensions (e.g., socioeconomic status, size, and makeup). Thus at one end of socioeconomic range was a classic, inner-city ghetto school with a 97 per cent nonwhite enrollment (74 per cent Black and 23 per cent Spanish speaking), whereas the other end included neighborhood schools from relatively affluent suburban districts. The schools also ranged from large buildings with enrollments of 1,000 to small neighborhood schools with less than 150 children. There were pure primary grade schools (kindergarten through third grade) and full elementary schools (kindergarten through seventh grade). The amount of professional time available to PMHP also varied considerably from school to school and from district to district. The most intensively saturated school had a half-time psychologist and social worker, whereas the less well-endowed schools had roughly one-fifth of a professional team's time. Given these major differences in structural and professional resources among participating schools, it was clear that a variety of program adaptations had to be developed. Although we expected that the various programs would share common goals and ways of deploying personnel, we also knew that program specifics would have to vary across settings. Thus PMHP was about to become a confederation of like-minded models, each with its own profile and personality. But before that could happen, a number of key program decisions had to be made.

The first of these, largely structural, concerned the basic program-staffing concepts to be used in the expanded PMHP. The pattern that finally evolved in all project schools was to use portions of the time of a mental health team—i.e., a school psychologist and social worker plus "X" number of aides (approximately ten in most cases) for each pair of schools.

Our first estimates about the amount of nonprofessional time needed were little more than best guesses, based on our experience during the aide pilot project. We were quite sure that we could not have a stable, broad-gauge program if we depended exclusively on volunteers. Volunteer programs would limit the availability of aides to children, create high turnover rates, and require a great deal of training of new personnel. Our intent is neither to demean volunteerism nor to suggest that there can be no place for volunteer aides in programs such as PMHP. To the contrary, there may be circumstances in which volunteer aides are the only possible sources of help and merit serious consideration. This entire issue is considered more fully in Chapter 11. For the moment, however, the important point is that we chose not to go the volunteer route in 1969.

Once the decision was made to hire aides, half-time status made good sense since most of the women in our prospective pool of aides wanted time for homemaking and child-rearing responsibilities. We believed that employing aides on a half-time basis would allow them to be in the schools often and predictably enough to establish stable, continuous relations with the children. As a first approximation, five half-time aides were typically assigned to the primary grades of each PMHP school. To work within the structural organization established for professionals, the basic project units thus became pairs of schools with district-assigned professionals plus ten half-time aides. The main exception to the half-time rule for aides was in the inner-city school, where full-time aides were hired because of the large number of children in need and also because half-time positions were inappropriate for women who had families to support.

Past experience suggested that the program's foundation in a school would be strengthened by a "get acquainted" period before aides began seeing children. This would allow professionals to learn more about the school's needs and ways of operating and to become better known and, hopefully, more trusted by school personnel. Thus professional training and the recruitment and training of nonprofessionals for the expanded project were planned for the period between September 1969 and February 1970, before the program's direct child service activities started. During the six month "tooling up" period, professionals were to prepare schools, orient personnel, set up appropriate referral systems, and arrange space for the project with whatever help was needed from project staff. The last three months of the school year (spring 1970), during which the program was in full action, was a "debugging" period. We hoped that this approach would ready the project for full-scale operation when the schools reopened in the fall of 1970.

The rest of this chapter describes our professionals and nonprofessionals and how they were selected and trained.

PROFESSIONALS: SELECTION, CHARACTERISTICS, AND TRAINING

Professionals were not hand picked for the expanded PMHP. Specific procedures for identifying PMHP professionals varied from city to county schools. In the county schools there was virtually no freedom at all; once a school was chosen as a project school by the district, the psychologist and social worker assigned to that school automatically became part of the PMHP team. These professionals were simply advised by their respective districts that they would be involved in the new program. The situation was somewhat, though not entirely, different in the Rochester City School District. Customarily, each year the district's mental health administrators gave professionals an opportunity to express assignment preferences among schools and special projects. In 1969 PMHP was included on this preranking list. The district professionals ultimately selected for PMHP were chosen from among those who indicated *some* interest in the project; indeed such an assignment varied from a first to perhaps a fourth or fifth choice.

The initial group of 12 PMHP professionals—six teams consisting of a psychologist and a social worker, three assigned to six city schools and three assigned to six county schools—had varied backgrounds. As a group, they were well trained and relatively experienced, averaging 13 years of prior professional work and seven years of prior school mental health experience. All their previous experience, however, had been in traditional school mental health roles.

Given their extensive background and experience, the prime training goals for professionals were to develop a clear rationale for early detection and prevention programs and to communicate as much as possible about the specifics of PMHP as an alternative approach to school mental health services. Professional training meetings were held weekly for six months. An outline of the curriculum was prepared beforehand and distributed to group members. The major topics covered during these meetings included the following:

1. A review of the major aims, methods, and prior findings of PMHP.

2. Current problems facing the mental health fields.

3. The nature and use of conceptual models in mental health.

4. Alternative uses of professional time in the mental health fields in general and in the schools in particular.

5. Systems analysis and modification.

6. Mental health consultation and crisis intervention.

7. The relation of the curriculum and the learning process to human development.

8. A review of specific projects that used nonprofessionals as help-agents.

9. Recruitment, training, and supervision of nonprofessionals. (This unit was the core of "metatraining," i.e., training professionals to train nonprofessionals.)

10. PMHP's actual operations, including specific roles and activities of professionals and nonprofessionals, preparing schools for programs, record keeping, relations with school personnel, and space and equipment needs.

11. Research evaluation of a community program such as PMHP.

For each topic the group was given a series of suggested readings. Curriculum modification and reshaping took place periodically as the group's interests and needs dictated. At the end of the formal training sessions, five additional meetings were added at the professionals' request to consider specific behavioral approaches and their use in the schools as well as the diagnosis and treatment of perceptual and learning disabilities. Informal training meetings with professionals continued on an average of twice a month for the next several years of the program. These later meetings focused on practical program issues such as which children should or should not be seen, the mechanics and problems of record keeping, effective methods of aide supervision and the optimal use of consultation. The meetings also dealt with professionals' concerns about the effectiveness of program components, demands that were seen as excessive, and concerns about specific program elements (e.g., screening for intelligence) that some considered inappropriate or useless.

Professionals varied in their reactions to training. Although most found it useful, conceptually and pragmatically, several were impatient with the training, saw it as "school work," and considered it to be unimportant compared with the real, important business of getting the program underway.

NONPROFESSIONALS: RECRUITMENT AND SELECTION

During the planning period for the project's expansion and while professional training was taking place, PMHP received a fair amount of publicity through radio, television, and newspaper stories. As a result, many women inquired spontaneously about working as child aides. Other applicants were identified over several months through an announcement, distributed to some community professionals, that specified the attributes of an ideal aide and solicited nominations of qualified interested women. Project staff made specific inquiries at several inner-city antipoverty agencies to identify potential applicants for positions as aides in inner-city schools.

About three months before the program began, all applicants received a letter that identified the 11 prospective PMHP schools and requested background information about the applicants as well as a ranking of schools they would prefer as prospective work settings. Based on the applicants' preferences and the number of positions available (range: six to eleven) in each pair of schools, applicants were assigned to various school pairs and were told that they would be interviewed jointly by the team assigned to the school in which they had asked to work.

Final decisions about accepting candidates as aides, in our view, had to be made by school personnel since they would be working with and supervising the aides on a day-to-day basis. The school interviews, conducted by six different psychologist-social worker teams from four school districts, necessarily reflected the needs of both the district and the specific school. Typically, they lasted about one to one and one-half hours and covered a variety of topics such as the candidate's current life situation, family background, previous employment history, reasons for wanting to work in PMHP, and a discussion of her skills and interests as these related to work with young children. The decision to hire a candidate was made jointly by the team members after the interview ended.

Briefly, the composite sample of aides can be described as follows: The women were in their early 40s (the range was 19 to 67), were married (two were unmarried), and had three children (the range was one to eleven children). Although the group was predominantly middle-class in background, about 15 per cent were Black or Spanish speaking and had inner-city backgrounds. The latter were assigned full-time to the inner-city school settings.

So that project staff and professional personnel would better understand the characteristics of the women selected as aides, interviewers were asked to rate each candidate independently on 18 seven-point scales at the end of the interviews. The following attributes were rated: (1) personal warmth, (2) enjoyment in working with children, (3) concern about others, (4) acceptance of individual differences, (5) ability to work well with others, (6) independence, (7) reliability, (8) adaptability, (9) overall level of adjustment, (10) openness to new knowledge, (11) psychological-mindedness, (12) interest in PMHP, (13) effectiveness of child-rearing, (14) empathy for children, (15) ability to express appropriate affect, (16) openness in the interview, (17) how well the professional liked the candidate, and (18) an overall estimate of the candidate's potential effectiveness as an aide. Although these were the specific characteristics that were rated for each interviewee, others were important to interviewers in determining a prospective aide's acceptability. Examples of the latter included the ability to accept hostility without responding in kind, a reasonably nonjudgmental attitude, and the capacity to understand and work within the framework of a dyadic relationship. Similarly, other nonrated characteristics were used as negative predictors of an aide's success. Thus candidates with strong, highly intellectualized attitudes about school reform who communicated a readiness to charge into the school, à la Carrie Nation, to clean up "corruption," educate teachers, and set people straight were not likely to be chosen.

Formal research analysis of the aide-rating data was reported in a study by Cowen, Dorr, and Pokracki (1972b), who found that the psychologists and social workers agreed fairly well in their ratings of the 18 characteristics. The 56 women who were offered aide positions had significantly higher ratings on all 18 characteristics than the 43 women who were turned down. But the differences between the two groups were attributable to the fact that the accepted group received extraordinarily high ratings on all characteristics rather than to poor ratings for the rejected group.

The aide selection study indicated how the selected candidates differed from their nonselected applicant peers. An additional question of considerable interest was: How do aides differ from demographically comparable women in general or volunteer women in particular in characteristics that might rationally be expected to affect their performance as aides? This question raised several delicate research problems. To study it properly required that the evaluation take place during one, narrow, ten-day time span: i.e., *after* aides had been informed that they had been hired, to assure them that the testing was not going to be used for selection, but *before* training started, so that their responses could not be influenced by information or attitudes imparted in training. The study became the subject of a doctoral dissertation by Sandler (1972), who reasoned that specific qualities or attitudes would be important both in initially attracting women to aide positions and in their being chosen for the job. His aim was to develop a test battery to reflect such attributes and to compare the aide group to a demographically similar group of volunteers. Sandler's first cluster of measures included personality factors and interpersonal relationships. He used Jackson's Personality Research Form, tapping 20 basic personality characteristics, and Hogan's Empathy Test for this purpose. He also developed a "clinical-response styles" test that described ten hypothetical interactions between an adult and a child who was involved in a troublesome problem situation. The adult's job was to rank the appropriateness of four response options provided for each of the ten situations. These options had been prekeyed to reflect controlling, nurturing, understanding, and rejecting responses. By adding up the sum of the aide's ranked responses, four scores were derived—one for each dimension.

On the assumption that interest patterns also represented an area that might differentiate PMHP aides from other volunteers, Sandler included a classic interest test, the Strong Vocational Interest Blank as another basic measure for the study. He also used a semantic differential attitude measure (Osgood, Suci & Tannenbaum, 1957), which covered several areas potentially related to effective aide functioning: including schools, teachers, principals, mental health workers, children, emotionally disturbed children, children who are slow learners, myself, and homemaking. By rating each of the nine concepts on a series of bipolar scales (e.g., good-bad, helpful-harmful), a picture of the respondents' attitudes toward work-relevant areas is obtained. The full test battery, which required three to four hours to complete, thus included representative measures of personality and interpersonal relations, interest patterns, and attitudes towards schools and school personnel, children, and oneself.

For a control group, Sandler used 89 demographically comparable volunteers, identified in cooperation with several local agencies that staffed community volunteer programs. The heart of the study was the comparison of the personalities, interests, and attitudes of the aides and the volunteer controls. Important differences between these groups were indeed found. With regard to the personality dimensions, aides were significantly more affiliative and nurturing than controls, significantly less aggressive in their interpersonal relationships, and less inclined to be "lone wolves." Aides also had significantly higher empathy scores. Each of these five differentiating qualities augured well for the aides' effective functioning; their common thread was that they suggested effective interpersonal relationships with others.

Equally informative were the significant differences between the groups in terms of general and specific interests. Aides had significantly stronger interests than did controls in the teaching and social service areas, including such specific occupational activities as guidance counselor, YMCA recreation leader, English teacher, social worker, and public health nurse. In contrast, aides were significantly less interested than controls in the technical-scientific areas in general and in specific occupations such as dentist, chemist, mathematician, science teacher, engineer, accountant, and navy officer. Clearly, the aide group's dominant pattern of interests fits the theoretical profile of an effective helping person. Finally, several attitudinal dimensions also differentiated aides from the volunteer controls. Aides had significantly more positive attitudes toward elementary schools, teachers, principals, mental health workers, mental health (as an abstraction), children, emotionally disturbed children, homemaking, and themselves as people.

An additional, related study (Dorr, Cowen, Sandler & Pratt, 1973a) identified six basic factorial clusters from the original aide test battery: interest patterns, attitudes, extroversion, helping-orientation, social class, and scientific orientation. It was found that aides scored significantly higher than controls in terms of social interests, positiveness of school-related attitudes, and helping orientation. These data confirmed Sandler's earlier findings.

The above studies generated several important conclusions. First, the selected group of aides received unusually high scores in humanistic orientation and helping potential. Moreover, the group's discriminant profile of personality qualities, interest patterns, and attitudes, in contrast with the volunteer controls, corresponded well with the prevailing image of the attributes of effective helping persons. Thus we believed that we had succeeded in attracting as aides women who were, a priori, well qualified to meet the demanding challenge of bringing effective help to young, maladapting school children.

TRAINING OF NONPROFESSIONALS

It was desirable and appropriate for professionals to train their own nonprofessionals since they best knew their own strengths and interests, what they wanted to emphasize, and their school's particular needs. Moreover, training subgroups of ten seemed ideal in size, and having professionals lead the training would provide a good opportunity to promote cohesion and a common sense of direction with the new aides.

Project staff participated in nonprofessional training in several ways. It prepared a lengthy training manual (of about 100 pages), including some 20 pages of case history materials, as a training resource for professionals. The manual was written for the "most extreme instance," i.e., for a professional who had never led a training group and lacked a clear idea of what training should include. The manual was offered as a resource that professionals could use, revise, or reorganize as they saw fit.

It was written for a series of 14 two-hour training sessions to be conducted in parallel by the several training subgroups over a two-month period. The manual's introduction identified the need for training nonprofessionals and the professional's role in such activities. This was followed by a broad outline of the training sequence. The bulk of the manual, however, consisted of a series of suggested outlines for specific sessions. These usually began with an overview of the session's purposes and scope, recommendations about who should attend, and suggestions for the session format, all followed by a more detailed outline of the content to be covered. Suggestions for voluntary reading and references to the literature were provided for most sessions.

To provide all aides with some common background, the project staff conducted the first two training sessions before professionals started their subgroups. The first session considered the development of the mental hygiene movement, including the contributions of persons such as Clifford Beers, and recent changes in social philosophy that have helped to crystallize attitudes in this area. Past efforts to deal with mental health problems were reviewed, as were the traditional roles of specialists, such as psychiatrists, psychoanalysts, clinical psychologists, and social workers. Limitations and failings of traditional mental health approaches were also briefly considered. The fact that current mental health problems markedly exceeded the professional resources available for solving them led to more specific discussions about the basic concepts of community involvement, the use of nonprofessionals, and prevention of mental disorder. These discussions pivoted around four essential points: (1) that the aides' projected role was designed to meet a genuine social need, (2) that there were both theoretical and pragmatic justifications for this role, (3) that the specific program being developed was part of a broader evolutionary trend in mental health, and (4) that all parties concerned should expect some initial uncertainty and lack of clarity concerning their roles.

The second training session, also conducted by project staff, was to acquaint aides with earlier PMHP efforts, both to justify the expanding program and to develop a sense of continuity with the past. The session began with a review of PMHP's early history, including its initial rationale; its first early identification and prevention efforts; and a concrete description of early program components, e.g., Red Tagging procedures, use of consultants, and professional roles. As best we could, we tried to envision the rough profile of the aide role and candidly considered some, as yet unresolved problems in articulating that role. During this session, the aides received several basic "messages": the challenge we all felt as this phase of the project was about to start, the importance we attached to the evolving aide role, and the need to be open and tolerant about inevitable uncertainties and ambiguities.

The remaining 12 training sessions were conducted by the respective teams in the school in which the aides would actually be working. This part of the training was designed to encourage aide participation and discussion; catalyze a way of viewing children's problems; and reduce normal anxiety about the unknown, prospectively demanding role of being an aide by ever closer approximations to the actual work situation. The next section outlines the main content of these later training sessions.

In the third session the aides were oriented to the special characteristics of the particular school to help them understand the specific environmental features that would inevitably affect their work with children. It was recommended that principals and one or more school or neighborhood resource persons should be present at this meeting to talk about the neighborhood, its socioeconomic and ethnic composition, its problems, living conditions, resources, and existing relationships between the school and the community.

The fourth session dealt with the range and types of mental health problems found in specific schools. Recommended participants included the mental health professionals, aides, principals, and teachers. The proposed format of the session was to mix didactic case history materials with discussion to stimulate further the aides' psychological orientation and to encourage them to formulate preliminary views about their possible roles in dealing with such problems. Typically, the fourth session began with a presentation by the principal about how he viewed the school's mental health needs. Next, the professionals spoke about the psychological environment in the classroom and about specific classroom behavior problems, using actual case materials whenever possible. Consideration was given to how teachers dealt with such problems and how their efforts were constrained by the needs of other children and/or by limitations of their training.

The fifth session, the first in a series of observational meetings, was designed to give aides initial exposure to the classroom. This included an initial aide-teacher contact and permitted aides to observe directly how teachers interacted with children, how children looked and behaved in class, and some normal problems of the classroom environment. Aides were told to focus on whatever caught their interest and to keep specific behaviors, interactions, and issues in mind for later group discussion. Aides went to classrooms in pairs for 20 or 30 minutes and then, after switching partners, moved to a second class for a similar period. A discussion session ensued, involving the full aide group and the team. After that, aides and professionals met over lunch with the teachers whose classes had been observed for still more discussion of the morning's events and an integration of the teachers' and aides' views.

The next three to five sessions, depending on the needs and preferences of individual subgroups, dealt broadly with personality development, maladjustment, and parent-child relationships. The purposes of these sessions included catalyzing a further sense of psychological-mindedness in aides, providing concepts and vocabulary that might be useful to aides in later interactions with professionals, and giving aides whatever additional confidence might come from further intellectual understanding of children's behavior problems. Illustrative case history material and films about normal and abnormal development were used during these sessions.

The broad topic in the next series of sessions was the normal, well-adjusted child. The point was stressed that particular subcultures had their own standards and norms. For example, school achievement is highly valued in some, but not all subcultures; the ability to defend oneself and fight well is highly valued by and adaptive for some groups but not others. Thus the point was made that the subculture's adaptive demands must be considered when evaluating the adequacy of a child's adjustment to that culture. The need to consider each child as an individual with a unique genetic and environmental background was also discussed. The point was made that although aspects of "healthy" personality can indeed be identified, no one child should be expected to show all these characteristics. Moreover, it was pointed out that skills and competencies show up on a "more-or-less" rather than an "all-or-none" basis.

The next topic considered was the parent-child relationship, facilitated by the use of movies and/or case history materials. The importance of family influences in shaping the child's personality and psychological development was emphasized. Later the focus shifted to the typical problems of childhood. The format for this session was much the same as for preceding ones, except that the use of several specific films (e.g., *The Quiet One* and *Feelings of Rejection*) was recommended. Classic types of faulty parent-child relationships, such as parental rejection, overprotection, and domination were considered in this unit. Each syndrome and its major consequences were described. Attention was also directed in this session to the developmental problems of early childhood such as feeding, toilet training, difficulty in sleeping, and so-called nervous habits.

Later training sessions were more practical. For example, one session focused on the child aide's role and was designed to give aides a clearer, more realistic picture of exactly what they would be doing. In addition to the professionals and new aides, participants included several experienced aides from the initial group, which by then had been with PMHP for five years. Unquestionably, the participation of experienced aides was the single most instructive and therapeutic aspect of the entire training sequence. Veteran aides were women with whom the newcomers could identify. Moreover, by virtue of having "been there," they could respond spontaneously to many pressing questions by drawing on their own experiences and, in so doing, provide much comfort and reassurance to new aides.

It was not that professionals couldn't answer the same questions; rather, their answers might seem more distant or intellectualized. Although the professionals were admired and respected by new aides, they tended to be seen as better trained and thus different. When, for example, a new aide raised a "dreaded" question about work with children (i.e., one that anticipated a real situation that might come up and she was afraid she might not be able to handle it), the veteran aide might naturally and knowingly comment to a peer: "Oh, you remember when *we* were at the beginning stages and worried about something like that too?" This kind of spontaneous reaction in effect communicated to the new aide that: "Your fears are normal and understandable; we've 'been there' and we felt the same way, but *now* we feel quite comfortable in that situation." Thus including experienced aides in some training sessions was a highly facilitating component of training.

Some of the content considered in this session included the nature of the aide's role, including its emphasis on a committed relationship; the importance of encouraging children to express feelings, helping them to develop the coping behaviors and mastery skills needed to strengthen their confidence and security, and serving as an adult model; and the place, and importance of setting limits. Also emphasized was the need for aides to rely heavily on their knowledge, reflexes, and natural styles of interaction. They were assured that support and assistance would be available to them at all stages of the process (e.g., for referral decisions and progress evaluations) through professional supervision via consultation and/or informal contacts with school personnel.

This phase of training also considered ways for aides to assess their own effectiveness with and helpfulness to children, such as direct observation of the child's behavior, changes in the aide-child relationship and in-session activities, feedback from relevant sources of information such as teachers and parents, periodic progress-evaluation conferences with team members, and supervisory sessions with the professionals.

The next several sessions, all involving teachers, focused in greater depth on the aide's relationship with teachers and other school personnel and provided an introduction to teaching techniques. The purposes of these sessions included defining the aide's role more fully for teachers; establishing contacts between teachers and aides and encouraging further exchange of information between them; and clarifying the specific functions of the team, aides, and teachers as they related to the shared objective of helping children. Program purposes were reconsidered in depth, and mechanisms for smooth operation of the program (e.g., coordination of aides' and teachers' schedules) were discussed. A second session in this sequence introduced aides to the academic side of the child's experience. Teachers spoke about curriculum, academic goals, and classroom management problems and how they tried to handle them. An introduction to teaching and remediation techniques was provided, though the aide's role was not structured primarily as tutorial. Basically the session was designed to promote the fullest possible role clarification, assuming that the more completely this could be done beforehand, the more likely it would be that all parties could do their job of helping children most effectively. Once again, the reciprocity between learning difficulties and psychological problems was stressed.

A final lengthy clinical session capped the training experience. By then, almost everyone was anxious to get started. Either a classroom observation, a film, or a detailed case history was used to start this meeting, depending on the subgroup's resources and preferences. The clinical material was used as a springboard for considering the causes of a child's problems and how they might show up in school and for developing formulations about the child's needs and an hypothetical plan of intervention.

Thus in a telescoped training program of 12 to 14 sessions, aides were given a view of the program's purposes and their place in it; some basic concepts of early child development, both normal and abnormal; a closer view of their own role and the roles of others in the new program; and observational-clinical experience and opportunities to discuss these experiences. Since we had decided to go with aides' natural reflexes, life-styles, and prior experience, rather than massive training and formal clinical experience, this was as far as formal training went. As the program was

about to start, the aides varied in their readiness to begin
working with children. Some were champing at the bit and
couldn't wait to get started; others waited in nervous antici-
pation for concrete challenges that they feared might ex-
ceed their abilities and resources. Nevertheless, with the
conclusion of formal training, it was time to discover
whether we would sink or swim.

The "Debugging" Period

There is little question that by March 1970, the system
as a whole was in a state of heightened readiness for the
expanded program to start. School personnel had already
heard much about the "phantom program" through
briefings by project staff and school mental health teams.
They were eager to have concrete help brought to the many
youngsters who had by then been identified as needing
assistance; each school had an ample slate of referrals. We
had hoped that aides might be able to start slowly, perhaps
with two or three youngsters, so that they would be able to
adapt to their new role without excessive pressures. However idyllic this plan, it was ill attuned to the realities and
temper of the moment. School-based people were so anxious to get started that within two weeks after the program
was launched, 225 children were being seen by aides. Thus,
within the first month of the program, aides were seeing an
average of more than six children each.

During the debugging period (mid-March to the end
of the school year in mid-June) subgroups tried out many
different approaches and began to discover the ones that
best suited them. Thus the program model developed
differently in different schools. Several schools piloted, as
befit their needs, rather unique uses of aides' time. For
example, in inner-city schools, where there were sharp barriers against communication between the home and school,

aides were effectively used as ambassadors between families and a school system heretofore seen as alien. Individualized patterns of aide supervision also evolved. Some
teams used only individual supervision, whereas others
worked in small or large groups. Teachers, principals, and
other school personnel learned different styles of participation in project activities consonant with their interests,
needs, and time. Project staff encouraged exploration of
diverse patterns for seeing children, supervising aides, and
allocating time during the pilot period in hopes that this
would permit schools to identify approaches that best
suited their circumstances and at the same time maintain
PMHP's overall philosophy and thrust.

A report by Cowen, Dorr, Sandler, and McWilliams
(1971a) describes PMHP utilization patterns during the
debugging period. Fifty-six aides saw 329 children for a
total of 7,583 contacts—an average of about 23 contacts
per child. Thus roughly 9 per cent of the primary graders
in the 11 project schools received individualized educational and/or interpersonal help. Notwithstanding the
brevity of the trial period, different utilization patterns
were evident. For example, in one school, children were
seen for an average of 38 contacts during the three-month
period; in another, many more children were seen for an
average of only 12 contacts each.

Several important conclusions emerged from this early
trial period. First, the program, as conceptualized, would
indeed "fly." Aides were, in the main, comfortable in their
new role, approached it with enthusiasm, and felt subjec-
tively that they were helping children. Second, the brief but
intense trial period reminded us, once again, of the great
unmet need for school mental health services. Nearly 10
per cent of all primary grade children in the participating
schools had been identified as needing additional help,
were referred to the program, and were seen. That this all
happened so quickly confirmed what we had seen as highly

probable all along: that a program of this type, based on the half-time services of nonprofessional child aides, could geometrically expand the reach of helping services to young children in need—hopefully in ways that would forestall development of later, more serious maladaptation.

The debugging period also helped us to identify, almost as a preview of coming attractions, areas of program malfunction in which problems were either already evident or seemed likely to occur. Some of these resulted from the project's leap from a controlled, finite entity in one school to a vast, sprawling operation. PMHP's new cast included, not only its central staff, but also a dozen school professionals, school district pupil personnel directors, school superintendents, members of school boards, scores of teachers and other school personnel, and thousands of children and parents. Given the sheer number and diversity of involved parties, it was virtually impossible to communicate adequately with everyone. Thus misunderstandings and frustrations developed because the project's aims and methods could not always be explained adequately to the many people affected by it—each of whom was entitled to such information. Many teachers, for example, were fuzzy about exactly how the project worked and about the youngsters for whom it was really intended. A frequent consequence of the lack of communication is the sense of alienation or exclusion that it can produce. PMHP's early period of expansion did not escape that fate.

Another problem arose in several understaffed settings. Demands and expectations in areas such as recruitment and training of nonprofessionals, teachers' meetings, parents' meetings, and aide supervision far exceeded the professionals' available time. And beyond that, the new way of operating required by PMHP was frustrating to some professionals, accustomed to traditional ways of functioning. Some found that they were uncomfortable with or simply did not enjoy one or more key PMHP professional roles (e.g., supervising aides). For them, the project required too much of a change in long-established, security-breeding modes of professional operation. This problem was sharpened because staff did not always clearly spell out the specifics of the professional role in training. The project's "teaming" of two professionals (a psychologist and a social worker) created other problems. If one member of a team did not wish to or could not perform certain functions, it increased the other's burdens and became a source of friction. Moreover, as might be anticipated, when experienced, thoughtful, and sometimes strong-willed professionals are paired, each may have his own very personal experiential history, ideas, pet notions, competencies, and preferred orientations. As a case in point, some of the professionals in our first group were educationally oriented while others were more psychologically or psychodynamically oriented. Some were parent oriented; others, child oriented. Some liked and others resented day-to-day administrative responsibilities. A further complication and source of pressure on professionals came from the different concepts of what PMHP could offer that originated with teachers, principals, and other school personnel in various settings. Although some of these problems were minor and readily worked through, others required an ongoing, at times agonizing process of discussion, accommodation, and compromise over an extended period before the project could function smoothly and effectively in a particular school.

The preceding overview deals only with the debugging period, an extremely important if highly frenetic time in PMHP's development. The two most important lessons learned during this period were that, one, the expanded project looked as if it would work and, two, there were many problems, some serious, that required attention and successful resolution if it was truly to function well. PMHP's subsequent growth and expansion, including changes in its size, scope, format, and procedures, has been more gradual, in comparison with the lightning-quick developments of the debugging period. We turn to that part of the story in the next chapters.

6

Basic
Project
Elements

In the spring of 1970, PMHP passed from a protected pilot-demonstration project to one that had to survive in the real world of school district priorities, budget hearings, and other competing programs. Between 1970 and 1973, PMHP grew from 11 to 13 to 16 schools in Rochester and Monroe County. During that period, we arrived at a better understanding of the needs of the individual schools and school districts and learned much about modifying programs to conform to situational realities. Such modifications, as previously noted, transformed PMHP into a federation of like-minded programs rather than a group of carbon-copy replicas. In one sense, we became a franchise operation—the Kentucky Fried Chicken of school mental health. Although personnel, facilities, and ways of conducting the program varied from place to place, we sought to maintain maximal quality of service under all circumstances. The indispensable common denominators of the PMHP approach also became clearer during this period.

An emphasis on young children and efforts to work preventively with them have always been central to PMHP's focus. Such an orientation, for us, assumes effective mechanisms for identifying school maladjustment early. The early detection and screening procedures that PMHP has found useful are discussed below. Once identification takes place, some form of intervention must be provided. The reader is by now aware of PMHP's investment in and utilization of nonprofessionals as the prime direct service agents with children. The aides' training and job functions have already been considered in a context that emphasizes their potential for expanding geometrically the reach of helping services. Another truly important aspect of PMHP is the redefinition of the school mental health professional's role from that of a provider of direct service to a small number of children to that of trainer, supervisor, and consultant for school personnel who have ongoing daily contacts with many more children. The main purposes of this chapter are to flesh out these components as they emerged in the expanded project and to provide a clearer image of the full program in action.

PROFESSIONAL ROLES AND THE SCREENING PROCESS

Early detection and screening have always been integral to PMHP. We have assumed that such identification is central to any system that seeks to bring early effective help to maladapting school children. In PMHP's first phase, as already noted, the team invested much of its energies in early identification. They used their special professional skills to gather pertinent information about each child (e.g., group diagnostic evaluation, interviewing mothers) and, through a team approach, integrated such data into a meaningful diagnostic picture of the child's strengths and weaknesses.

In traditional roles, school mental health professionals function primarily in a crisis-oriented "on-call" way. When teachers have specific concerns about children, either because they present behavior problems in class or because they are not profiting from their schoolwork, they ask the team to locate the source of the child's difficulties and to recommend solutions. Thus, in a case-by-case *ad hoc* way, the psychologist administers an assessment battery, the social worker interviews the child and/or his family, and together they interpret their findings to teachers and other school personnel to help them be more effective with the child. All too often, there is an unavoidably long delay between the teacher's request and the professional's initial actions. Equally often, even after evaluations are completed, few viable solutions to the problem surface. If time permits, the more ambitious professional may try to work directly with the teacher to help lessen her management problems with children whose learning or behavior problems interfere with classroom activities. Sometimes referrals are made to a remedial program within or outside the school system. This rather classic definition of the mental health team's role allows little time for direct intervention with children or for systematic in-service training for teachers. The discrepancy between the professional resources available and children's needs is simply too great!

PMHP, however, offers an alternative role model. The aide program provides professionals with a mechanism of direct intervention that permits major redefinition of their roles. They now become responsible for gathering systematically much of the information needed to identify children at risk and work closely with and support the aide's attempts to minimize risk. They are also a more integral part of the teacher's in-service training, helping her to become more sensitive to children's needs and to procedures for dealing appropriately with them. Ideally, by working with children early in their school careers, the need for later, more extensive workups and outside refer-rals is reduced, thus giving the professional more time to devote to the intervention process via aides and to consul-tation with teachers.

One aspect of the PMHP screening involves gathering and collating extensive data on first grade children. The team reviews each child's school record, the comments of kindergarten and first grade teachers and then does group screening and parent interviewing. Each year in early Octo-ber, the psychologist administers intellectual and personal-ity measures to groups of 10 to 15 first graders. The testing is done in the child's classroom, and whenever possible the teacher serves as a proctor. The California Test of Mental Maturity has been used for intellectual assessment and the Goodenough Draw-A-Man (DAM) has been used for an initial personality assessment. The particular instruments used are less important than the fact that some measures are used to assess young children's cognitive and psycho-logical status. Other tests would doubtless serve these pur-poses as well. Administering the tests also gives the psychologist a chance to observe the children clinically. Their behavior, feelings, and attitudes can be noted and integrated into a final formulation of the child's current status. For example, the psychologist might observe that a child has difficulty following directions or is distractable, immature, overly dependent, withdrawn, or aggressive during testing.

The test situation thus offers a small work sample that provides a microcosmic glimpse of the child's approach to classroom demands and his reaction to success or failure. The results of the intelligence tests provide an estimate of academic strengths and weaknesses and often indicate a discrepancy between the child's ability and his actual func-tioning. The more projective Draw-A-Person Test often suggests hypotheses concerning the child's self-concept and his interpersonal style, maturity, or dependency. The results of the psychological screening and the hypotheses that are generated in the process are shared with the social worker, who can use the information as focuses during interviews with parents. The psychologist is also able to consult with and offer helpful suggestions to the teacher on the basis of such information. Sometimes too, the screening data provide the psychologist with early information about the need for further diagnostic work or referral to an outside agency. If the child is later referred to PMHP, the team can use the test data in planning the aims and tactics of an aide intervention and in supervising the aide.

The school social worker is also importantly involved in early screening. A good professional working relationship between psychologist and social worker is indispensable to PMHP's smooth operation. It is essential that the two share responsibility and information, that they respect each other personally and professionally, that they observe their own and each other's professional prerogatives and limits, and that neither usurp the other's role. As a team they are able to add to each other's screening information. The social worker, for example, can focus the interview with the child's mother to help the psychologist better understand his test findings as well as hunches and unanswered questions that arise from the test data.

Although the social worker's overall role in PMHP emphasizes a positive approach to early identification and prevention of children's educational, social, and emotional problems, his contacts are primarily with significant adults in the child's life—parents, teachers, aides, and the school principal. The social worker has relatively few direct casework contacts with children, although he may observe some of them in class, both to understand the maladaptive behaviors described by the teacher in her referral and to be able to respond affirmatively when a parent asks: "Have you seen my Jimmie? Do you know what he looks like?"

As part of the screening process, the social worker's impressions of a child's family and his environment establish a useful perspective against which the psychologist's and teacher's inputs can be viewed, because the parents' attitudes toward a child and toward the importance of his mastery of the school situation surely contribute significantly to his actual behavior in the class. Interviews with parents also allow the social worker to play the preventive role of reinforcing positive child-rearing practices and suggesting alternatives for negative ones. Thus the social work interview helps to develop a good working relationship between the team and the family. Moreover, the interview provides the social worker with important information that may be helpful in the occasional situation where referral of the child or a family member to an outside agency may be indicated.

The Social Worker's Interview with the Mother

During PMHP's first stages, the social worker's interviews with mothers of first grade children were structured as a part of a routine "get-acquainted" process. They were designed to acquaint mothers with PMHP's presence in the school, describe the project, alert her to the services available to the family through the project, and assure her of the project's continuing interest in her child throughout his school career (Trost, 1968). Although prior knowledge of a child's problems was sometimes available, such information was not typically brought up in the initial interview unless the mother did so herself. If that happened, she was encouraged to talk about the problem as she saw it, including her feelings and how she might deal with it. At the end of the interview, at which time tentative casework impressions had been formulated, these mothers were typically offered another appointment to discuss their concerns further. In the meantime, the social worker agreed to explore with the teacher how she saw the child in school and how the school might help with the problem.

This relatively nonthreatening, non-problem-oriented, initial interview with all first grade mothers is a luxury that few social workers have in PMHP's present structure. Drastic limitations in social work time mean, in effect, that the worker is only able to see the mothers of referred children. Accordingly, many mothers are seen in more of a crisis atmosphere when it is necessary to elicit specific, pertinent information about the child and his family and obtain the mother's permission for an aide to work with the child. Ideally, under less pressured circumstances the social worker can establish a better relationship with a mother—one that will enhance her cooperation in a later helping process—if he can get her to come to his office, where she can put her best foot forward.

In most instances, mothers have been asked to come to the school for social work interviews. This tests their interest and motivation for help; provides a neutral setting for the contact; makes for fewer interruptions; affords a respite for many mothers from home duties, thus allowing them to feel more relaxed; and makes for more efficient use of the social worker's time. If, for some reason, a mother cannot leave the home because she has a small child or transportation problems or if there is no convenient interviewing space in the school, a home visit is an alternative. Some project social workers prefer to give the mother the choice of coming to school or having the worker visit the home.

Interview formats and styles vary somewhat with different workers and also as a function of the mother's readiness to discuss her child's problem. A PMHP "Mother Interview Outline," developed by project staff, is available to all social workers. This schedule outlines the types of information ordinarily obtained in the interview. After describing the program briefly, the worker typically shifts to a series of questions about the child's medical and developmental history. This serves as a relatively good warm-up for further exploration of more sensitive family relations and also provides information that is useful in forming casework impressions. Illustratively, the mother's responses to questions about the child's allergies, hospitalizations, eating habits, and toilet training might point to problems of dependency, separation anxiety, hostility, or rejection. Discussion about parent-child relationships often leads to the mother's portrayal of how the child is seen at home, how he is handled, how she and her husband relate to one another, and how their relationship may bear on the child's present difficulties. The mother's own school experiences are also considered. These are often important because they may suggest residual positive or negative attitudes toward the school or toward education in general, failure to motivate a child for learning, or pressures on a child to achieve.

Ideally, the interview with the mother should occur before the child is assigned to an aide. For one thing, it is a good way to obtain the mother's permission for the child to participate in the project. More importantly, it rounds out the psychologist's test interpretations, provides data that are useful in selecting an aide who will be well suited to work with the child, helps the aide and team to set goals, and often provides a framework and sense of direction for aide supervision. If aide-child contacts are to be maximally productive, they should be programmed, not only to meet the child's school needs, but to take into account his life history and home and community experiences. If it is impossible to interview the mother before the child is assigned, her permission for his participation can be obtained by phone, with the understanding that she will be seen in the near future.

Screening Devices for Teachers

Although group psychological screening of first grade children and social work interviews remain important aspects of PMHP's screening, changes in the project's basic format during the expansion period called for adaptations in the total screening process. Both expansion of and consequent variations in available professional resources were at the root of these changes. Originally, with a full-time project psychologist and social worker, intensive social work interviews with mothers of all first grade children could be held. However, this can no longer be done in a new PMHP school that has only one-fifth of a social worker's services. In such understaffed schools, at best only the parents of a limited group of identified vulnerable children can be interviewed: i.e., those viewed as having school adjustment problems and as likely candidates for referral to the aide program.

Group psychological screening of first grade children early in the school year continues, but the program's expansion has made pressing the need to develop teacher-administered screening measures that would yield early objective data for all youngsters. Early in the expansion period, much effort was invested in developing such instruments. One aspect of PMHP's rapid growth was that it was now a much less personal entity. We simply did not know teachers and were in a poor position to inveigle them into devoting large amounts of time to filling out screening data. It was therefore essential to develop measures that were (1) brief, so as not to impose excessively on the teacher's time, (2) objective, reliable, quickly scorable, and thus amenable to providing rapid feedback of information, and (3) above all, relevant to the teacher's basic classroom mandate of educating young children.

Two screening instruments, the (AML), originally used by Bower (1960) and his associates in a series of studies in California, and the Teacher Referral Form (TRF) were either developed or further refined during the full action period and have become integral aspects of PMHP screening and early diagnosis. Copies of these two measures, as they are now used, can be found in Appendixes 1 and 2. A more detailed account of the research steps involved in their development is presented in Chapter 8.

For the moment, it can be said that the AML is a brief, 11-item, quick-screening device for teachers to use in identifying primary graders' school maladaptation problems. The measure is extremely concise, requiring only about 30 seconds per child to complete, or 15 to 20 minutes for an average-sized class. The TRF, though similar in scope, format, and objectivity to the AML, is somewhat lengthier and more complex. It consists of three major sections. Part 1, the most important, lists 41 possible classroom behavior problems that the teacher rates for absence or presence and, if present, for intensity. Part 2 lists several family background factors (e.g., parents separated or divorced), which the teacher is asked to rate in a similar manner if she believes the factor is contributing to the child's classroom difficulties. Part 3 consists of three seven-point rating scales reflecting how well the teacher knows the child, how likeable she considers him to be, and how serious she considers his school adjustment problems to be. The TRF requires about three minutes per child to complete, or about one and one-half hours for an average-sized class.

Factor analytic studies of these two measures, based on large samples of primary graders, indicates that they have generally comparable factorial structures; each reflects three prime dimensions of school maladjustment: acting out problems; shyness, timidity, and withdrawal; and learning disability. The major practical difference between them is that we have increasingly used the AML as a rapid mass screening device, whereas the more comprehensive sophisticated TRF is used more often as a diagnostic-prescriptive tool.

Thus PMHP's early detection and screening component is as important today as it was 15 years ago. We still consider group intelligence and personality screening to be an integral part of the overall process, as is the social work interview with mothers of vulnerable children. Although the latter are restricted to fewer mothers these days, this constraint is caused by limited resources rather than ideological preference. Finally, we have done much to further the development and effective use of mass-screening and diagnostic instruments completed by teachers and have begun to use such data to formulate prescriptive interventions for children.

CLINICAL CONFERENCES

Once again, it should be emphasized that with PMHP's expansion to many settings, it is no longer possible to describe a standard set of practices that characterize the project. Practices vary enormously as a function of different professional backgrounds and inclinations, school needs, and, most importantly, available resources. Thus the descriptions of PMHP clinical conferences in this section are little more than modal approximations.

Assignment Conferences

Once collected, the screening data provide a basis for reviewing a child's problems and for making decisions about what can be done to help him. This essentially is the goal of the assignment conference, in which the school psychologist, the school social worker, aides, and one or more teachers are typically involved. Depending on the child's problem and the school's way of operating, others, e.g., the principal, may also be present. Indeed, less central persons, such as the nurse, reading teacher, lunchroom monitor, busing monitor, music teacher, or gym teacher, may be invited if the child's difficulties touch situations in which they are involved. Sometimes a senior PMHP consultant also attends assignment conferences, especially in new settings. Under such circumstances, the consultant can serve a useful modeling role.

Assignment conferences pile up early in the school year, when decisions must be reached about identified children and how program resources will be used for the year. In some settings, three, four, or even five full days are set aside in October and November for a series of assignment conferences. A typical format for these conferences is to have a teacher spend a block of time with the team and aides, discussing the children she has preidentified as potential candidates for PMHP because of their classroom behavior. This format is made possible by bringing substitute teachers into PMHP schools for a full day. The substitute relieves three or four classroom teachers for time blocs of approximately one and one-half hours, which permits the latter to participate fully in the assignment conference. This practice lends dignity and importance to the conference and avoids imposing on the teacher the extra burden of giving up lunch hours or time after school for the meeting. Realistically, extra meetings often produce resistance in teachers if perceived as another "voluntary" obligation in an already heavy schedule.

The assignment conference brings together concerned parties to share information gathered from multiple perspectives about the child's current situation and his adaptive problems. Sharing such information permits participants to reach a better understanding of the sources of the child's difficulties and, along with that, to develop an intervention plan that best fits his needs. The teacher briefly describes the problems she has seen in the classroom, the psychologist reviews the screening and group testing data, and the social worker apprises the group of the family situation as gleaned from her interview with the mother. This is not a fixed, ritualistic procedure in which, for example, five minutes are allocated for the psychologist's report and five more for the social work interview. Instead, time allocations per child and among participants depend on the nature of the problem and the sources of information. The psychologist's statement might take only 30 seconds in some instances, whereas the social worker might take ten to fifteen minutes to describe relevant aspects of the family situation. On the average, about 20 to 30 minutes is spent per child. Thus in a typical two-hour assignment conference, five or six youngsters can be reviewed. However, the notion that guides the assignment conference is: Given the fullest possible current view of the child and his problems, what "best guesses" can be made about the interventions or modifications that can most improve his school experience?

In many instances, the major decision of the assignment conference is for the child to be seen regularly by an aide. However, this is not always the case. For example, the data may suggest that the major source of the child's problem resides in some aspect of the classroom situation. If so, a decision might be made that the preferred approach would be to modify classroom practices A, B or C. Hypothetically, then, a child may be doing well in most ways, except for one or two specific but annoying aspects of his classroom behavior (e.g., chronic testing of limits, not strictly enforced by the teacher). In such a case, the assignment conference plan might call for firmer enforcement of class limits by the teacher as a first approach, leaving open the possibility that if this doesn't help, other approaches can be considered later. There are also instances in which the assignment conference concludes that the child's core problems rest in a home characterized by high standards and excessive pressures. The conference might decide that the social worker should meet with the mother to review the home situation and to determine whether it can be modified constructively, short of assigning the child to a one-to-one aide relationship. If that parsimonious approach does not work, the alternative of assigning the child to an aide remains open. Nonetheless, the modal assignment-conference decision is to assign the child to be seen regularly by an aide.

Although the assignment conference provides a reasonably clear picture of the child's problems, PMHP thus far has, quite frankly, not fully capitalized on such information in developing different prescriptions for intervention with different children. That issue came into sharp focus only recently, through the development of a framework based on a "pure-type" referral problem (Lorion, Cowen & Caldwell, 1974b). Thus we found that children's school adjustment problems could be classified primarily as acting out, shy-anxious, or suffering from learning disabilities and that among the three groups, shy-anxious children had the most favorable intervention outcomes. Retrospectively, this finding was understandable. First, aide selection favored women who were warm, giving, and motherly. Moreover, aide training was relatively nonspecific, emphasizing the need to develop a committed human relationship with children. If aides are selected for their warmth and ability to give in the first place and are told to be loving without more specific suggestions for differential helping approaches with different problems, they are likely to be most effective with the children who stand to profit most from a warm, permissive, mothering relationship.

At the start of this book, we said that the PMHP story was an open unfinished one; nowhere is that point better illustrated than for the "pure types" question. We simply have not used the fairly rich body of diagnostic and referral information available with maximal effectiveness. In other words, we now believe that there is enough information at referral to understand a child's problems quite specifically and to translate those understandings into differential intervention prescriptions. What is needed—and this development now has a high priority—are differential prescriptions, particularly for children who act out or suffer from learning disabilities, that speak more realistically to "where they are" at referral and point to more effective modes of intervention than past ones. All that we have learned in PMHP over the years, both clinically and empirically, confirms the importance of clear, accurate, early, diagnostic screening information. What we are now learning is that such information must be used in even more individualized ways to increase the efficiency of subsequent interventions.

Progress Conferences

Progress meetings are a second important type of PMHP conference. Such conferences typically take place at mid-year, although they may be initiated at any time to review what has been happening with the child in his aide contacts and in class. The frequency and length of the progress conferences depends on a setting's resources. They are almost always held in well-staffed settings and are less frequent in poorly-staffed ones. Progress conferences are generally attended by those who attended the assignment conference. They tend to be briefer than assignment conferences since there is less need to review the original input data. The teacher, who has observed the child's classroom behavior daily, and the aide are the prime "data reporters" in the progress conference. Questions that structure the conferences include: How well are we doing with this child? Are the particular problems for which he was referred easing up? What changes in strategy and intervention practices could help in better achieving agreed-upon goals? Sometimes the progress conference judgment is that things are indeed going well and that the problems for which the child was originally referred are less pressing. In such cases, a decision may be made simply to continue on course. In other instances, however, there may be little or no progress or even reports that the child is doing more poorly than before. In such cases, the group must decide whether slow initial progress could have been anticipated (e.g., because the child is still testing the climate of trust) or whether it indicates a need to change the plan of intervention in class, at home, and/or with the aide.

A disconcerting, but sometimes instructive aspect of the progress conference occurs when discrepant reports of the child's status are provided by different observers. The teacher, for example, may present a picture of a classic "Dennis the Menace": the child has no interest in schoolwork, disrupts class procedures, annoys other children, and makes life miserable for her. The same child may be described by the aide as an angel—so much so that she is puzzled about why he even has to be seen. In instances of this type, a frequent reaction of the reporting parties, not to mention other conference participants, is that someone must surely be crazy! However, as such situations are pursued more concretely, it often turns out that both reporters are correct. What has been overlooked (and it is sometimes very helpful to make the discovery) is that the two reports reflect different behavioral situations with different adaptive demands. A child has an aide all to himself, but he must compete with 30 others for the teacher's attention. With the aide, the child is free to pursue whatever activities he wishes to, but he must meet specific, sometimes stringent, adaptive requirements in class. Awareness of the fact that the child's behavior must be considered in the light of the different realities and adaptive demands of different situations is often helpful both to the teacher and the aide. It may allow the teacher to break away from the simplistic view that the child is naughty and accept the fact that he is capable of different, more socially acceptable behaviors under some circumstances. By the same token, the aide may come to understand that the angelic behavior she sees is specific to a particular, sheltered, safe, interpersonal relationship, which the child must eventually transcend to meet the more realistic adaptive demands of the classroom.

Thus the progress conference serves the useful purposes of allowing involved parties to take stock of a child's progress and, if needed, to introduce correctives that promise more favorable outcomes.

Termination Conferences

Typically, during the last two weeks of the school year, termination conferences are held. In terms of structural organization, termination conferences are similar to the earlier assignment and progress conferences. Thus mental health professionals, aides, teachers, and other school personnel come together for fairly large blocks of time to consider what has happened with children referred to PMHP during the year. From a blend of such data, decisions are made about future courses of action. In many instances, those who attend the termination conference decide that the child has made good progress and that he no longer needs to be seen through PMHP. For other children the judgment is less clear cut. Thus it may be decided that although the child has made some progress, it would be best, if only as a precaution, to see him briefly at the start of the next school year. With still other youngsters, there may be little if any indication of progress, and a decision is made to continue to see them during the next school year.

Again illustrating PMHP's "unfinished story quality," accumulation of clinical experience with termination conferences, plus supporting research data, add to our awareness of areas of project ineffectiveness. Several of these areas have been noted in a recent paper on PMHP "regularities" (Lorion, Cowen & Kraus, 1974a). One phenomenon we have observed and have been disconcerted by is that most PMHP children who terminate do so during the last week of the school year. It is almost as if somebody waved a magic wand on June 10th or 15th and transformed the child from a state of maladaptation to one of adaptation. In fact, we know that growth and development do not follow such a curve. Many youngsters who are terminated at the end of the school year have made considerable progress during the year and could, in all likelihood, have finished much earlier. The "system," however, tends to maintain them! It is as if there were an unspoken understanding, whereby teams and aides agree that "once we start a child in PMHP, we are committed to work with him for the full school year." If resources are allocated to see youngsters over several years in a system with finite delivery potential, this necessarily withholds services from other children who might profit from them. PMHP's research findings (Lorion et al., 1974a) indicate that children are most likely to profit from the aide program during the initial year of contact. Those seen over several years do not do better than those seen for shorter periods.

Several possible explanations of why children are kept in project over several years can be imagined. One is that school mental health teams and aides require more certainty of "cure" than is needed. Another is that project people are reluctant to let children try their own wings early—an interpretation that is supported by the fact that children who have improved are not terminated during the school year. Another factor that may operate to keep children in the project for a full school year or multiple years, is the "mother" self-concept of many aides. One negative consequence of seeing oneself as a mother is that it can make for difficulty in giving up a child. This self-image was probably overly reinforced, both in the way the project staff defined the aide's role during training and later in consultation and supervision.

Consultation

Consultation has developed as a mental health approach because of several interrelated, serious problems facing the field, not the least of which is that the need for help far outstrips helping resources. For a number of reasons, ranging from attitudinal to geographic to economic, many people with psychological problems are unable to see mental health professionals. Indeed, only a modest fraction of the psychologically distressed come to the "official" care agents formally designated, by textbooks and common public knowledge, as society's healers for such problems. More often, psychologically upset individuals take their troubles to a trusted, sympathetic person in their immediate environment who will listen. Thus there is a sharp difference between society's *de jure* code that annoints mental health specialists to deal with emotional and psychological problems and *de facto* practice. This point is well documented in the report by Gurin et al. (1960), which indicates that roughly 42 per cent of society's emotional problems are brought to clergymen, another 29 per cent to family physicians, and less than 20 per cent to all mental health professionals combined. Some mental health professionals react to such data with concern and alarm, fearful that people who are not qualified to handle such problems are in fact doing so. Others, recognizing that this state of affairs is a necessity, have evolved approaches that work within the framework of reality.

Consultation is one such mechanism. In the face of social reality, the mental health consultant's job is to bring knowledge and expertise to those inevitably called on to deal with psychological problems as part of their everyday functioning. In so doing he hopes to strengthen the caregiver's ability to deal with such problems more realistically and effectively. By upgrading the mental health skills of the caregiver, the consultant contributes to a geometric expansion of society's helping resources. In that sense, it can be argued that the effective use, even of relatively small amounts of time in mental health consultation, can be more socially utilitarian than using the same time to see individual patients.

Although the preceding speaks to the general goals and methods of consultation, its applications have been somewhat different in PMHP. When the expanded project started, its school mental health professionals already had many requisite skills and experiences needed to run the program. The major problem was that they had always used these skills in different ways than those called for by the newly emerging role. Thus, although many of their new professional activities were to be materially different from those of the traditional school mental health worker, these new activities and job demands were known only abstractly to the professionals. Accordingly, an initial objective of PMHP staff consultation was to demonstrate and model new professional roles. Although such "modeling" was seen as important in PMHP's early expansion stages, it was hoped that ultimately the professionals would assume independent consultative roles.

There are two groups of PMHP consultants: (1) senior PMHP staff members, including the chief psychologist and chief social worker and sometimes the director and the research coordinator, both of whom happen to be clinically trained, and (2) a roster of senior clinical consultants and consultant trainees including postdoctoral candidates in psychiatry and psychology and graduate students in psychology and social work.

Scheduling formats have been worked out so that both groups of project consultants make regular visits to schools either cross-sectionally or longitudinally. Cross-sectional refers to the situation in which the consultant visits many schools, each no more than two or three times per year; longitudinal refers to a situation in which the consultant visits a limited number of schools in depth many times during the school year. Each of these approaches has its advantages and limitations. Although cross-sectional consultation allows the consultant to contribute to many more school programs, it limits his ability to get to know school personnel well, to understand the structure of the school in depth, or to be entrusted with relatively serious problems. The longitudinal approach facilitates the latter objectives, but it restricts the spread of a consultant's knowledge and skills across many settings. Clinical experience over the years suggests that school settings prefer and feel they can derive more from longitudinal consultation, even though this means that some consultants will not be available to them. Accordingly, we have gravitated more and more toward longitudinal assignments for senior staff and outside consultants. Each year, several predoctoral and postdoctoral students are in training as consultants with PMHP. Past practice has been to "attach" trainees to senior consultants for a period of time, continually assessing the development of their consultative skills. As these skills mature, trainees function more independently in school settings.

We have conducted several surveys of the scope and content of PMHP's consultation activities. Presently, PMHP brings more than 250 consultative visits per year to participating schools, averaging about 15 to 20 visits per year per school. Content analysis of these visits suggests that three major things take place: (1) clinical case consultation on the specific problems of individual children, (2) staff or personnel consultation, dealing primarily with problems of professionals or nonprofessionals that pertain to their PMHP role responsibilities, and (3) program consultation, having to do with PMHP's effectiveness in the eyes of participating personnel, school administrators, or school-district representatives. These three roles are not entirely discrete or separable, and in fact they are often intertwined during a consultative visit. Nevertheless, they are the main discriminable components of PMHP's overall consultation services.

Based on this breakdown, about two-thirds of PMHP's consultation consists of clinical case consultation, i.e., looking in depth at specific problems raised by referred children. Such consultation covers many different substantive problems, which are posed at varying levels of generality or specificity. Examples of issues covered in consultation sessions include setting limits for aggressive children, specific interventions for children with learning problems, handling termination, and so forth. More specific problems that aides have raised include the following: what to do if a child asks to be seen more often, how to handle questions children raise about whether or not the aide sees other children, how to deal with gifts from children, what to do if a child wants to bring a friend to a session, how to deal with the situation in which the child refuses to leave the classroom. Many such problems come up concerning cases that the aide is having difficulty handling. Such concerns, of course, also come up in the aides' regular supervision with the professional team. Consultation often deals with the especially perplexing or enriching types of situations that crop up in all settings.

The remaining one-third of the consultative sessions are about equally divided between the other two functions noted above: staff consultation and program consultation. Staff consultation deals primarily with the concerns that program personnel have about their roles and effectiveness: i.e., how they deal with children and how they feel about their performance or interpersonal relations with staff as these factors relate to program effectiveness. In contrast, program consultation deals with evaluation of program strengths and weaknesses and with tactical or logistic changes needed to increase its effectiveness. Program consultation necessarily touches people other than those directly involved in the program's day-to-day operation: e.g., school principals and school district administrators to whom the program is accountable.

In the past we have not always discriminated sufficiently among clinical case consultation, staff consultation, and program consultation. Because of our failure to do so, schools have viewed staff and outside consultants too similarly. Understandably, their metric for determining which problems to bring up with whom is the consultant's availability. In other words, if school personnel have a problem, they will raise it with whomever happens to be in the building in consultant's clothing—regardless of his stated role on an abstract organizational chart. Ideally, program-related problems should come directly to senior PMHP staff members, whereas outside consultants should be used in more clinical roles that are as independent of primary administrative or program-related responsibilities as possible.

To sharpen this discrimination, the different consultative roles have been more clearly articulated in our current program. Administrative changes have also been made to increase the likelihood that program concerns will be brought directly to PMHP staff consultants, while outside consultants will be used more consistently as clinical case consultants. Both the reasons behind these changes and how they actually work in practice are considered more extensively in a later chapter.

Supervision

Earlier discussions about child aides stressed the fact that the women selected for this work were chosen because of their life histories, personality makeup, and experiential background rather than because of prior formal education or training. We assumed that well-qualified women would thus be identified and that they would be given a limited amount of prior training to help them function more effectively on the job. Hopefully, the engineering of the aides' later work experience would encourage continuous, on-the-job development. For such growth to occur, considerable emphasis had to be placed on ongoing supervision of aides by professionals. In training professionals for PMHP, we stressed the importance of supervising aides and proposed specific minimal standards for supervision: two hours a month of individual supervision per aide and one and one-half hours per month of group supervision. In practice, however, several important variables govern the frequency and effectiveness of supervision. Principal among these are the professional resources available in the schools. If, for example, professionals have only five hours a week to spend in a PMHP school, they cannot devote most of that time to supervising aides. A second factor that influences the amount and quality of supervision is how the professional sees his own skills, interests, and abilities. Whereas some professionals enjoy and are at home with supervision, others find it alien and unpleasant and have little interest in it. In practice, then, there has been much variability in the extent and quality of aide supervision in different PMHP settings. Some professionals are extremely conscientious in discharging supervisory responsibilities; others attach so low a priority to it that aides feel they are not getting enough supervision and become resentful.

Supervisory formats also vary a good deal from setting to setting. Whereas some professionals do regularly scheduled individual supervision, a few prefer to supervise individually on an as-needed basis, others emphasize regular group supervision, and still others prefer a combination of individual and group supervision. We have not insisted on specific supervisory formats because we recognize that such decisions are linked closely to individual styles and preferences. We have, however, continually emphasized the importance of supervision if aides are to grow on the job and thus be able to provide more effective services to children. On the whole we cannot say that supervision in PMHP has been overwhelmingly effective. For the reasons already indicated, supervision has not gone as well as we had hoped in some settings. The lack of serious, tight supervision has in fact been a source of concern for many aides and has prompted staff to introduce special, compensatory discussion meetings for aides.

This description of our experience with aide supervision has implications for other districts that wish to develop PMHP-type projects. If supervision is as important for aides' growth as we have implied and resources for it are not available within the project, then efforts to find alternatives should be made. This will help to avoid situations in which aides continue to repeat errors and fail to grow for lack of input and challenge from others who are knowledgeable. But it is also fair to say, even for a relatively well-staffed program such as PMHP, that although we clearly see the importance of aide supervision, we have not succeeded in developing fully satisfactory mechanisms for providing it.

OTHER PROJECT MEETINGS

Ongoing Professional Meetings

The preceding sections described PMHP's basic "in-school" meetings and procedures; this one considers non-school-based PMHP meetings that are part of the project's current format.

When the initial round of professional training ended early in 1970, biweekly training and discussion meetings for professionals were initiated and have continued regularly throughout the project's most recent phase (1970–73). Some of these have dealt with content or approaches that go beyond PMHP's primary focus. For example, there have been several on behavior modification techniques with young children and several others on the special problems of children with learning disabilities. Other meetings provide new inputs about clinical procedures or research findings in a discussion format. As professionals filter out new information that seems relevant to their everyday problems, they transmit it to aides for direct application in work with children. Professional meetings also provide a forum for discussing everyday problems in conducting PMHP. Given the program's scope, these questions are numerous and varied. Examples, which differ across settings and personnel, include: What should be done if referrals are not coming in fast enough? What can be done if there are too many referrals? Which children are best suited for group assignments? What can be done if teachers, principals, or other school personnel are uncooperative or resistant to the program? Which children are reached by the program with more or less effectiveness? At other times, the meetings have dealt with even more practical matters such as needs for and utilization of space, the equipment and materials needed to conduct an effective program, how often children should be seen, and the criteria to be used in referring children to community agencies.

Several topics that are centrally related to the emerging role of a PMHP school mental health professional have come up repeatedly for discussion. Principal among these are consultation and supervision. Discussions about consultation dealt with such matters as optimal frequency; focuses for consultation sessions; preferences for having specific consultants at particular schools; concerns, at times, about the ineffectiveness of consultation; and perceived needs to cover new topics or materials in consultation sessions. Discussions of aide supervision were understandably frequent because this activity is so central to the professional's role in PMHP and to the program's integrity. These discussions were far ranging and included, for example, requests for suggestions about specific supervisory techniques, consideration of similarities and differences between consultation and supervision, expressions of concern by the professionals about the lack of time available to them for supervision or about their discomforts in the supervisory role, and the relative merits of case-centered versus consultee-centered supervision.

A number of the professional meetings "took off" from presentations of PMHP research findings. Since PMHP research has had a practical, program-related focus, many of its studies have produced findings with direct program implications—either reinforcing existing practices or pointing to new alternatives. Such translations were facilitated by the research staff's willingness to sift through large bodies of data, first, to distill those with program-related implications, and, second, to write reports about them that could be easily assimilated by nonresearchers.

Several examples will concretize the point. Among PMHP's most meaningful research studies in terms of professional feedback value are its annual reports on utilization of resources. Such studies handily summarize information about the number of children seen in each school and in the program as a whole, the number of consultation contacts with schools, the distribution of PMHP children by grade and by sex, and frequency of contacts with children in different settings. Thus the research staff can draw a composite picture for service people of how PMHP, deliberately or otherwise, has allocated its resources. Such data provide a needed matrix for aligning and comparing one's images of what a project *should* be like and what it is actually like. Utilization surveys can, for example, show that in setting A, aides see an average of six or seven children for 40 to 50 contacts each, whereas in setting B, aides see an average of ten or twelve children for

20 to 25 sessions each. Such data inevitably raise the question of whether differences in practice are related to the differences in children's needs and problems or to preconceived beliefs on the part of professionals and aides about optimal service patterns.

The following examples will further illustrate the point. The research team reported over several consecutive years that roughly two out of three PMHP children were being seen twice weekly by aides. When such a descriptive fact is followed, as it was in this case, by the additional finding that frequency of contact was unrelated to positive outcome (indeed, if anything, related negatively to outcome), then the group must reconsider the relationship of the program practices that have evolved, sometimes by default, to the program's key objectives. Presentation of this set of findings, as might be expected, elicited some defensiveness but also a good deal of discussion about possible constructive change in program practices. In addition, without prior explicit planning, it turned out that more than 95 per cent of all PMHP children who terminated in a given year did so during the last week of the program. The issue that this discovery raised for the professionals was whether such precipitous termination really reflected how children improved or betrayed a nonverbalized but real assumption that once a child started in PMHP, he had to continue for the full school year, no matter what happened. Furthermore, we discovered from the utilization studies that about 40 per cent of all PMHP children were being seen over multiple school years—again, by accident rather than by plan. When coupled with the additional fact that a child showed the most improvement during his first year in the project, this datum too provided food for discussion by professionals about possible revision of basic practices.

A somewhat different illustration of the same basic point can be found in the example cited earlier that withdrawn children seemed to profit much more from the program than did acting-out children or those with learning disabilities. When the research group reported this to the professionals, attention was necessarily directed to interventions that might be more effective with the latter two groups. The question regarding "pure-types" that we have tackled in PMHP is a special instance of a broader issue in human service intervention: How can helping services best be adapted to the particular problems of particular individuals? This question is just as real and appropriate for the broad field of psychotherapy (Garfield, 1971) as it is for PMHP. To answer it requires, first, that sensitive assessment procedures be developed to identify specific problems and, second, that the effectiveness of intervention procedures for different problems be determined empirically. The ultimate goal, for PMHP and for other interventions, is to develop problem-intervention taxonomies that encourage selection of intervention "matches" to maximize outcomes for all. To do so, however, a step is required in which research findings and their implications are digested and then translated into consumable form for program personnel.

This section has not attempted to consider the full range of research findings identified by the PMHP research team for consideration and discussion by professionals. Our purpose was merely to emphasize that this has been an important component of the professional meetings and to illustrate how it has been done. The points to be underscored are that the PMHP research team engages practical problems, distills their findings into understandable, discussible essences, and brings them back to professionals and district administrators to review as a basis for program modification. Thus PMHP is not a static project. It changes, hopefully in realistic and constructive ways, in the light of critical self-scrutiny. In that context, the professional meetings stand as an important vehicle for presenting findings and considering program alternatives. Without the professional's understanding of the empirical basis for program change and without his cooperation in this process, there can be little program growth.

Finally, the professional meetings served as a forum for gripes, grievances, and expression of concerns about perceived program malfunctions. Often such concerns pivoted around the professional's understandable view that the demands placed on him exceeded his available time. Supervision provides a case in point. In our earlier consideration of this topic, we neglected to mention that discussions about supervision among staff and professionals sometimes consisted of a tug-of-war between the two groups. The basic message emitted by staff was: "Fellahs, you've got to take this supervision stuff more seriously and do a lot more of it!" The response of some professionals, in effect, was: "But we just don't have enough time for supervision; there are simply too many other demands on us to run the show!" Other concerns were expressed by professionals: for example, many had doubts about the usefulness of the group testing data, particularly intellectual appraisal. Some argued that the data obtained from intelligence tests duplicated data that was available to them through their regular home-district testing programs; others, often with justification, complained that the tests were not scored sufficiently early to be useful to them; and still others complained that the data were invalid for the groups with which they were working, or for particular children.

The following exemplifies a very different concern expressed by professionals. An aide, either because of an initial error in professional judgment when she was hired or because of a current difficulty or crisis, was not doing her job well or, even more serious, did not seem well suited to the program. Such situations precipitated conflicts in the professional who knew that the aide was not right for the program but, because he had worked closely with her for so long, was unable to face terminating her.

Depending on the temper of the moment and the content being considered, professional meetings ranged from the highly involved, almost electrically charged, to a rather routine, humdrum, boring discharge of responsibility. Although such meetings served a valuable purpose in PMHP's development, it may be less important for other similar projects to have them for as long or as often as we have had them.

Ongoing Meetings with Aides

In addition to the meetings for professionals, regular meetings have also been held for PMHP aides, over and above consultative sessions in the schools. As suggested previously, a practical problem that developed as PMHP unfolded in diverse settings was that there was not enough professional time in some schools to provide for adequate supervision of aides. This led to some frustration for aides, who understandably felt they were floundering or not growing sufficiently on the job. In turn, this frustration, expressed directly or via senior aides, translated into pressure on PMHP staff to provide closer supervision. This posed a delicate dilemma: on the one hand, the staff did not wish to undercut the school-based professional; on the other, the aides' need for supervision was real.

Open discussion of this problem with professionals led to a decision that staff should provide additional aide supervision. Accordingly, a plan evolved for regular but voluntary supervisory-discussion meetings for PMHP aides to be held at project headquarters rather than in the schools. On the average, about 40 per cent of the aides turned out for these meetings, which were led by a senior outside consultant with special interest in this activity. Two major directions developed in these sessions. First, aides brought up difficult problems of child interaction and management for which they had not been able to obtain supervision. These were discussed by the group as a whole and by the consultant, who added his own inputs. A second thrust developed as aides began to express some feelings of inadequacy in certain areas of child handling, and specific requests surfaced for the consultant to present materials in areas where such shortcomings were felt. This was profitably done and often generated involved discussions by the group. In the main, these supplemental sessions were felt by all to serve a useful purpose.

In a somewhat different direction, further ad hoc training meetings for aides have developed as we identified, through additional field experience with the project, areas that needed further development. For example, from the time that the aide program started in 1964 until 1970, aides saw children individually. Clinically, it became clear to us that there were some youngsters who had problems (such as poor peer relationships or undersocialization) for which a group experience seemed more appropriate than an individual one. This led in 1970 to the development of a special training curriculum for aides who wished to start child groups (Terrell, McWilliams & Cowen, 1972). The curriculum included consideration of the goals and objectives of the group approach, its techniques, and its special advantages and limitations.

Aides were told about the proposed extension of training and had the option of participating or not, as they preferred. Thirty-one of the 57 PMHP aides opted to take the additional group training, and 24 of the 31 actually ran one or more groups that year in their home schools. Consultation and supervision of group work was provided by project staff. By the end of the school year (1971), the practice of having aides see small groups of children in addition to seeing children individually was established in the schools. Since then about 10 to 15 per cent of PMHP's contacts have been with small groups of children.

Another regular set of meetings is held for the senior aides. Typically, these meetings are conducted jointly by the project's chief psychologist and social worker as single two-and-one-half-hour monthly meetings. Senior aides have a special position in PMHP, both in terms of their roles and responsibilities and the challenges that the job raises (Cowen, Trost & Izzo, 1973b). Granting the considerable variability of the senior aide role in different settings, one important, common function was as a resource person for other aides. Thus senior aides were, in part, day-to-day trainers of new aides and were most often the persons available to provide information and answer questions. Not infrequently, senior aides were invited to observe a new aide and offer comments and suggestions to help sharpen her role and perfect her techniques. In addition to those "clinical" functions, the senior aide often did key administrative jobs (e.g., arranging agendas and preparing materials for consultants' visits; arranging school conferences involving teachers, aides, and other school personnel; and arranging actual work and room schedules for seeing children). In the latter sense, the senior aide was "an extra pair of hands" for professionals and helped to relieve them of certain responsibilities that would otherwise have taken up even more of their limited time. Specifically, most senior aides were assigned to three or four schools, spending about a day in each. Thus, as a group, senior aides had a rather broad perspective of the project's functioning. The fact that they were assigned to multiple schools also provided them with excellent points of contrast. It permitted them to make observations about the program's effectiveness or ineffectiveness in different settings as this related to the school's resources, personnel, philosophies, and interpersonal relationships.

The reality of the senior aide's situation was such that she was often called on to take actions or to make judgments that would in many quarters be seen as "professional." The fact that the senior aide was in a good position to identify problems called for a forum in which such problems and her stance with regard to them could be considered. The senior aide meetings served those purposes. A critical and frequent issue that came up in some guise during these meetings was that the senior aide was often trapped by a dual set of responsibilities and allegiances: her responsibility to the program in a particular school where she was assigned and her responsibility to the project itself, to which she reported. This sometimes put her in serious conflict. If she failed to report deficiencies in a particular program, she risked reinforcing its unsatisfactory elements. However, if she reported the deficiencies, she might be branded as an informer. But the availability of discussion-supervisory meetings for senior aides was important, for their personal growth and development, and for establishing the communications needed to identify program strengths and weaknesses and ultimately for increasing its effectiveness.

Meetings for Principals and Teachers

Periodic meetings, about twice a year, have also been held with PMHP principals. These meetings, which recognize principals' important role in PMHP, consider their current perceptions of the program and the problems they see in its operation. Principals are extremely important in any school. Their style and philosophy determine the school's operating profile and strongly influence how the project is construed and carried out. Principals have typically been enthusiastic about having PMHP in their schools; indeed, for some it has become something of an elitist badge of honor which is sometimes "lorded" over principals of non-project schools. In addition to eliciting useful views about the program, these meetings have also helped to provide principals with a current reading of program activities and previews of anticipated changes.

Another important meeting is the teacher workshop, held once a year. Teachers have almost daily contact with PMHP professionals and aides in discharging their everyday school responsibilities. They are also frequently exposed to PMHP consultants. Early in the school year, they participate in PMHP orientation meetings for school personnel conducted by the school mental health professionals. These contacts notwithstanding, teachers do not always have an accurate detailed picture of PMHP's aims and procedures. For that reason, we invited schools to designate teacher representatives and conducted a three-to-four-hour workshop for them. This workshop was held in a congenial atmosphere at project headquarters and included a lunch for the participants. It reviewed, in capsule form, PMHP's purposes, personnel, and ways of operation, including consideration of the variations needed to make the program viable in different settings. Teachers' questions and group discussions were encouraged to build a full, clear, accurate picture of the project. Teachers who participated in the workshop thus became on-site resource people or PMHP ombudsmen in their home schools.

In practice, teacher discussions of PMHP often take place in informal settings, such as the teachers' lounge during a coffee break. Although many of the teachers' questions about PMHP are directed to the team, this does not always happen. Thus, if each school has at least one teacher with a rich exposure to PMHP's concepts and procedures, she can serve as a readily available source of information for other teachers.

PMHP Staff Meetings

We have held regular monthly consultants' meetings for some time now. These meetings for all staff and outside consultants who actually visit schools provide an opportunity to bring back and to review with peers the problems and interesting challenges that come up for consultants. Consultants' meetings bring to the group's attention a broad array of program concerns from various school settings and a view of how problems cluster in certain settings. They also make clear the fact that consultants too have idiosyncratic styles and preferences. Some, for example, heavily emphasize clinical case consultation, whereas others are more concerned with the ongoing events of a consultative session. These meetings thus help to keep consultation skills "sharp." They update project communication and keep the group aware of the pulse of its activity and the trouble spots of the moment.

Two other meetings have been and continue to be basic to PMHP's operation: staff meetings, originally attended by all senior and junior staff and trainees, and research meetings, attended by all staff and research technicians as well as graduate students, undergraduates, and volunteers who are doing research.

Staff meetings are broad and far ranging in scope. Attending these meetings for a full school year is perhaps the best way to get a comprehensive picture of PMHP's inner workings. Matters considered at staff meetings range from basic policy issues about future PMHP directions, general reviews of program effectiveness, specific consideration of the current problems of the participating schools, and implications of research findings with regard to changes in program practices, personnel problems, and consultation-format schedules at one extreme to practical, mundane concerns such as ordering equipment and supplies, planning for a teacher workshop or principal's meeting, or purchasing television equipment for training and research at the other extreme.

As the project grew, staff meetings became more unwieldy because the staff gradually broadened to include a number of people with less central connections to the project's mainstream. Accordingly, more recent staff meetings had to give over major portions of time to announcements of information already known and digested by a smaller, more central, senior staff group. This change in our structure limited the staff meeting as a forum for dealing with significant project related issues and eventually led us to develop other mechanisms for dealing with such issues.

Regular weekly meetings dealing with all aspects of the research operation have also been an important aspect of PMHP's structure for many years. These meetings offer an opportunity for people to present notions, however neonatal or loosely formulated, about PMHP-related research studies that they would like to do or to have done. Such presentations are often little more than "blue-skying" framed by the hypothetical question "Wouldn't it be nice if we could study . . . ?" The research meetings frequently generate interesting, important, and doable research studies. Other focuses for these meetings, after potential research studies have been identified, include the development of specific research designs and the consideration of problems of methodology and instrumentation, which sometimes lead to studies that develop techniques needed to investigate variables of concern to participants. The meetings also consider alternate strategies concerning data collection, problems of experimental control, and other basic research issues. While studies are in process, individual investigators typically present interim summaries of research findings to the group framed in terms of questions such as "Are the data in hand sufficient to answer the question we raised?" "Do the findings thus far suggest a need to broaden the research base?" "What other analyses are needed to clarify interpretation of the data?" and so on. Still later, the findings are reviewed in terms of publishability and, more particularly, in terms of their implications for modifying PMHP practice. Many PMHP studies reported in the literature reflect exactly that practical orientation and have, as already noted, led to important revisions of PMHP practice. Because PMHP research studies are so varied, regular attendance at the research meetings inevitably exposes participants to a broad range of practical and methodological problems in research design and is thus a valuable training experience. Given the fact that we are involved in studies of outcome, prediction, selection, performance-characteristics, process, referral qualities of children, and the complex interactions among many of these variables, the range of exposure is broad indeed.

The reader does not need to be highly sophisticated or a mathematical wizard to realize that the sheer number of PMHP meetings staggers the imagination. By describing these meetings in detail, we do not intend to suggest that all of them are essential; rather, we do so to document how our particular experimental model unfolded and developed. This process obviously reflects the interests, the styles, and the resources of the Rochester experiment rather than the assumption that all such meetings are essential to the proper conduct of a project of this type. In the last analysis, PMHP's heart and soul consists of a few basic concepts, which happened to blend in particular ways. These concepts are (1) widespread, systematic early detection, (2) the use of nonprofessionals as helping agents in ways that geometrically expand the reach of helping services, (3) a focus on young children that will hopefully capitalize on their plasticity and modifiability, and (4) a change in the role of the professional from a person who renders direct helping services to one who recruits and trains nonprofessionals and acts as an educator, consultant, and supervisor. If these are sensible concepts, they can be operationalized in many different ways, given the realities of different resource systems.

This is true even within our own program, where some schools have considerably more professional resources than others. Conceivably, some aspects of our program could be omitted elsewhere. For example, our research, which has been extensive for many years, requires much time and effort from many people. We felt this to be extremely important in the program's development since, before PMHP could appropriately be used by others, documentation of its workings and effectiveness seemed essential. We do not assume that *all* replication programs need to invest in such a research component. New programs could properly develop as service programs by drawing upon PMHP's research findings and those of related projects that lend justification to this development.

A point that cannot be sufficiently underscored is that PMHP's particular pattern of meetings is not essential to the program. Program decisions by groups that wish to establish conceptually related approaches must be predicated on a realistic assessment of their resources. The challenge is not how to duplicate meetings that happened to serve the ecology, history, and resources of PMHP, but rather, given the new setting's resources, how best to achieve the goals of early detection, to use nonprofessionals as effective help-agents, and to expand services geometrically to early detected, vulnerable school children. Necessarily, this will require decisions about program priorities that reflect resources as well as local needs and problems. Fuller discussion of this issue and more specific suggestions about priority allocations appear in a later chapter.

7

PMHP's
Current
Structure

The most important challenge during the later phases of the expansion period was how to move from a circumscribed program in one small geographic region to an approach with greater impact on delivery of school mental health services across the country. That challenge shaped our current structure and determined our new course. In response to it, PMHP has been structurally modified in our geographic area, and a systematic effort is underway to disseminate the approach nationally. These developments are the main focuses of this chapter.

PROGRAM DIRECTIONS

Changing needs and times, together with PMHP's accumulated experience led in the fall of 1973 to a new, considerably more complex organization. The project heretofore always a homogeneous entity, at least structurally, was located in 17 schools in Rochester and the three adjacent county districts by spring 1974. Among the latter, all of one county district's elementary buildings were PMHP schools; a second county district had five PMHP buildings, all small, neighborhood schools; and the third had a single large PMHP primary school with 900 pupils.

The project now included three discrete components: CORE schools, consultation schools, and national dissemination. PMHP's new structural arrangement is depicted graphically in Figure 2. It will be helpful to keep that structure in mind during the descriptive account that follows. Contrasted with the project's earlier structural representation (see Figure 1), Figure 2 shows how PMHP has grown and changed.

CORE Schools

Four schools are designated as CORE schools. Actually there are five schools, since two small neighborhood primary schools (with 100 pupils each), in the county are fused as a single unit. Two of these are in the RCSD, and one each is in two county districts. Fundamentally, CORE schools are saturated program units, set up to permit optimal project representation and to favor smooth, effective functioning of the program. The CORE format was worked out in prior discussions with appropriate school district administrators, school principals, and the respective school mental health professionals, all of whom were enthusiastic about the new role. Each CORE school has the half-time services of knowledgeable, experienced, PMHP school mental health psychologists and social workers. In the RCSD, a single psychologist and social worker staff the two CORE schools as a full-time assignment. Both county CORE schools have half of a psychologist's and social worker's time; the other half is assigned to other district functions. Each CORE school has five experienced, well-qualified, half-time child aides with strong past-performance records.

FIGURE 2. ORGANIZATIONAL STRUCTURE OF PMHP, 1973-1974

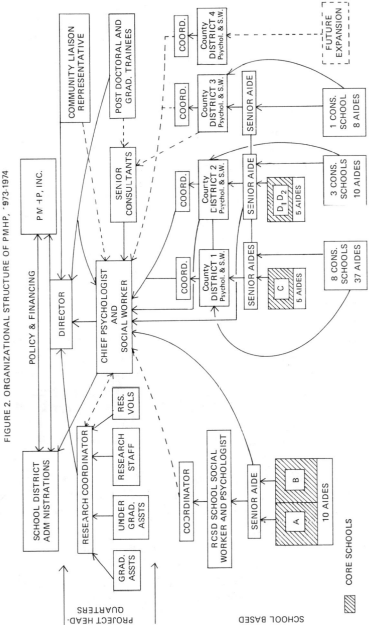

Basically, CORE schools are laboratory-demonstration-research settings. PMHP staff has greater control over programs in those buildings and greater certainty that key PMHP activities (e.g., aide-supervision) will take place. The "contract" with CORE schools also allows for diverse research activities. CORE psychologists and social workers are considered to be extensions of PMHP staff, and one staff meeting each month is held with CORE personnel to deal exclusively with conduct and management of the program in those settings. Moreover, "how-to-do-it" training sessions, dealing with gut project functions for district coordinators (see below) are also available to CORE professionals.

Since the project's procedures are assumed to be best represented in CORE schools, these schools serve as a base for parent districts to exemplify PMHP procedures for those with less background and experience. Thus a new PMHP school with less well-trained and less experienced personnel can gain first-hand experience with basic PMHP practices (e.g. referral conferences, group supervisiory meetings with aides) by observing and participating in such events *in vivo* at a CORE school. Similarly, CORE schools are prime visitation sites for national workshop participants. And as districts elsewhere implement programs and want concentrated PMHP internship experiences for their school mental health professionals, qualified people are placed in CORE schools for short-term internships under a CORE team's supervision.

Finally, CORE schools are locuses for innovation. As clinical experience and research findings in PMHP build up, some program practices are shown to be more effective than others. Thus exploring new approaches and/or modifying old ones is important. A point already cited in the finding (Lorion et al., 1974a) that seeing children twice weekly produces no better outcomes than seeing them once weekly. Doubtless, the project's reach could be extended appreciably by seeing more youngsters less often. Such findings have been discussed extensively with CORE personnel, with the objective of field testing program modifications in these schools.

CORE schools are designated in Figure 2 by hatched lines. CORE professionals and senior aides report to two different sets of people—to their respective district pupil-personnel service directors and to PMHP's chief psychologist and social worker. Overall, PMHP staff has more extensive and closer contacts with CORE personnel than with personnel from non-CORE settings.

Consultation Schools

All PMHP schools, other than the CORE group, are presently called consultation schools, meaning several things. One important difference between CORE and consultation schools is in their professional staffing patterns. Whereas we have "tampered" with normal district staffing patterns in the CORE schools to assure the half-time services of a psychologist and social worker in each, this is not done in consultation schools. Such schools have whatever staffing pattern is typical in the parent district. Thus the amount of professional time assigned to a PMHP consultation school may range from as little as four or five hours per week to as much as 12 to 15 hours, depending on the district's circumstances and resources. But, in general, consultation schools have less saturated service programs than CORE schools and thus their conference and supervisory activities are more diluted. The point to be emphasized, however, is that in consultation schools, the amount of professional time is determined by district needs and normal professional assignment practices rather than by PMHP staff preferences.

Second, consultation schools are freer than CORE schools to develop in terms of their own needs and stylistic preferences—i.e., to develop "as they must." This means several things in practice. They are free to use or not to use basic PMHP procedures and instruments. For example, even though PMHP has heavily used the TRF as a screening and teacher-referral device in the past, consultation schools are free not to use it or to substitute another screening procedure if they wish. In addition, consultation schools may decide not to use process forms to record the events of the aide-child interaction and aide supervision, or they may decide to substitute assessment procedures other than the California Test of Mental Maturity and the Draw-A-Man test in their group psychological-screening battery. Several consultation schools have done exactly that (especially if their parent districts happen to be using similar measures) because, understandably, they find it more convenient to be part of a homogeneous format.

Consultation schools have few research obligations or commitments. Since in practice they assume PMHP to be effective, they do not typically go through annual research and evaluation cycles. Instead they concentrate their more limited resources on program services. Should they wish to have formal program evaluation or to do other project-related, nonevaluative research, PMHP staff furnishes the necessary assistance and consultation. PMHP staff, however, still provides training and consultation for new professionals coming into consultation schools.

Thus, although consultation schools maintain ties with PMHP's central operation, the federation is weaker than the one with CORE schools. An important aspect of the consultation school program is the move toward decreasing and ultimately severing the ties to central PMHP staff. We assume that if PMHP indeed offers a viable alternative for delivering school mental health services, the ultimate initiative for and direction of such programs should reside *within* school districts. Thus, as part of the consultation school's development, PMHP staff has attempted to build in growth mechanisms that will allow districts to assume increasing responsibility for and leadership of the program. This is another reason why it is appropriate for consultation schools to be increasingly involved in determinations concerning project formats and procedures. It is realistic that things be done this way if the project is to fit district needs and resources well several years hence.

An important administrative step, taken to facilitate development of the consultation school concept, was to have each participating school district appoint a project coordinator. This was to be a relatively senior district person, who would be trained in basic PMHP functions and assume increasing responsibility for discharging the maintenance and leadership roles needed for the project to become an independent, district entity. It is fitting that the four people appointed as program coordinators by the respective districts differ in their within-district roles and positions. In the RCSD, the coordinator is the district's chief of psychological services. Two other coordinators are senior mental health professionals who were in PMHP line roles for several years. And, in the fourth district, the coordinator is a supervising teacher with relatively little prior background or experience with the project. Since three of the four participating districts are affiliated with a larger Board of Cooperative Educational Services (BOCES) system that includes other county districts which in the past have expressed interest in starting PMHPs, the BOCES chief psychologist and chief social worker were appointed as PMHP coordinators for that parent system.

It is clear that the several coordinator's roles are "shaking down" somewhat differently. Several districts got off to faster starts than others with respect to such factors as the amount of contact the coordinator had with central PMHP staff, the functions for which he was willing or able to be trained and to assume responsibility, and so forth.

Moreover, it is still unclear, while the symbiotic link with the project's central headquarters remains in force, whether the coordinator's role will go beyond administrative and training responsibilities to include power and authority functions such as those involved in hiring and firing. Creation of the district coordinator positions had also introduced occasional role complexities, as can be seen in Figure 2. Thus, in the RCSD, one county district, and the BOCES unit, PMHP staff has no control whatsoever over coordinators, except for whatever voluntary control the latter wish to have exercized over them. Such a relationship is indicated by dotted lines in Figure 2. The relationship between the other two county coordinators and PMHP staff is even more complicated because of the accidental fact that they both double as a CORE psychologist or social worker in their home districts. As CORE professionals, they are partly accountable to senior PMHP staff; however, when wearing their district coordinator's hats, they have the same voluntary relationship to the project staff as do the other coordinators.

The appointment of coordinators was more than just an administrative formality. It was motivated by the conviction, stated previously, that if the project was to endure, it must ultimately be the districts' "show" to run. Accordingly, PMHP staff took the position that whatever PMHP procedures and practices were teachable should, over a brief period, be taught to responsible district personnel— in this case the coordinators. It seemed that the chances for a project's survival would be enhanced by a planned, but gradual and sheltered transfer of responsibility from project to district headquarters.

Thus PMHP staff identified key program elements and developed a series of training exercises, including individual modeling sessions for certain activities and a group seminar for coordinators, designed to strengthen their hand for program leadership in the districts. Among project activities suited for direct modeling was the interviewing and selection of new aides. Given the project's imminent expansion to new schools and the fact that future expansion and aide turnover would require new rounds of training, this seemed to be an essential, concrete, starter activity. Despite the fact that PMHP staff had written extensively about aide selection, we believed that by modeling live interviews with prospective aides and by providing immediate postinterview feedback and evaluation, a richer, more meaningful learning experience could be provided for coordinators. Accordingly, the project's chief social worker, who had heretofore been exclusively responsible for initial interviews with prospective aides, arranged joint screening interviews with district coordinators during the summer of 1973. This helped to make a previously abstract procedure more concrete. As coordinators gained experience in the new role, it was easier for them to interview and select aides on their own and to train other district personnel in interviewing guidelines and the criteria for aide selection.

During the fall semester, 1973, project staff conducted a crash course for district coordinators in the "nuts and bolts" of PMHP's operation. CORE professionals were invited to attend and participate in these sessions. Since all chose to attend, the training group included ten people. The meetings were designed to review concrete program practices and were built around the following theme: If it's teachable, let's try to teach it! Since there was much to be covered all at once, the first six or eight group meetings were held weekly. Later the group moved to biweekly meetings, and by the end of the first semester, the meetings were held monthly, with a corresponding shift in focus to the new program's operational problems.

Some of the topics covered during the initial intensive phase included the following:

1. Clarification of the project's new structure and organization, including detailed consideration of the different "contracts" (two-way sets of commitments and

obligations) between PMHP and CORE as well as consultation schools,

2. Psychological assessment procedures used in PMHP for initial intellectual and personality appraisal, and equivalents that could be used in consultation schools,

3. Teacher screening and referral devices,

4. In-depth review of the purposes and procedures of the social workers' contacts with parents,

5. Detailed consideration of procedures for selecting aides, including the focus and content of the initial screening interview and a review of the rating scales for aide characteristics that have been used in past selection rounds,

6. Review of procedures for training aides: i.e., the content covered and the relation of the initial formal training to later on-the-job training,

7. Specific consideration of PMHP program components, such as the initial assignment conferences, mid-year progress conferences, and end-of-year termination conferences,

8. Consultation—including the use of program consultants (PMHP staff members whose prime concerns are with the smooth, effective conduct of the program and the modeling of program elements) and clinical or outside consultants (mental health professionals who are closely associated with PMHP and provide program enrichment through clinical case consultation on especially complex or unusual cases),

9. Supervision of aides, emphasizing both its importance for continuous, on-the-job growth as well as specific techniques for individual and group supervision, and

10. Research data, presented in a practical program-oriented way concerning the question: What do these findings tell us that might suggest program modifications? For example, the fact that better outcomes were found for shy-anxious children than for acting-out children or those

with learning problems (Lorion et al., 1974b) led to discussion and suggestions about how standard PMHP interventions for the latter two groups could be improved. This discussion resulted in a small pilot program, using specific behavioral approaches for establishing self-control in impulsive children, that is now being carried out by a group of interested aides in two county schools. Similarly, the finding that much of the improvement of project children occurs in the first rather than later years (Lorion et al., 1974a) suggested the need to explore precontracted, short-term (e.g., six-, eight-, or ten-session) interventions for some children. This orientation is especially appropriate in view of the scarcity of resources in our own and other settings. We approached "new practices" by first "hearing" our research findings and trying to translate their implications specifically into new program directions. We have, however, approached such change conservatively. Rather than try to overhaul PMHP's basic structure, we have opted for mini pilot programs, when interest and need so dictate, to establish "beachheads" of new practice that, if demonstrably effective, can later be more broadly incorporated into the larger project.

As suggested in the preceding section, the thrusts of the coordinator training sessions are to transmit the usable knowledge we have acquired, build toward increasing district autonomy, suggest new ways of approaching service delivery, provide the direction and modeling needed to initiate new practices, and offer supportive resources to districts in their effort to advance the program's service and/or research components.

The preceding goals, although difficult to achieve, are very important for several reasons. First, the ultimate mode of operation envisioned for the project—one of district autonomy—is essential, given the realities of today's pinched education budgets and the growing scarcity of outside moneys to support innovative school mental health projects. Increasingly, the question school district mental health personnel must face in one or another form is: "How can we get more mileage for less money?" Second, even though consultation school versions of PMHP are more dilute and autonomous than the original, these schools still have better contact with central PMHP staff and more program information than would new districts from other parts of the country, starting from scratch. Thus, if PMHP variants are to be implemented elsewhere, the model should be demonstrably workable in our geographic area, even with considerably less central involvement of PMHP staff than in the past.

An important practical issue not yet considered is how the relationship between PMHP and consultation schools works from an administrative-budgetary standpoint. Consultation schools now operate essentially on a pay-as-you-go basis. At budget time, a "contractual" arrangement, reflecting the school district's current program status and needs, is worked out between PMHP Inc. and appropriate district fiscal and administrative officers. The contract specifies the nature and amount of program-supporting services to be provided by PMHP staff. These items are "priced out," and their sum represents the amount paid by each school for the service package. Thus a typical consultation school contract for 1973–74 might include the following items: (1) eight "program consultation" visits (one per month) by the chief project psychologist or social worker, (2) eight clinical consultation visits (one per month) by outside PMHP consultants, (3) training sessions for district coordinators, (4) training sessions for new professionals in project schools, (5) training sessions for new child aides (6) six to eight seminar sessions for child aides, (7) informational meetings for teachers and principals, (8) periodic consultation with district administrators (e.g., superintendents, school board members, pupil personnel coordinators, and business managers) pertaining to various program components, (9) research consultation on projects of interest to the school, (10) provision of instructional material, training manuals, and assessment instruments, (11) availability of the central project's library and audio- and videotapes of project procedures, and (12) phone consultation, as needed, with senior clinical project personnel.

Although the foregoing is a typical "contract," it is, for several reasons, not uniform for all districts. First, contract services are limited by the available PMHP resource pool, so there are situations in which some contract elements are detached and met through other resources. Thus, in one district, which joined the program late in the year, both program and clinical consultation are handled by an outside consultant—a person who had spent a full postdoctoral year with PMHP and is thus familiar with its operations. (This arrangement is depicted by the oval on the district line in Figure 2.) Second, contract terms must reflect a given program school's situation. A veteran school may require relatively few consultative visits, whereas a new school may require extra supervisory time to help new personnel learn about the program's day-to-day details. Finally, as consultation schools gain more experience and develop more district leadership and autonomy, they require fewer supporting services from central PMHP staff— a fact that should be reflected in the annual contract. Conversely, because PMHP staff devotes less time to veteran districts (because their potential for more autonomous program conduct has grown), it has more time and resources to extend the program to new districts that wish to start programs.*

---

*Since this section was written, a major administrative change, reflecting the move toward district autonomy envisioned in the text, did in fact, take place (9/74). BOCES I appointed its own full-time PMHP coordinator, Mr. Gene McCabe. This means that the four separate county coordinator roles depicted in Figure 2 are now collapsed into a single role and a single person.

National Dissemination

As PMHP came slowly to the view that the new model offers an effective, scope-expanding alternative to traditional school mental health delivery systems, the question of how other districts around the country might best harvest our experience moved into sharper focus. PMHP's first ten years were entirely sheltered, restricted as they were to a small pilot-demonstration project, and even in its first three years of expansion, the project was confined to the Rochester, New York, area. Although, particularly during this later phase, we received many requests for reprints, training manuals, and test instruments and although several former students had, in their post-trainee job placements, started kindred programs, relatively little had happened to promote systematic adoption of this seemingly utilitarian delivery system. Our experience was not unlike the more general finding of Shore (1972) that less than 10 per cent of the important changes in service delivery practices can be traced to information obtained via the printed word.

Doubtless, grant programs, no matter how careful their screening and review procedures, yield only a small fraction of projects with socially significant payoffs from among the relatively large numbers funded. Worse yet, because dissemination-utilization mechanisms are so underdeveloped, a substantial proportion, even of these few successful projects, become archival. Organizations that had generously supported PMHP through its slow, difficult developmental phases rightfully became concerned about the need to disseminate project findings and to promote more widespread utilization of the model elsewhere. With this objective in mind, a trial run, designed to encourage new PMHP utilizations, took place in May 1972. The backbone of the experience was a week-long live-in workshop, described in more detail later, that dealt with PMHP's rationale and practices. That model became a prototype for the more serious, systematic dissemination effort that comprises the third major component of our current activities.

The key initial decision made in planning a national workshop concerned who the appropriate target people should be. Since our aim was to root similar programs in new districts, it seemed that school district personnel, influentially involved in the delivery of school mental health services, were the ideal targets. Our internal bookkeeping system was such that we had on hand relatively complete listings of requests received over several years, for reprints, training manuals, and testing measures. From these lists, we selected people with school district addresses, assuming that this would provide a group with some prior interest in and information about PMHP. Approximately 75 such persons were contacted and informed of the workshop. Additionally, workshop announcements were sent out to about 60 university and/or agency-based mental health professionals, known to have strong school mental health interests. The latter group was not invited to participate directly, although as it turned out some did apply; rather, they were asked to call the workshop to the attention of qualified personnel in school districts in which they were working.

The original mailing contained three documents: (1) a cover letter, roughing out in general form the workshop's projected nature and purposes, the content to be covered, the criteria to be used in selecting participants, specific information about procedures for applying, and deadlines, (2) a three-page synopsis of PMHP's rationale, evolution, and current format to insure that prospective applicants would be familiar with the program's specifics and could thus judge whether or not to apply, and (3) a two-page application form that had to be filled out and submitted two months before the workshop. In addition to routine identifying data (e.g., name, home address, home telephone number), the application required the following information: actual job title and name of employment setting; educational background, including degrees received and dates; description of current job, including major roles and activities; a summary of past experience in school settings; and a statement presenting the applicant's reasons for wanting to participate in the workshop. The final, most complex item called for a statement by a responsible administrator from the applicant's home district verifying the candidate's position and commenting on the district's interest in implementing PMHP. This item was included both to insure that a highly placed district administrator knew about PMHP and wished the candidate to participate in the workshop, and to provide a rough preliminary assessment of the district's interest in and potential for program implementation.

In the approximately six weeks between the time the workshop announcements were distributed and the final deadline for submitting applications, about 50 applications were received. These varied in terms of factors such as professional background, job status, and geographic location of the candidate. Since we could only accommodate about ten school districts, we were forced to sharpen criteria for selecting the final group. These criteria fell into two main clusters: the candidate's personal qualifications and the attributes of the group as a whole. Among the former, we were less concerned with personal background and training qualifications and more with characteristics such as the strength of the district's commitment to implement PMHP, the applicant's familiarity with and interest in the program, and his position in a district's power structure—i.e., his potential for bringing about change in service delivery methods. We also sought to choose a maximally balanced group with respect to geographic diversity, professional background, type of school district (e.g., urban and rural, large and small), and problems represented. Grant funds were available to cover participants' travel and living expenses. Although districts were told that only one representative could be supported, they were given the option of sending a second person if they would subsidize his travel and living expenses.

Although some candidates (e.g., university faculty, students, temporary school district employees, and mental health professionals not associated with schools) were eliminated from consideration, final selection among the remaining well-qualified applicants was difficult. In the end, ten school districts that best met the individual and composite criteria were selected. These included Philadelphia, Pa.; Des Moines, Iowa; Austin and Ft. Worth, Tex.; Louisville, Ky.; Ansonia, Conn.; Ann Arbor, Mich.; Fairbanks, Alaska; Minneapolis, Minn.; and Lawrence, N.Y. Four of the ten sent a second participant at their own expense, for a total of 14 participants. The group included individuals with backgrounds in psychology, social work, and education.

The workshop program was intensive, including 40 to 50 hours of formal meetings and discussion in a span of six days. Overall, its main objective was to provide participants with as clear and detailed a picture as possible of PMHP's rationale and procedures. The workshop had a practical flavor; it was aimed at providing concrete information and materials to ease implementation for districts with such interests.

For several months before the workshop, project staff prepared, reviewed, screened, and edited 28 videotape film clips of basic project events to be used for the conference and later, as the backbone of a PMHP videotape film library for training and dissemination. These tapes covered "gut" PMHP functions such as individual and group supervision of aides; consultation sessions; referral, progress, and termination conferences; aides actually working with individual children or groups of children; and discussions about PMHP with aides. From these raw materials, several illus-

trative tapes, reflecting diverse project activities, were selected for use in the workshop.

Conference participants arrived on a Sunday afternoon, and a reception center manned by PMHP was kept
open during that period to allow staff and participants to
get acquainted and begin informal discussion. Thereafter,
things proceeded hectically in the following sequence. The
first day's sessions included an introduction of participants
and a description of their school districts' ways of operating, resources, and problems; a conceptual overview of the
mental health fields today and their problems, leading to a
development of the rationale for PMHP; a specific overview
of PMHP as it had unfolded; and a video-tape of an assignment conference.

On the morning of the second day, participants, in
small groups of three or four, visited project schools for the
first time to see the program in action and to meet with line
program personnel. This was followed by a luncheon session, during which participants shared and discussed their
school observations and raised issues and questions growing out of the morning's experience. Later that day a discussion session was devoted to topics associated with
setting up a project of this type in a school: e.g., selection
of site and personnel, orientation of school personnel and
parents, use of aides, and consultation. The last exercise of
the second day involved the viewing of a video-tape of aides
working with individual children and a small group.

The third morning included a series of "in-parallel"
meetings in which small groups of participants met directly
with small groups of aides to learn firsthand about the
aides' role. These meetings were followed by a discussion
and question session among PMHP staff and participants to
develop a clearer, more detailed view of the aides' role.
There were two major sets of afternoon meetings on the
third day. The first involved school district pupil personnel
directors and school principals, who provided an administrator's-eye view of the project. The second involved the

lay members of PMHP Inc., our supporting citizens' group, who discussed practical issues pertaining to project "survival" (e.g., fiscal matters, public education, and the like). The third evening, the workshop's midpoint, was the occasion for a social gathering involving participants, staff, school personnel, administrators, and corporation members. This was not only a pleasant and relaxing change of pace, but it also provided opportunities for unusual mixes of people and for conference participants to pursue, less formally, areas of special interest to them.

The fourth morning witnessed a second school visit by participants, again in small groups. This visit coincided with an actual consultation session conducted by a senior PMHP consultant, followed by a discussion among consultants and participants about the objectives, tactics, and outcomes of the session. The fourth afternoon included a meeting between groups of participants and several senior aides to learn more, firsthand, about the senior aides' role and a meeting with PMHP staff to discuss and ask questions about that role. The last event of the afternoon was a discussion session based on film clips of individual and group supervision of aides.

The fifth morning was devoted entirely to the subject of school mental health consultation. Several videotapes illustrating the diversity of content, focus, and consulting style in such sessions were used, followed by small discussion groups led by the consultants who were involved in the taped sessions. There were two afternoon sessions on this day: one dealt with the place of evaluation and research in PMHP and included a brief presentation of some key project findings; the other was a more open-ended, freewheeling, discussion session designed to allow participants to zero in on issues that they felt had not yet been sufficiently considered.

The final meeting on the sixth morning was a plenary session involving all participants and PMHP staff. This session allowed the participants to integrate what they had

learned, to consider how this new information could contribute to programming in their home districts, to consider
the resources and problems that they might realistically be
expected to have in such an effort, and to begin to plan
jointly with staff for concrete follow-through.

Based on participants' on-site comments as well as
later, more reasoned, written follow-up comments, there is
reason to believe that the workshop, in the main, "went
well." Participants ended up with a reasonably clear, realistic view of PMHP; some understanding of what it takes to
put a project of this type together; its opportunities and
danger points; some ideas about how the project's underlying objectives must be applied realistically in the light of a
particular district's needs, problems, styles, and resources;
and a concrete introduction to PMHP's specific methodologies, training procedures, and assessment devices.

We do not mean to say that the workshop was flawless.
Some things, in retrospect, clearly were wrong. A case in
point is the breakneck pace inflicted on the participants,
including workdays that often started just after 8:00 A.M. in
the morning and lasted until 6:00 P.M. in the evening. In
our zeal to impart "essential" facts, we failed to respect
well-known psychological principles about the conditions
required for effective learning. It is doubtful, for example,
that participants profited much from any session held from
4:30 to 6:00 P.M. Several participants felt that there should
have been more emphasis on program troublespots, on
practical matters associated with rooting and sustaining a
project of this type, and on specific recommendations as to
how the project could be tailored to suit situations where
there were fewer or different resources.

National dissemination of PMHP is an integral aspect
of our current program, and we view the intensive live-in
workshop as a key starting point in this approach. At the
time of this writing, we had just completed a second national workshop, held in January 1974. Notwithstanding

Rochester's bad winters, we again had more than 50 applications. The quality of the applicants was high, and there were even fewer obvious rejects than during the first round. Again, using the criteria of the school district's interest and commitment and the candidate's potential for influencing mental health delivery approaches, a participant group of psychologists, social workers, and educators was selected from 11 school districts: Bath-Brunswick, Maine; Charlotte, N.C.; Seattle, Wash.; Denver, Colo.; St. Louis, Mo.; Camp Hill (Harrisburg), Pa.; Honolulu, Hawaii; Tallahassee, Fla.; Ridgway, Pa.; Grand Rapids, Mich.; and Bloomington, Ill.; Heidelberg, Germany (U.S. Army School District). The group once more included people with diverse professional backgrounds, the participant districts ranged from large urban ones to rural areas, and special ethnic and minority problems were well represented. The program's format included much of the same content as that covered in the initial workshop. But it was presented at a less frenetic pace and thus fostered better learning conditions.

Two other features, both designed to promote implementation, have been built into the new program. There are provisions for on-site follow-up visits by senior PMHP staff members in those districts implementing the program. Presumably there is a period after the workshop during which participants take back to their home districts a set of new learning and possible implementation plans. These must be considered in terms of the district's procedures and time schedule by responsible district personnel and hopefully lead in some cases to a concrete implementation plan. In the course of early district-level exploration, such tentative plans will almost certainly raise practical issues and identify problems that must be overcome. At some point in this sequence, which will doubtless be different for different districts, an in-depth site visit from a PMHP staff person may help to resolve some of the practical problems and facilitate the implementation. Indeed, within the first two months following the 1974 workshop, three such fol-low-up site visits had already been made.

A second element, also designed to encourage implementation, is the opportunity for short-term (one week to one month) internships in CORE schools. As districts move ahead in their plans to develop related programs, additional practical issues will surface. Although such issues may have been touched on during the workshop, experiencing firsthand how the project works can enhance the chances of launching a new program successfully. Thus the short-term internship is designed to permit the district person to work in a PMHP school while simultaneously participating in several rounds of PMHP staff, training, and research meetings and having the opportunity for in-depth discussions about matters that are relevant to the program with local PMHP line and staff personnel. The internship program has already become an actuality; two districts have sent both a psychologist and a social worker to PMHP since the 1974 workshop. The simultaneous presence of four internes from two school districts was a good plan. It consolidated and accelerated learning by providing opportunities for mutual support, discussion, and on-the-spot feedback and planning.

It is difficult for several reasons to "count" new PMHP implementations accurately. For one thing, we simply don't hear about some of them. There are marginal instances in which related projects have sprung up without ever coming in direct contact with PMHP. Other programs may result from individuals contacting PMHP in person or by phone, without participating in a workshop; or the idea might have spread through distributed reprints and materials. At the time of writing, about six to eight mini-PMHPs apparently had developed in various places around the country as a result of workshop or training experiences with us. Indeed, in one instance (Sandler, Duricko & Grande, 1974), formal research evaluation of a similar program yielded interesting and significant data concerning effectiveness. Another half dozen or so program implementations appear to be well along the way to being launched, and up to ten additional districts are in various early stages of exploring how to start a project of this type.

The ultimate importance of rooting workable, utilitarian, new, school mental health delivery systems should not obscure the complexity and difficulty of that task, touching as it does on the adaptability of new approaches to the realities of different settings and resources, the extent to which such programs must compete with other worthy ones for scarce funds, and the involvement and commitment of individuals and their ability to modify entrenched ways of doing things. Despite these potential adversities, PMHP is committed to developing new utilizations of the model in diverse settings. The project's current structure—involving saturated CORE schools as training, research, and demonstration centers; consultation schools, in which the thrust is toward developing district-based leadership and autonomy in program conduct; and the national dissemination component, designed to help other districts reap the benefits of our hard come-by experience—appears to comprise a sensible, realistic fourth stage in PMHP's natural evolution.

8

The
Research
Operation

The main thrust of the book thus far has been to describe PMHP's service programs. In doing so, several examples of ties between service and research have been given. Although PMHP is primarily a clinical program designed to bring effective helping services to young children, it has sought continually to evaluate its effectiveness and to establish a data base from which more could be learned about child development, children's adaptation to school, and school adjustment problems. The present chapter focuses on the research operation. We shall review the studies PMHP has done, their main findings, and some research issues that have surfaced as the project has become a complex, community-based, service-justified entity located in diverse school settings.

The idea that we hope to communicate in this chapter is that PMHP has forged a unique blend of service and research into a marriage that, though rocky at times, has basically been fruitful. Notwithstanding the different, sometimes competing goals and methods of service and research, we have established a way of living in which both objectives develop in mutually respecting, supportive ways. PMHP's research has been far removed from the quiet dignified academic atmosphere of the university laboratory, more and more so with the project's growth over time. Without the ivory tower's insulation and protection, we have become increasingly aware of the difficulties of "real world" research and of evaluating live service programs— issues that will be considered in later sections of this chapter.

One hazard of evaluative research for program personnel with vested interests is that it can expose program weaknesses or failings. As such, it can readily be viewed with apprehension or mistrust. Optimally, research calls for careful, systematic acquisition of data, controlled conditions, and a genuine effort and commitment of time on the part of many people. Among those who do not grasp the immediacy or relevance of research findings—and these points are indeed sometimes difficult to grasp—research demands can generate resentment and resistance. Although such reactions are part of his reality, the researcher cannot allow them to determine his decisions about how research should be done. That would leave out an important part of the picture. Just as one can contrast the optimistic and pessimistic views of those who describe a glass of water as half full or half empty, one can also emphasize the positive or negative side of research.

Systematic evaluation of a program helps to isolate effective and ineffective components and thus to maximize the likelihood of its success. Equally important, research can assure those who provide services that they are meeting their responsibilities to children. One of the most difficult challenges for service providers is to assess the consequences of their efforts objectively. The careful balance between service and research developed by PMHP was designed as a safeguard against the danger that a conceptually attractive alternative to traditional school mental health services might replace such services because of its logic, rhetoric, or glamor rather than its empirical findings. School mental health programs will be improved only as their strong and weak points are identified, noneffective ones are dropped, and needed changes are made in others.

SCOPE OF PMHP-RELATED WRITINGS

Much has been written about the PMHP experience. One can, for example, compare those writings that deal with core PMHP elements with those that consider related offshoot programs, general issues of child development and school adjustment, or training issues. Another way of ordering PMHP-related writings is to distinguish between empirical studies and descriptive accounts or discussions of training implications that grow out of the project experience. Based on the latter distinction, one can report nearly 50 PMHP or PMHP-related empirical studies straddling diverse areas of content.

Although the main purpose of this chapter is to summarize the project's research, it may be helpful first to cite some of its nonresearch writings. There have been a number of descriptive accounts of the full project or some aspect of it written during PMHP's history (Cowen, 1969b; Cowen, 1972; Cowen, Dorr, Izzo, Madonia, and Trost, 1971; Cowen et al., 1973b; Cowen and Lorion, 1975a; Cowen and Zax, 1969; Izzo, 1968; Izzo and Trost, 1968; Terrell et al., 1972; Trost, 1968a, Trost, 1968b; Trost, 1968c; Zax and Cowen, 1967; Zax and Cowen, 1969; Zax, Cowen, Izzo, Madonia, Merenda, and Trost, 1966). One descriptive article (Cowen, 1968b) reports on closely related programs that have grown out of the PMHP experience. Several additional papers (Cowen, 1969a; Cowen, 1970; Cowen, 1971a; Cowen, Chinsky & Rappaport, 1970;

PMHP Manual, 1970) focus on PMHP's implications for training in the mental health fields. And another group of conceptual-theoretical writings, removed from day-to-day project operations, nevertheless were shaped in important ways by the PMHP development (Cowen, 1967; Cowen, 1971b; Cowen, 1973; Cowen, Gardner & Zax, 1967; Cowen & Zax, 1967; Zax & Cowen, 1972).

The remaining 50 or so PMHP-related writings are directly based on empirical studies. Several of these are reports of conceptually related programs that share the structural qualities of using nonprofessionals as helping agents with target groups that need interpersonal assistance. In all these programs, the professional serves as a trainer, consultant, and resource person in ways that geometrically expand the reach of helping services. This group of programs has come about by transporting or extending the PMHP model to other areas as a means of probing the approach's generality. One illustration of a broad program generalization of this type is found in the comprehensive study of the use of college students as socializing agents with chronic hospitalized schizophrenics (Rappaport, Chinsky & Cowen, 1971). Less far afield, data have been presented which show that retired people (Cowen, Leibowitz & Leibowitz, 1968) and college students (Cowen, Carlisle & Kaufman, 1969; Cowen, Zax & Laird, 1966b), like child aides, can bring effective helping services to young school children in need. "Tuned-out" high school students have also been used effectively as help-agents with maladapting primary graders (Clarfield & McMillan, 1973; McMillan, 1974; McWilliams & Finkel, 1973).

In several of the "offshoot" programs just described (those using retirees and "tuned-out" high school students) the help-agents themselves are people who are disenfranchised or alienated. In our society the retiree is often turned out to pasture, so to speak, in hopes that he will graze quietly and unobtrusively. Society's "set" toward retirees is typically one in which the battle is considered won if nothing is heard from them; consistent efforts to harness the wisdom and experience of retirees in socially productive ways are rare. Though the substantive problems of "tuned-out" youth are different, they parallel those of retirees structurally in that young people are also in a situation in which neither their energies nor resources are used in personally or socially contributory ways. In a different way, they too are left to graze.

The value of using socially disenfranchised groups in human-service roles is that the operation of the "helper" therapy principle is facilitated (Riessman, 1965). This principle suggests that among the most useful, personally therapeutic things that can happen to socially disenfranchised individuals is for them to become involved in situations in which their own actions and interventions bring genuine help to other human beings in need. In the programs described here, those other human beings happen to be maladapting primary graders. If isolated social groups such as retirees, "tuned-out" high school students, and others can be cast into meaningful helping roles in the human services, the resultant programs can encourage the simultaneous, mutually supportive resolution of complex social problems—the alienation and anomie of the helper and the maladaptive behaviors of those he helps.

Another derivative program should be mentioned in which college students serve as help-agents with inner-city toddlers, identified through routine examinations at well-baby clinics as having slow linguistic, personal, and social development despite the absence of adverse physiological or neurological indicants (Jason, Clarfield & Cowen, 1973; Jason & Kimbrough, 1974; Specter & Cowen, 1971). Although this program is substantively different from PMHP, emphasizing as it does the specific ingredients of enrichment, stimulation, and language modeling, and the shaping of prosocial behavior, it is nevertheless conceptually related. A major link exists between the two programs in the area of early detection and the view that the sooner intervention procedures are started, the more promising the prognosis. That being so, it is natural to look for situations in which even earlier applications of early detection and intervention can be undertaken. The rapid, dramatic, positive changes brought about by extremely early intervention with inner-city toddlers underscores the potential fruitfulness of this approach.

RESEARCH STUDIES

This section summarizes PMHP's empirical studies, done over the past 15 years. The aim of the section is simply to provide a broad picture of what we have studied and found. Although we are aware of certain methodological and design problems that have plagued some of these studies, particularly during the recent period of expansion, the section's strategy will be to overview the data without intruding these research issues and problems. This is a decision of convenience rather than repression. It is simply more parsimonious, more compact, and easier to follow this way. A later section of the chapter considers the methodological and design issues that shape and limit the conclusions to be drawn from PMHP's studies of outcome.

The group of some 40 empirical investigations most closely related to PMHP's main thrust include methodological and test-development studies; studies of parents', teachers', and aides' perceptions of the project; studies of selection and performance characteristics of aides, studies of the aide-child interaction process; studies of the project's overall structure and scope; partial or overall evaluations of the project's effectiveness; and studies of issues related to child development and school adjustment that grow out of the project's data base.

Methodological Studies and Test Development

At several points in PMHP's history, it has been necessary to modify existing instruments and techniques or develop new ones to assess variables that have been considered central to the project's service operations or research evaluations. Some early test developments are described in the project's first evaluation report (Cowen et al., 1963), which included child-adjustment and performance scales and teacher-reaction measures. One study from that era (Cowen, Izzo, Trost & Monjan, 1964) describes the use of a quasiprojective measure, the Secret Stories test, used only in the initial round of PMHP evaluation studies. Another illustration of early methodological work is the study by Beach, Cowen, Zax, Laird, Trost, and Izzo (1968), which helped to pinpoint specific family history correlates (e.g., mothers' and fathers' attitudes and the nature of the mother-father relationship) of the global Red Tag judgment made about school maladapting children.

More important, especially recently, has been the development of several rapid, reliable, objective measures used both for mass screening and referral and, later, for evaluating the progress of PMHP children. Although some type of measure for early detection and screening has been used since the project began (Cowen et al., 1963) and the interrelations among several of these early measures have been explored (Cowen, Dorr & Orgel, 1971), the past several years have witnessed an intensified effort (briefly noted in Chapter 6) to refine early detection and evaluation procedures to a far greater extent.

The first of the two measures to undergo such intensive study was the AML, an 11-item quick-screening device for teachers—a test that we did not develop. The original AML research came from a series of studies conducted in the 1960s in the California State Department of Education (Bower, 1960; Van Vleet & Kannegieter, 1969), but much additional work with the instrument has been done by the PMHP research staff (Cowen, Dorr, Clarfield, Kreling, McWilliams, Pratt, Pokracki, Terrell & Wilson, 1973a). Factor analysis has shown that five of the test's 11 items (odd-numbered items) deal with aggressive or acting-out behaviors; another five (even-numbered items) deal with shy, withdrawn, internalized, moody behaviors; and one (item 11) deals with learning problems. The teacher rates the frequency of occurrence of these 11 behaviors on five-point scales ranging from "seldom or never" to "all of the time." The instrument yields four scores: Acting Out, Moodiness, Learning Disability, and a total AML or Maladjustment score. Since the behaviors rated on the AML are relevant to the teacher's everyday classroom observations, it is both easy and meaningful for her to fill out the form.

A coordinated series of AML research studies (Cowen et al., 1973a) (1) shows that the scale and its subscales are reliable, (2) presents item-item and item-scale correlations as well as factor analysis data, (3) develops norms for primary graders by grade level, (4) tests for AML differences by grade level and by sex, (5) shows that the measure correlates reasonably well with other known, valid, but lengthier school adjustment scales, and (6) demonstrates that the full AML scale and its several subscales discriminate clearly and in the expected directions between children referred or not referred for help to a school mental health project because of their school adjustment problems. Thus the AML, although fairly narrow and superficial, is sensitive and discriminating and thus is very useful as a rapid mass-screening device.

The second referral measure used in PMHP is the TRF, developed initially in several studies reported by Clarfield (1972, 1974). Since the TRF has already gone through several minor structural modifications, we shall only describe the test's current format. Three major subsections comprise the total TRF measure. Part 1, the largest and most important of the three, includes 41 items, each reflecting a classroom behavior problem, which, if present, the teacher is asked to rate on a five-point intensity scale. Part 2 includes a half-dozen or so family problems (e.g., parental separation or divorce) to be similarly rated if the teacher believes the factor is contributing to the child's school adjustment difficulties. Part 3 is made up of three global seven-point rating scales reflecting how well the teacher knows the child, how much she likes him, and how well adjusted she considers him to be in class.

A comprehensive series of TRF reliability, factor analysis, normative, and validity studies has been completed. The factor structure of this measure is stable and reliable and closely resembles that of the AML. Thus there are three major factor clusters consisting of 14 Learning (L) items, nine Acting Out (A) items, and seven Shy-Anxious (SA) items. Thus, like the AML, the TRF yields three factor scores and a total maladaptation score based on the weighted sum of all items checked with regard to the child. The TRF discriminates clearly between referred and non-referred children and is sensitive to different types of problems. A major TRF normative study was recently completed that provides separate norms for boys and girls, urban and suburban children, and children at different grade levels (Lorion, Cowen & Caldwell, 1975).

The TRF provides more of an in-depth picture of the child than does the AML and has some diagnostic value beyond the more superficial type of screening that the latter measure offers. Thus, unlike the AML, which has only one learning disability item, the TRF learning cluster has 14 items and offers a much richer assessment of that important dimension. Another illustration of the TRF's usefulness can be found in Clarfield's (1972) original study developing the TRF. He reports that regardless of the specific reason for a child's referral to PMHP, 70 per cent of the children referred had a check mark next to the following (learning cluster) item: "poor concentration and limited attention span."

Thus PMHP has placed much recent research emphasis on refining assessment devices that offer rapid, accurate, objective data on children's school adjustment problems, i.e., determine "where they are at" based on language and concepts that are meaningful to the teacher. If the prime need is for mass, initial screening of very large numbers of young children, the AML is especially useful. However, if more detailed, refined, diagnostically oriented inputs are needed to plan specific interventions, a broader, more sophisticated assessment procedure such as the TRF seems preferable. In programs such as PMHP, where both objectives are important, the AML and TRF can be used in complementary, mutually supportive ways.

In addition to their use in screening and referral, both the AML and TRF have been used as measures of program outcome. Structurally, this has been done in two ways. One is a simple pre versus post comparison in which the first measure, describing the child's current status, is taken before the intervention starts and the second when it ends. The arithmetic difference between pre and post ratings is used as the index of change. An alternative is to use the test as a measure of change by structuring postprogram instructions in such a way that raters describe changes on each item over a fixed time period covered by the intervention.

The AML and TRF, alone or together, appear to do a reasonably good job with respect to the purposes for which they were designed: i.e., to measure the nature and extent of children's school problems and changes in them over time or as a result of intervention. However, the measures betray the prevailing orientation of the mental health fields toward pathology and its alleviation. There is also another, historically neglected side of this problem. In addition to symptomatology, it is not only appropriate but important to look at children's strengths and resources. Conceivably, children at any level of pathology could have different assets and resources. Moreover, the presence of certain strengths might help, not only to predict outcomes, but also to determine which intervention would most help a particular child. Another practical reason for trying to assess children's resources is that some people, including teachers, feel more "at home" talking about children's strengths than about their problems.

It thus seems that a fuller picture of PMHP's accomplishments or failings and a more effective set of interventions could result from a referral-outcome framework that also measured children's resources. With this objective in mind, Gesten (1974) has just completed the development of a methodology for assessing young school children's assets. His measure, the Health Resources Inventory, consists of 54 positive, mastery behaviors of primary grade children (e.g., "has a lively interest in his environment," "defends his view under group pressure," "tries to help others") that can be rated by teachers. Preliminary findings with this measure suggest that it is reliable, it correlates negatively with problem behaviors, and it has a factorial structure consisting of five principal dimensions: (1) peer sociability, (2) learning orientation, (3) frustration tolerance, (4) gutsiness, and (5) ability to follow environmental rules. This methodological development may be an important addition to past PMHP assessment frameworks—one that can meaningfully expand the project's early detection and screening framework as well as its evaluation base.

Teachers' Views of PMHP

Although teachers' judgments about children's classroom behavior have been central to PMHP's research—especially in the project's referral and outcome studies—one specific study (Dorr & Cowen, 1972) addressed the separate question of how teachers view the project. Since this research was done during the project's expansion phase, when PMHP numbered more than 100 teachers in 11 schools, a broad range of teacher responses was anticipated. But because teachers stand to benefit from PMHP as a result of both the improved behavior and functioning of children seen by aides and the project's consultation services, teachers' perceptions of PMHP's effectiveness represent one index of the project's success. To get an idea of teachers' perceptions, a questionnaire was developed to measure their feelings about (1) the accessibility of PMHP professionals, (2) the degree to which they felt informed about PMHP, (3) the extent to which they felt that PMHP had helped them to deal more effectively with children, and (4) how they compared PMHP to other school mental health programs they had known.

Teachers gave highly favorable ratings on all four of these items. The item comparing PMHP to other programs received the highest ratings. Since the allocations of professional time varied considerably from team to team, the relationship between the amount of professional time available in a school and the teachers' reactions to PMHP in that school were also studied. More professional time related to higher teacher evaluations on all dimensions except for "child help"—a finding that suggests the need to improve communication in settings with limited professional time.

Research with Aides

The project's expansion led to a sudden major increase in the aide pool, making possible a series of research studies that could not have been done in phase two, when there were only six aides. Because several of these investigations have already been described in detail in Chapter 4, they will be considered only briefly here.

The study of Cowen et al (1972b) that was based on data obtained during selection interviews with aides showed that the women chosen for the program received high marks on the full range of interpersonal styles and skills rated by interviewers. A second study (Sandler, 1972) pinned down the characteristics of the selected aides more precisely. This investigation was based on a comprehensive test battery assessing personality and interpersonal relations, vocational interests, attitudes in areas related to the aide role, and clinical skills and sensitivities. The battery was given to all new aides during the short period after they had been hired but before training started. A control group in this research consisted of demographically and socioeconomically comparable women who were engaged in volunteer activities that did not involve school children.

Consistent differences between aides and controls were found on variables such as style of interpersonal relationships, interests, and attitudes. Thus aides had significantly higher empathy, affiliation, and nurturance scores than controls and significantly lower aggression scores. Their vocational interests were more oriented toward teaching and social service occupations and less toward scientific or managerial activities than those of controls. Aides also had more positive attitudes than controls about concepts relating to mental health, the schools, and to themselves.

Since this battery of characteristics was comprehensive —indeed unwieldly because it yielded more than 100 separate scores—it was confusing and difficult for the nonresearcher to interpret. Thus a means was sought for reducing the test results to a simpler form. With this goal in mind, a factor analysis study was undertaken, based largely on Sandler's data (Dorr et al., 1973a). This procedure yielded six dimensional clusters: (1) cultural-intellectual interests, (2) attitudes toward children and other concepts related to the aide role, (3) extroversion-introversion, (4) "helping person" needs and interests, (5) social class, and (6) scientific interests. In comparison to the con-

trols, the aides had significantly stronger cultural-intellectual interests, more positive attitudes toward job-related
concepts, and stronger "helping person" characteristics.

In sum, these studies suggest that PMHP aides are
warm, motherly, empathic women who have strong, positive views about mental health and are drawn to interpersonal helping activities. In terms of face validity, these
qualities are certainly desirable for a person who works
closely with young, maladapting school children. They not
only show up in formal evaluations of aides, but are also
strikingly apparent to visitors who meet and talk with aides
and see them in action. For many outside visitors, the aides'
interpersonal skills, sophistication, and overall effectiveness are among PMHP's truly distinguishing qualities.

Another important question about aides is how they
change as a result of training, on-the-job experience, and
supervision. A study by Dorr, Cowen, and Sandler (1973b)
examined this question. Aides and controls took two of the
short tests from the original battery (the attitude measure
and the test of clinical interaction styles) after six months
of training and on-the-job experience. The main findings
of this study were that aides, when compared with controls,
were more understanding and less rejecting over time
when dealing with children's questions and assertions.
These findings, together with the aides' continuing strong
preference for nurturing responses and positive attitudes
toward their role, suggest that these initially highly qualified women improved even more with training and experience. Neither their natural warmth nor positive feelings
about their work had waned.

We have already noted clinically that professionals'
first reactions to the abstract idea of an aide program were
very positive. However, since there can be differences between programs as abstractions and as facts, we evaluated
professionals' judgments about aides in a formal research
study (Dorr and Cowen, 1973b). Thus, at the end of each

of the project's first three years of expansion, professionals were asked to rate all aides on a Professional Evaluation Form that tapped 16 variables: (1) perceptiveness with regard to children's problems, (2) formulation of plans for dealing with children, (3) warmth with children, (4) flexibility and resourcefulness with children, (5) effectiveness with withdrawn children, (6) effectiveness with aggressive children, (7) effectiveness with children who have learning problems, (8) ability to maintain objectivity, (9) enjoyment in working with children, (10) attitude toward supervision, (11) utilization of supervision, (12) relations with teachers, (13) relations with aides, (14) likeableness as a person, (15) reliability and professionalism, and (16) overall favorability. All ratings were made on five-point scales ranging from "excellent" to "very poor." At the end of the first year, the professionals' ratings were very high, and they remained that way over the next two years that the evaluations were made. These data suggest that the role of the PMHP aide remains viable in the professionals' eyes, that aides continue to be interested in and excited by project activities, and that they do not "burn out" over time. The latter interpretation is supported by the relatively low annual turnover rate among aides.

Overall, the research with aides has been promising. Professionals think highly of aides initially and maintain their regard, based on aides' actual work behavior. Aides, chosen for their good mothering qualities, give on-the-job evidence that supports the wisdom of the selection process. And at least one study suggests that aides grow through training and experience while at the same time retaining their natural warmth and compassion.

Process Analysis

A question frequently asked about aides is "What do they actually *do* when they are with the children?" At a clinical, case-history level, this question is the major focus of the next chapter. Here we shall only briefly describe some recent, objective data about the aide-child interaction process (McWilliams, 1971, 1972). McWilliams first developed a two-track process-analysis framework to define the major goals and activities of aides' sessions with children. The activities section included seven major categories of interaction: educational-tutorial activities, social conversation, problem conversation, joint competitive activity, joint cooperative activity, aide-active time, child-active play, and child-solitary play. The goals section set 11 goals for aides to aim at such as strengthening the child's academic background, building a relationship with the child, and freeing up behavior. Aides checked their goals and the amount of time they spent in various activities during one session, every two weeks, and over the year. A study using senior aides as observers showed that these ratings were reliable.

Content analysis showed that overall, aides spent about 65 per cent of their time with children in some play activity: competitive, cooperative, or child-active, aide-passive. Fifteen per cent of their time was devoted to social and problem-oriented conversation and another 15 per cent to educational tutoring. More recent process surveys indicate a substantial drop in the tutoring category—probably unfortunately so. There were differences in activities and goals across settings. Thus urban schools, especially those located in the inner-city, appropriately spent more time on tutoring than did suburban ones, whereas the converse was true for socialization and building of relationships. The most frequently stated session goals were those of helping the child to make independent choices (21.5 per cent), strengthening his academic abilities (15.0 per cent), building a close relationship (14.5 per cent), and helping to build his confidence (11.0 per cent).

Children with acting out, withdrawal, or learning problems had somewhat different aide-interaction experiences.

Thus children with learning problems spent far more (three times as much) time in tutorial activities than did the other two groups. Similarly, acting-out children logged significantly more time in conversations about their problems than did the two other groups. There were also differences in aides' stated goals among the several types of referral problems. For example, the goal of academic strengthening was mentioned far more often for children with learning disabilities, while the goal of learning to express feelings was mentioned most frequently for youngsters who acted out.

Relationships between aide characteristics and process measures were also found. Illustratively, the less extroverted aides allowed children to choose activities more often and attempted to foster relationships, build confidence, or engage in competitive activities with them less often. Similarly, aides with strong helping needs avoided taking an active role with passive children, and aides with very weak scientific-mechanical interests engaged more often in friendly conversation with children in attempts to build relationships with them and to "loosen them up."

McWilliams' findings suggest that aides engage in a broad range of activities with children and that activities during sessions relate both to the nature of the child's problems and to the aide's personal characteristics.

Studies of Outcome

For PMHP, indeed for any human-service helping intervention, the ultimate "bread-and-butter" question is: How well does the program work? PMHP has been keenly attuned to this question from the start and has conducted a continuing series of outcome-evaluation studies during its 17-year history. By almost any metric imaginable, these are highly varied studies. They have been done at different stages of PMHP's evolution and thus deal with somewhat different projects. Some studies have a short-term, others a long-term focus. They differ in the criteria used, the sophistication and rigor of design, the presence or absence of control groups, and, in the crassest sense, just how good or bad the findings are.

Since the two major evaluations of PMHP's earliest developmental stage (Cowen et al., 1963; Cowen et al., 1966a) were reviewed in Chapter 3, they will be considered only briefly here. Both early studies compared an experimental (project) school to demographically similar control schools on a variety of criteria, including school records, performance indexes, teachers' behavior ratings, self-reports, and peer evaluations. Though somewhat different measures were used in the two studies, there was considerable overlap between them. In each case, the main evaluation was done in the third grade: in other words, when the program had been in effect for three years. The two studies also compared the development of early identified, maladapting (Red Tag) and nonmaladapting (Non-Red Tag) children during the first several school years.

With respect to program effectiveness, the two studies did not yield comparable findings, though they had some directional consistency. The first (Cowen et al., 1963) showed no more than several directional indications of PMHP's early effectiveness. Thus data from that study hardly provided a resounding confirmation of the program. The second study (Cowen et al., 1966a), based on a new group of children and another cycle of experience, yielded consistent data testifying to the program's effectiveness. Project children, directionally, did better than controls on virtually all the outcome criteria—significantly so on nurses' referrals, achievement test scores, achievement-aptitude discrepancy scores, teachers' ratings, and self-reports of anxiety. This second study suggested that the program, as initially conceived, made reasonably good sense; the findings provided a "go-ahead" for further refinement and expansion.

With respect to the early school histories of Red Tag versus Non-Red Tag children, the data from both studies, again especially the second, added up to a compelling sum. If left alone, by the end of the third school year early identified vulnerable children were seriously behind their non-vulnerable peers in all aspects of school functioning and adaptation: health measures, performance measures, teacher and professional judgments of behavior, and peer ratings. The clear message was that these children were so far behind in all ways after three school years that they had to have immediate, effective help if they were to "cut it." This awareness was the main factor that led us to establish the initial aide program.

Beyond the clear fact that Red Tag children, did significantly less well during the first three school years, additional studies were carried out to examine the long-term effects of early maladaptation in school. These investigations, done years after the original studies, were based on the same subjects later in their school careers. A study by Zax, Cowen, Rappaport, Beach, and Laird (1968) compared the subsequent elementary school careers (through seventh grade) of two consecutive-year samples of Red Tag and Non-Red Tag children evaluated by PMHP in the primary grades. Using a broad range of measures including subsequent achievement, classroom behavior, school records, and peer evaluation for both samples, children in the initial, early detected, Red Tag group were found to have significantly poorer, later school records than their peers, suggesting that early ineffective school behavior portends continuing, serious difficulties.

A later related study (Cowen, Pederson, Babigian, Izzo & Trost, 1973c) confirms this point even more dramatically. Through the comprehensive Cumulative Psychiatric

Register, available in the Rochester area, it was possible to track the subsequent histories, over an 11-to-13-year period, of three consecutive, yearly samples of children initially classified by PMHP as Red Tag or Non-Red Tag. The Register contained entries of relatively more serious mental health contacts involving clinics, hospitals, and private practitioners. Whereas about one out of three children had initially been classified as Red Tag, more than two out of three of the children who later appeared in the Register came from the Red Tag group. In other words, using Register entries as a major criterion of later serious adjustment problems, the vast majority of persons who appeared in the Register are known to have had early school adjustment problems.

A second, highly intriguing finding of this study also bears mention. For reasons unknown to us (except perhaps for man's hoarding instinct), we saved, for more than ten years, the original third grade test data from our very first samples. It was thus possible to identify a group of 60 persons, whether originally experimental or control children, who later appeared in the Register and to match them precisely for age, sex, grade, teacher, and school to Non-Register peers with comparable third grade test data. The question we studied retrospectively was: Which test indexes, had we known of them before the fact, would have discriminated between children who did and did not have later, serious psychiatric problems? The criteria were the same as those used in the earlier outcome studies: school record, aptitude, achievement, behavior rating, self-report, and peer evaluation. The findings were surprising. Whereas most measures tended, directionally, to discriminate as expected between the groups (i.e., poorer early adjustment for the later Register group) only one cluster sharply and consistently differentiated the Register and Non-Register groups: peer sociometric ratings. Thus the judgments of nine-year-old peers about their fellows were the most accurate of all test predictors of later psychiatric problems. Perhaps this finding reflects the intuitive wisdom and sensitivity of the young child. Or perhaps it suggests that nine-year-olds, when they detect early differences in peers, continue to behave toward them in ways that reflect those perceptions, thus adding to the target child's difficulties and increasing the likelihood of later, more severe problems.

Several studies of outcome from PMHP's second phase, already reviewed in some detail in Chapter 4, will be considered only briefly here. The first (Cowen, 1968a) compared the effectiveness of the aide program, after-school day care program involving college students, and a no-program control group. Two sets of criteria were used: (1) behavior ratings by teachers for all groups and (2) parallel ratings by aides, only for those children in the program who were seen by aides—rather than by college student volunteers. The study's main findings were that the groups seen by aides and college students were judged by teachers to have improved significantly in comparison with the controls. The group seen by aides improved the most, followed by the group seen by students, with no improvement in the control group. Aides' ratings, restricted to the aide-seen group, also showed significant pre-to-post improvement in the children.

Another study (Cowen et al, 1972a), based on data from stage two, focused on long-term rather than immediate adjustment criteria. This was a follow-up study based on interviews with mothers of children who had been seen several years earlier by PMHP aides. Mothers and interviewers independently did a series of nine seven-point ratings assessing changes in the child since the intervention in salient areas such as educational performance; getting along with parents, teachers and friends; and degree of happiness. The two sets of ratings correlated well. Both mothers and interviewers agreed that the children had improved significantly in these areas. Cowen (1971c) summarized most of the studies of outcome from PMHP's first two stages in a separate report.

Later Studies of Outcome

The largest and most varied PMHP studies of outcome come from the project's third, i.e., expansion period. Because of PMHP's growing diffusion and sharpening research constraints, issues that will be considered more fully in the last section of this chapter, these latter studies depend heavily on the judgments of teachers and aides, often lack control groups, and are in general less rigorous methodologically than earlier ones.

An early study from this period (Dorr & Cowen, 1973a) was based exclusively on aide-evaluation data. Since aides have regular contacts only with project children, a control group cannot be developed for such a study. The prime measure used in this research was a Child Behavior Change Scale, which included ten negative attributes (e.g., angry, withdrawn) and five positive ones (e.g., trusting, cooperative). For two consecutive-year groups, aides judged twice—once at mid-year and once at the end of the year—how much the child had changed in terms of the 15 characteristics since the program started. For both groups they also provided three global ratings, using seven-point scales, for educational, behavioral, and overall change. Aides perceived significant improvement in the children on virtually all individual items and on the global scales. An interesting sidelight of the study is that aides more often expressed their judgments that improvement had taken place in terms of increases in positive behaviors rather than in terms of decreases in negative behaviors.

A later broader, phase-three study (Cowen, Lorion, Dorr, Clarfield & Wilson, 1975), provided data that support the preceding findings. In this study, teachers' and aides' pre and post judgments about child behavior were obtained for relatively large samples of PMHP children and controls with roughly similar initial problems. For reasons already noted, teachers' judgments could be obtained for the controls, but aides' data could not. Teacher measures used in this study included the TRF and AML, as described previously. The main assessment device used by aides was the Aide Status Evaluation Form (ASEF) (Clarfield, 1972), a measure that exactly parallels the TRF, including assessment of acting out, shy-anxious, and learning problems, except that it is filled out by aides rather than teachers. Teachers indicated that project children did better than controls on 17 of the 24 AML and TRF indexes. Pre-post comparisons within the project group indicated significant improvement on virtually all criteria following the intervention. Aides indicated significant, indeed overwhelming improvement for project children on all dimensions analyzed.

Overviewing the composite of all findings from PMHP's outcome studies, they are, as indicated at the start, uneven. This is true concerning the crispness of their design, the richness of their methodology, as well as the content and persuasiveness of their findings. In fact, at this very moment we are faced with an acutely embarrassing set of findings, based on an as yet unpublished study conducted in 1973. Although this study again shows pre to post improvement for the PMHP sample, it offers no evidence whatsoever that the experimental groups improved more than control groups. Indeed, on the basis of some criteria the controls improved more! Conceivably these findings will never appear in a journal, in some measure because journals have built-in biases against publishing negative results. They are nevertheless there and are part of our history.

The point to be emphasized in this discussion is that the PMHP research team has brought many pitchers to the well, and in several instances the handles have broken. The project's record in terms of outcome is not one of unqualified success. Yet the weight of the findings support the conclusion that the program brings effective helping services to children in need. Moreover, the project has been willing, far more than is ordinarily the case in evaluating school mental health services, to "put its neck into the noose" of objective scrutiny. In that sense, its record is as good as or better than most efforts to evaluate the effectiveness of helping interventions. And as we shall see in the section to follow, PMHP's willingness to explore the ins and outs of the outcome question has generated research that points to useful new directions and practices for the program.

Limited Studies of Outcome

The project's expansion stage also prompted several indirect, less than comprehensive studies of outcome. One measure of project outcome, though not the most central, is its scope or reach. Indeed one of PMHP's *raisons d'être* is to increase sharply the amount of high-quality service brought to school children in need. Two studies of PMHP utilization patterns (Cowen et al., 1971a; Cowen, Lorion, Kraus & Dorr, 1974) suggest that the project has met its goal of expanding services. The first study showed that during the project's initial three months, aides saw 329 children, or about 9 per cent of the primary grade enrollment of the participating schools, for more than 7,500 individual contacts—an average of 23 contacts per child. In the next three years of full project operation (Cowen et al., 1974), the numbers of children seen were 531, 555, and 709, respectively. The three-and-one-third-year composite service figures from the project's expansion period show that more than 2,100 children, about 11 per cent of the primary grade enrollment of PMHP schools, were seen for nearly 67,000 contacts. Thus PMHP succeeds in reaching a substantial proportion of children who have difficulty adjusting in school—a group estimated by Glidewell and Swallow (1969) to be 30 per cent of the total school enrollment. This percentage doubtless includes those children with more serious school adjustment problems. Although utilization data do not tell us whether PMHP resources are being used optimally (e.g., whether a potential pool of 25,000 child-serving contacts would yield greater benefits if 500 children were seen an average of 50 times each or if 2,500 were seen an average of ten times each), they do say that the model substantially increases the reach of helping services in comparison with traditional approaches to the delivery of school mental health services.

Although PMHP indeed entails some additional, relatively small cost increments (e.g., for aides), a cost-benefit analysis of the program (Dorr, 1972) suggests that its reach increment exceeds its cost increment anywhere from four- to twelvefold. The overall utilization data thus suggest that PMHP markedly expands services to youngsters who most need them, with only modest increases in cost.

Each of the outcome-related studies to be considered next deals with a narrower component of the outcome question. Thus Cowen and Schochet (1973), based on written PMHP end-of-year reports, identified two demographically comparable groups of project "terminators" and "nonterminators." Terminators were children, judged clinically by professional supervisors in the light of available year-end information, to have profited sufficiently from the program so as not to need an aide for the next school year. Nonterminators were children who were judged to need additional help or further evaluation. The two major findings of this study were that terminators had been less seriously maladjusted initially and that teachers' and aides' ratings at the end of the school year differentiated the two groups in a way that was consistent with the earlier clinical judgment "terminator" versus "nonterminator." Thus terminators were seen as better adjusted at the end of the year than nonterminators.

A later study (Lorion, Caldwell, & Cowen, 1975) tracked these same children through the next school year. The questions that motivated the study were how well the prior end-of-year clinical judgments and data held up and how well they generalized to a new class setting and a new teacher. The main findings of this second study were that the group designated earlier as terminators did in fact remain terminators—i.e., very few had to reenter the aide program the next year—and that the advantages ascribed to them by teachers in ratings at the end of the previous year held up over time in a class with a new teacher.

The last three studies in this group (Lorion et al., 1974a; Lorion et al., 1974b; and Lorion & Cowen, 1975) are reviewed only briefly here since they were already considered in earlier chapters, particularly concerning the topic of how research findings help to establish promising new program directions. The first study (Lorion et al., 1974a) examines the consequences of several key program "regularities" or practices that characterize the PMHP intervention. Specifically, relatively few significant differences in referrals and no significant differences in outcome were found among demographically matched children seen once, twice, or three times a week in PMHP. Indeed, directionally, children seen least frequently improved the most. Similarly, there were no differences in referral or outcome between children seen for a single school year and those seen for two or more school years.

The second study (Lorion et al., 1974b), an instructive one, describes the development of a "pure-types" methodology based on the TRF referral measure. The methodology was essentially a shortcut recipe for identifying children whose predominant early school maladaptation featured acting-out versus shy-anxious versus learning-difficulty factors. The study showed that the aide intervention was differentially effective for different children and was most effective overall for shy-anxious youngsters. Consideration of why this happened and its implications for future programming are reserved for a later chapter.

The third study (Lorion & Cowen, 1975) began by identifying children who were most or least helped by the PMHP intervention and tried to establish what would have been before-the-fact discriminants for these two groups. Although certain variables such as "repeat in grade" or "repeat in program," failed to discriminate between successful and unsuccessful children later, poorer outcomes were found among children who were older, had lower socioeconomic or urban backgrounds, and were initially more maladjusted. The findings of this study also point to areas in which program practices require modification and tailoring. A nontechnical paper reviewing the content and implications of several studies from this last series has been published elsewhere (Cowen & Lorion, 1974).

"Outgrowth" Studies

One consequence of PMHP's energetic, multifaceted research approach is that the project is a data repository that encourages study of issues that go well beyond the project's main thrusts. This section exemplifies that point. A series of investigations, spanning many years, has addressed the broad question of interrelationships among various personality, behavior, achievement, and performance measures used as PMHP criteria at various age levels. Thus a study by Zax, Cowen, Izzo, and Trost (1964) shows relationships between Bower's Thinking About Yourself self-concept scale and his Class Play sociometric instrument (Bower, 1960) and a series of intelligence, achievement, and adjustment measures among third grade children. Similarly, Cowen, Zax, Klein, Izzo and Trost

(1965) found that anxiety in third grade children related negatively to IQ and achievement test scores and positively high teacher ratings of maladjustment, large discrepancies in self-ideal, sociometric unpopularity, and frequency of physical complaints in school. A study of third graders by Yellott, Liem and Cowen (1969) identified a network of relationships among several teacher, peer, and self-measures of adjustment and behavior and also found relationships between such indexes and children's achievement level.

Liem, Yellott, Cowen, Trost, and Izzo (1969) found that clinical judgments of early vulnerability related consistently to maladjustment indicators on tests, teacher ratings of dysfunction, sociometric peer judgments, and diverse indexes of poor educational performance and achievement. A related study by Cowen, Huser, Beach and Rappaport (1970), based on parental attitudes and perceptions of child behavior, found that these measures also discriminated clearly between children who were or were not adjusting well in the early school years. Parental estimates of children's adjustment correlated closely with teachers' judgments, especially for girls, and modestly with peer estimates of child adjustment. Longitudinal stability, over a four-year span between third and seventh grade, of a series of aptitude, achievement, and adjustment measures in children was the subject of an investigation by Zax, Cowen, Beach and Rappaport (1972). Although at least moderate stability was found for all groups of measures, this was greatest for intelligence, followed by performance and adjustment indexes, respectively.

A recent study by Felner, Stolberg, and Cowen (1975) illustrates paradigmatically another fruitful approach for studying child-adjustment issues, based on the availability of a large PMHP data pool. The TRF, described previously, deals primarily with behaviors that reflect acting-out, shy-anxious, or learning problems in the classroom. However, the measure also includes a second group of items having to do with family background or parent-child relational problems that the teacher checks if she is aware of their presence *and* if she believes that the factor contributes to the child's school adjustment difficulties. Examples of such items include serious health problems, family pressure to succeed, parental separation or divorce, foster home placement, death of a family member, and so forth. Preliminary inspection of the data submitted by teachers indicated that several of these items were indeed frequently checked.

Accordingly, Felner et al. (1975) identified two groups of children. Each of the children in one group had lost a parent through death. The parents of the children in the other group were either separated or divorced. Both groups were found to be more maladjusted overall than demographically matched controls. Moreover, the children whose parents were separated or divorced had particularly severe acting-out problems, whereas the children who had lost a parent through death had especially high shy-anxious scores. These significant cluster spikes remained, even after overall adjustment differences between the two symptom groups and their respective controls were parceled out. Direct comparison of the two groups, matched demographically and for overall adjustment, showed clearly that the children whose parents were separated or divorced favored acting-out behaviors whereas the children whose parents had died withdrew and became anxious.

This study suggests that certain variables, such as background, life history, and family style, can predispose the child to specific types of school adjustment problems. Such information has much potential value. It may help to identify strategies, both preventive and interventive, that can best serve specific children. The findings of Felner et al., (1975) have prompted a more systematic analysis (Lorion, Cowen, Kraus, & Milling, in press) of the relationship between background and family factors (e.g., economic difficulties, sibling rivalry, family pressure to succeed, over-protection, rejection, and so on) and school adjustment problems. Such life-history factors can also profitably be studied in terms of how they relate to the child's experiences in PMHP and to project outcomes.

Summary

PMHP's research investment has been heavy and enduring. Although we do not claim that this is the best or even the best-researched school mental health project, it may well be the most extensively researched. Moreover, PMHP's research program has been very broad ranging. Studies of outcome have been its most pivotal component. They have been diverse with respect to rigorousness, the range of criteria used, and the "goodness" or "badness" of the findings themselves. In the aggregate, however, the findings support the conclusion that the approach is workable and efficacious.

PMHP research studies have also helped us to understand the characteristics of child aides, how aides differ from other women, how they change on the job, and the nature of the aide-child interaction process. PMHP has done much to develop crisp, objective referral-screening devices and has completed a series of studies illuminating the nature, correlates, and stability of school adjustment problems. Beyond these direct project-related studies, PMHP has encouraged and served as a stimulus for broader, more general studies of child adjustment. PMHP's solid research component is an important factor that discriminates its approach from many other innovative, also doubtlessly contributory school mental health approaches, which without research and dissemination have had archival fates.

THE CHANGING RESEARCH SCENE

Slowly but steadily, we have become aware of important shifts in PMHP's research base. The project has continually expanded and deepened its community roots and moved away from its earlier laboratory-like insulation. In that process, it has experienced the research headaches of many other community-based projects. We developed enough concern about these problems, particularly those bearing on studies of outcome, to have put our thoughts together in a paper called "Research in the Community Cauldron: A Case Report" (Cowen, Lorion & Dorr, 1974). It is fitting and realistic that the final section of this chapter should consider the problems that erode sound experimentation in broad-based community projects.

Communication Problems

During the project's first years, it was based in a single elementary school and was carefully nurtured by its founders. Under such conditions, it was possible, with appropriate effort and imagination, to do experimentally respectable evaluations. Although PMHP's subsequent expansion from one to 11, then 13, and finally 16 schools was truly an exciting, gratifying experience, along with other happenings on the contemporary educational scene, the expansion complicated our evaluative efforts markedly. Even under the best of conditions, research studies are beset by ample problems and barriers. The "march of science" is painful and tedious. However, we soon discovered that careful, rigorous evaluation of a large community-service program, such as PMHP had become by 1969, was an agonizingly slow, complex, difficult, and at times infuriating process. Our experience between 1969 and 1973 educated us in what textbooks hadn't taught us. We learned in the "school of hard knocks!"

A basic dilemma in researching PMHP grew out of the project's philosophy, which encouraged program modification to fit individual team or school needs as closely as possible. The flexibility and diversity in the resulting loose federation of programs were seen as desirable because they were necessary to meet needs in individual settings. On the other hand, PMHP's geometric expansion, making for many idiosyncratic variations in the program across settings, significantly magnified design problems and impeded attempts to do methodologically sound research. Although PMHP's situation was, to be sure, unique, the issue we faced was the time-honored one of conflicting service and research needs.

Research evaluation has typically been given a low priority in service programs. This is understandable because those who provide services are often overwhelmed by the number of people in need and feel a responsibility to devote 100 per cent, sometimes 150 per cent of their efforts to service. Even in PMHP's early history, "family members" could be readily labeled as research or service types according to what their prime commitments were. But the family was small then, and each "camp" was sympathetic to and appreciative of the others' goals. Communication was excellent, and there were sufficient opportunities for service types to discuss and to understand the rationales and procedures of research. With expansion, however, differences between the service and research perspectives sharpened. Although central PMHP staff continued to view research and service as partners in a mutual endeavor, this convergent philosophy was not fully shared in the field. Many service people understandably focused on pressing school problems and, busy as they were, perceived research questionnaires as unnecessary burdens on their scarce time. At the same time, with program expansion, the relatively small research staff faced an enormous evaluative task, magnified by a shadowy demand from the field, and especially from school district administrators, for accounting. There were too many people and simply not enough time for detailed personal discussions and the development of shared understandings between the two groups. School contacts and visits by research team members became rare, and even when research staff did get to the schools they did not have enough time to explain questionnaires and research forms adequately.

Curtailed communication had negative consequences for the research effort. Needed cooperation on the part of professionals and teachers in the schools flagged. In some instances, data returns fell significantly below 50 per cent. If a form did not seem to contribute to the service effort, if its instructions were less than 100 per cent clear, and particularly if it appeared that filling it out would be time consuming, respondents either did not complete it or, worse yet, completed it quickly and carelessly. This further widened the rift between the two groups; each felt that the other did not sufficiently appreciate the importance of its efforts.

In the fall of 1972, the research staff expanded somewhat. Reopening field communication channels became a top-priority mission. Forms were modified to be as efficient and service oriented as possible, and their rationale was carefully explained in the accompanying instructions. Insofar as possible, personal contacts were used to encourage the genuine involvement and cooperation of field personnel. For example, in research planning meetings with service people, the decision was jointly made that referral forms had to be completed prior to a child's entry into the program. This decision followed extensive discussion of the service value of these measures for diagnosis, planning interventions, monitoring children's progress, and supervision.

Service and research personnel also negotiated an agreement about the research schedule and its data-collection points, a document that outlined in detail the studies planned for the school year and indicated which forms and information were needed by what dates. Service people later reported that this change alone greatly facilitated their participation since it allowed them to plan ahead and to set aside the time needed to complete the forms. Research personnel agreed to be available to consult with the school mental health teams. In this role, they were able to support the teams' efforts to communicate about PMHP with other school personnel. They were also able thereby to make the research operation a more personal and consequently more meaningful part of PMHP.

Our experience with problems of communication was instructive. Most of all, it forced us to accept the reality that our personal views about research were not basically shared by service personnel. We learned that the laudable abstract goals of science did not provide a sufficient rationale for service people to justify additional demands on their scarce time. Only when the parallel, long-term convergence of research and service goals became apparent and when the "ivory-tower folk" recognized the realistic constraints on service people's time did the atmosphere for evaluation and research improve markedly. Those interested in evaluating community-based service programs are well advised to consider our false turns. The basic prerequisites for genuine cooperation are consideration of and a willingness to discuss openly the problems one seeks to study and to be as flexible as possible about how to approach them.

Other Research Problems

Misunderstandings between service and research people were but one aspect of the total picture. Unfortunately, many other problems, some more serious, could not be handled simply by "beefing up" communication. The latter included problems of experimental control, problems in selecting appropriate criteria, and data biases that could not be controlled.

Problems of Control. In evaluating an intervention's effectiveness, an ideal design should include a group that has been exposed to the treatment and an otherwise comparable group that has not been exposed. The intervention's utility can be evaluated by studying differential change in the two groups, on appropriate criteria. An ideal way of forming a control group is to assign comparable subjects randomly to the two groups. In this way, the two groups will include initially similar individuals, with chance as the sole determinant of the subject's assignment to conditions. The control group is important because people change over time and their behavior is variable. It is vital to know whether changes observed after an intervention are caused by the intervention itself or, for example, by the mere passage of time or chance fluctuations. The use of a carefully selected control group helps the experimenter to determine which components of changes are related solely to the passage of time as opposed to the intervention, the latter presumably being of greater interest.

As noted previously, the ideal way to form a control sample is to assign subjects randomly to the two groups. In recent PMHP evaluations, however, this procedure could not be followed for several reasons. First, as emphasized throughout this book, PMHP is primarily a service program. Therefore, to withhold treatment from children for experimental purposes would have been unacceptable. Moreover, PMHP is a "guest" program in several host systems. In expressing a willingness to use this approach as an alternative to traditional school mental health services, the school systems appropriately asked that PMHP provide services for all children in need. The experimental elegance of denying treatment to certain children for control purposes was inappropriate and unacceptable to the schools. School systems are not autonomous units. They must continually respond to the immediate problems of children or risk vocal assault from school boards, teachers, and, most important, parents. None of these groups would have found random nontreatment of children acceptable. Finally, PMHP is but one small part of a comprehensive service-delivery package provided for school children. In that capacity, the project had neither the responsibility nor the clout to specify which children should or should not receive which services. Many PMHP schools have tutoring programs, reading classes, learning disability programs, or other help-oriented programs such as, the "Schools Without Failure" program. PMHP research staff cannot insist that such services be denied to children who happen to be in our control groups.

Thus the problem of testing the effects of PMHP is indeed complicated. We have had to do our evaluations without sufficient control over critical variables such as which children are assigned to the project, the kinds of problems for which they are referred, and the nature and extent of other services available to them. In other words, regardless of theoretical ideals and abstract canons of scientific rigor, PMHP has, more and more, had to accept things as they are and limp along with its research as best it can. In practice our situation has primarily required that we track and dampen the effects of as many of these "noise" variables as possible.

The attempt to locate appropriate control groups has thus called for maximum tolerance and flexibility. The strategy we decided to follow was to draw subjects from schools that were demographically comparable to project schools. Within those schools, we identified groups of children who were approximately the same as the PMHP sample in terms of age, grade, sex distribution, and school adjustment problems, hoping thereby to start our studies with roughly similar experimental and control samples.

Shortly it became clear that this had not happened and that we were in fact comparing children who had PMHP plus other experimentally unspecified programs to children who had been in more, fewer, the same number, or an unknown number of other programs.

The problem of other school programs, as implied previously, presents a mare's nest of potential biases pivoting on the question: "What *is* an experimental program?" PMHP evaluation would be purest if there were no other special programs or services in experimental or control schools. But since PMHP is set in the real world of education—a world of continuous experimentation with new programs—this "pure" case is never achieved. Most schools house many special programs, some of which are oriented toward the same areas as PMHP (e.g., academic skills, classroom behavior, and so on). When such programs are intermixed, it is well-nigh impossible to separate their specific contributions. This fact has important ramifications for comparisons of experimental versus control schools in PMHP. Typically, PMHP has been one of several special programs (e.g., DISTAR, or Glasser's Schools Without Failure) in an experimental school. Control schools have similar programs to upgrade skills, improve behavior, or repair dysfunction. Indeed, some control schools receive extra services because they do *not* have PMHP, as part of a "share-the-wealth" philosophy.

Thus, experimental versus control comparisons have in fact contrasted PMHP plus several other educational innovations or special services with overlapping clusters of three, four, or five related (non-PMHP) control-school interventions. Rapid program flux, with many short-lived programs and the continual introduction of new ones, complicates the problem even more. Although this is experimentally regrettable, it is, in educational as well as other social settings, part of the community researcher's reality.

Another concern that is simply an extension of the preceding one (even overlooking the problems presented by confounding educational innovations and special remedial programs and considering only school mental health services) is that comparisons of experimental versus control schools are still not comparisons of PMHP versus nothing because control schools have traditional mental health services. Experimental and control schools have roughly comparable amounts of professional time assigned to them. Moreover, professionals in experimental schools retain responsibility for an entire school, and portions of their time (variable from school to school, but averaging from one-fourth to one-third) are allocated to non-PMHP functions: e.g., work with children in the fourth grade and above or with teachers and parents; involvement in other programs, committee work, and all school meetings. Accordingly, even within the artificially restricted area of mental health services, recent studies of outcome have at best compared one service modality (PMHP) to another, which is heterogeneously and nonspecifically defined as traditional services.

Thus we became aware, early in the project's expansion period, that our evaluations would not provide tightly controlled, experimentally ideal evaluations of PMHP's effects. We had to settle for, at best, distant approximations of satisfactory research conditions. We realized that our situation also allowed for the systematic operation of certain biases, several of which will be reviewed more specifically later. For the moment, the key point to be stressed is that well-controlled research concerning outcome in community-based programs such as PMHP may be seriously weakened by conflicting, prepotent, program-related, realistic demands.

Problems of Criteria. Another growing concern in PMHP's research has to do with the criteria that should and can be used to evaluate the program's effects. In general, the expected outcomes of a human service helping program are more diffuse, less operational, and more difficult to specify and measure than those based on treatment of specific illnesses with drugs, for example. Thus children are referred to PMHP because they are having difficulty adapting to the classroom, a rubric that covers many problems including behavioral, interpersonal-familial, and academic-cognitive ones. Just what are the criteria by which one should evaluate the project's effects, and how are such variables most appropriately assessed? Do we, for example, establish specific frameworks for assessing each individual child referred to the program? Although this might be ideal theoretically, in that each child indeed has particular referral problems and goals, to do so for the large number of children involved in PMHP would be logistically impossible. Moreover, it would constrain generalizations about the program's effects for children in other school systems. Accordingly, we have opted to develop and use comprehensive measures for referral and outcome: for example, the AML and TRF. These instruments are designed to reflect broad areas of school maladjustment (e.g., acting out, poor socialization, and learning problems) uniformly.

The selection of criteria to evaluate outcome also depends on practical considerations such as: What is available? For instance, although PMHP is in good measure a mental health-oriented rather than a specific educational program, it might reasonably be expected to lead to academic improvements for children whose problems are in that area. Early in the project's history, we used report cards and achievement test scores to assess academic progress. However, recent changes in educational evaluation procedures, particularly their growing diversity, limits the usefulness of such indexes. For example, in many schools today, the old-fashioned A, B, C marking procedure has been replaced by global, general, prose statements about how the child is functioning. Indeed, in some settings grades have given way completely to check marks, stars, color codes, or other symbols that reflect the current social ethos away from objective numerical evaluation. The problem for the researcher is that there is no way to objectify and compare such diverse grading practices across schools. We are thus faced with the perplexing, challenge of how to compare the progress of children who receive check marks to those who receive red or blue marks to those who show growth in their ability to relate to peers or in any other similar descriptive category. No matter how desirable such changes and innovations in grading procedures may be from a social-educational perspective, they limit the researcher's ability to derive a general index of educational gain by which academic progress in project versus nonproject schools can be contrasted.

In an effort to circumvent this problem, we recently tried to revert, for experimental purposes only, to the Paleozoic practice of asking teachers to judge children along a hypothetical dimension of overall educational progress, using the abstract symbol "A" to reflect excellent achievement and ranging down to "E" to indicate unsatisfactory educational progress. Only a few teachers who were asked to provide such information were willing or able to comply. Most had worked so hard to get out of this "old-fashioned" mode of thinking that they could not bring themselves to reenter it. Some, more "contemporary" teachers had never used the approach and were reluctant to try it. Thus our "innovative" attempt to establish an artificial A, B, C grading system failed and was abandoned.

A second, also formerly used metric of academic progress is the standardized achievement test score. This approach, for different reasons, has also fallen into difficult times. In the first place, districts today tend to use their own individual achievement measures. Since these measures differ in terms of content and when they are administered, it becomes difficult to compare effects of the program across districts using this dimension. Moreover, the largest of our districts made a recent decision to provide the "right test for the right child." Not infrequently, it happened that there was no "right test." Thus as many as one-fourth to one-half of the children had no performance data whatsoever. As a result, a child in that district can be given one of several different tests or test forms or none at all, only if or when he is considered ready to take such a test. Although these policies too may be entirely sound from a socioeducational standpoint, for PMHP it has meant that performance tests cannot be used to compare groups because of the great variability in the tests used and when they are given.

In recent years, these realities have meant that there have been few if any objective educational indexes that can be used uniformly to compare project and nonproject children across PMHP schools or districts. This has forced us to depend more heavily on indirect measures of changes in children, particularly on the judgments of teachers, aides, and mental health professionals, who see children "in action" regularly. Although such inputs are relevant and appropriate, they also have their biases.

Additional Sources of Data Bias. The communication problems described earlier interfered with the process of acquiring data from teachers and aides. Since most PMHP children are six or seven years old, standard personality inventories cannot appropriately be used with them; the children are simply too young to read and understand the tests. Furthermore, because of the large numbers of PMHP children, even in a single school, comprehensive individual test batteries cannot be administered. The alternative has been to have teachers and aides complete relatively brief ratings of children's educational and behavioral status before and after participation in the program.

The aide, though a relevant observer of what happens to PMHP children, is far from an unbiased one. Just as the therapist is highly ego-involved in his patients' progress, often measuring his personal effectiveness in terms of how he perceives his patients' improvement, so aides judge *their* effectiveness in terms of children's progress. Moreover, being a PMHP aide, for many women, is a highly important activity. Aides thus form significant proproject cathexes, which may motivate them to see progress and positive outcomes in children with whom they work closely and under highly invested conditions for long periods of time.

The same issue applies, though perhaps in different ways, to teachers. The key consideration is that, for many reasons, it cannot always be assumed that respondents provide "objective" descriptions of children's behavior. Judges, whoever they are, may upgrade children because they like or believe in the project, or they may downgrade them for reasons having little to do with the child's behavior: e.g., because they resent having to complete research forms or because they are upset with a project staff member. Such distortions surely happen in specific cases, perhaps systematically in some settings, but they are difficult to pin down and remain as unidentified "noise" in the evaluation data.

Beyond the preceding problem of generalized bias, experimental and control teachers may have different biases. When teachers in the experimental schools are asked to rate a child's end-of-year behavior, there is no way of keeping from them the knowledge that the project's effectiveness is being studied. Hence, their ratings can reflect either an objective view of children's behavior or their personal attitudes, positive or negative, to PMHP. Control school teachers' ratings, however, are done in a simple pre-post context rather than within a PMHP frame. Thus they are asked to field the hidden question: "How good a job have *I* done with Johnny this year?"—a more personal evaluation that favors reporting positive outcomes. Although this difference in "set" might theoretically be circumvented by using classroom or videotaped behavioral observations made by judges unfamiliar with the child's experimental or control status, such procedures are costly and time consuming and could not be carried out in large-scale evaluation studies such as PMHP's most recent ones.

Experimental and control teachers also face different tasks when rating children at the beginning and end of the school year. Whereas experimental teachers refer children to a real, active program and submit live behavior ratings in that context, control teachers simply rate maladapting children. Although virtually all experimental children receive PMHP services, there is no control over the services provided to control children. Thus studies of outcome, rather than compare PMHP to *no* intervention, compare PMHP to loosely defined, traditional mental health services for controls.

Another source of data bias comes from the fact that in some PMHP settings (with an ample number of aides), "healthy" children are seen on a truly preventive, rather than reactive basis. However, there are no initially well-adjusted controls. Since children with good initial status are restricted in how much they can improve on post-program measures, children in control groups have more room to improve than those in experimental groups.

Still another problem of bias occurs because although end-of-year measures for both experimentals and controls are collected in June and all control premeasures are taken in December, experimental premeasures are submitted whenever the child is referred. Therefore, the evaluation period is shorter for some experimentals than for controls. Moreover, if there are seasonal differences in classroom behavior, these would show up differentially for experimentals and controls in pre ratings.

In summary, research on innovative, school-based, community mental health programs such as PMHP—indeed, in evaluating the effectiveness of new community programs in general—continues to be sorely needed. It must be expected that such research will be difficult to do, be beset by major methodological problems, and depart significantly from long-cherished "ideals" of clean research. At best, information will be gathered by slow, successive approximations, each approximation by itself lacking in laboratory precision. However, without a healthy respect for the intrinsic complexities of research demands in this trying area and a tolerance of ambiguity for less than airtight design, many truly significant programs will fail to develop *any* research substrata and many exciting questions about school mental health or other community programs will never come under investigation.

9

The
Children
We See

This chapter and the next together involve a major turn-about in the book's style and approach. In contrast to the prior factual, businesslike approach, Chapters 9 and 10 turn to the project's softer, more human side: i.e., to the lives and problems of young children. Chapter 9 examines this facet of the project, based directly on the case histories of a few of the many children PMHP has served. Chapter 10, in a similar vein, examines reactions to the project of other important members of PMHP's *dramatis personnae:* principals, teachers, parents, and aides.

Two of the most frequent questions addressed to PMHP staff are. "What kinds of children are referred to the project?" and "What do the child aides actually do when they are with the children?" This chapter deals concretely with these questions, and hopefully the case studies reported will provide the reader with a more personalized perspective of the range of project children's problems and aide activities.

The children described in this chapter are fictional. Their names and all identifying material have been coded to maintain confidentiality. In fact, some cases are composites of several children's records. But, however edited, we have tried to preserve as faithfully as possible, the true flavor of the PMHP experience for children.

POLLY

Polly first came to the attention of project staff when her first grade teacher asked for help in managing her in class. The teacher described Polly as a bright child who had no interest in school work and related poorly both to her peers and the teacher. Her language was infantile. She seemed completely self-centered. She often grabbed whatever she wanted and, if necessary, hit to get it. Her response to discipline was short-lived. She seemed bewildered when reprimanded, as if reproof were a totally novel reaction to her behavior. Much of the time she seemed physically exhausted; indeed she often napped at her desk. The teacher had tried everything from "loving to scolding to ignoring" but had been unable to reach her.

The social worker learned about Polly's family life during her home visit. Polly—the family called her "Angel"—was the only child of her father's second marriage. Several older siblings from his first marriage were married but still lived in the community. There was much adult activity in the home with family friends and the grown half-siblings, who were frequent visitors. Even when Polly was not the center of these activities, she received lots of attention from all the visitors, most of whom, even when they dropped in for a brief stay, brought her another beautiful toy or game. Her mother never left Polly with a "baby sitter." She usually took her wherever she went, only occasionally leaving her at the home of a relative or friend. Because the mother had an active social life, Polly was often up late at night. Each day she was driven to and from school to protect her from the "rough" neighborhood kids who walked to school. Overall, the mother described Polly as a happy child, *adored* at home by family and friends.

The mother told the social worker that she did not feel she could help to solve Polly's problems, which she attributed to the school and the teacher's attitudes. She did not want to be involved. It appeared that the mother unconsciously rejected the child and compensated by over-protecting her. The mother's primary activities revolved around her own friends and her step-children. She felt closer to them in age and interests and had more to share with them.

On the basis of the first grade test evaluation, the psychologist noted that Polly was well above average in intellectual potential. Although she clearly had the ability to do well in school, she was incapable of doing so because of her dependence and lack of self-confidence. The psychologist noted that she did a great deal of guessing on arithmetic problems and vocabulary and that she was impulsive. Although she displayed sadness and fear openly, she was rarely hostile.

During his classroom observation, the psychologist noted that Polly was especially restless when assigned to do "seat work" or when the teacher was doing things that didn't include her. On one occasion, for example, Polly went to the pencil sharpener three times in three minutes, grinding it slowly, deliberately, and loudly without eliciting a reaction from the teacher. She then went to the teacher's desk, sat in her chair, and pretended to be the teacher. When the teacher finally told her to go back to her seat and finish her work, Polly did so, smiling. But she continued to engage in other subtle attention-getting behaviors for the rest of the afternoon. The psychologist noted during this entire sequence that Polly's attitude was not at all hostile. She seemed on the surface to be an attractive child, trying to be cute in a quiet, nonverbal, almost adult way. She vacillated between being intellectually precocious and behaviorally immature. At times it was hard to think of her as a six-year-old. Polly desperately wanted the teacher's attention. It seemed as if little else mattered to her. For her part, the teacher simply did not know how to react to this intense need.

When the psychologist and social worker first met with the teacher, they described Polly as a frustrated, overly dependent child who was unable to do her own seat work, lacked appropriate socialization skills, and was in need of much adult reassurance. They painted the picture of a child who had little or no experience in relating to other children. In school she was surrounded by peers with whom she had to compete for the attention and approval of a single adult. All her energy was being directed toward that end. The team suggested that Polly be assigned to a child aide, but the teacher, with her newly acquired understanding of Polly's behavior, preferred to try to handle things herself in the classroom. "After all," she explained, "even though Polly's academic achievement is below her potential, it is more than enough to assure that she will be promoted to second grade."

Polly was not referred to the project the next year either. At the time, the second grade teacher was more concerned about several other children in her class who had severe academic problems and referred them to PMHP. She described Polly as an "acter outer" who was rejected by her peers. But since Polly was still able to do passing work, she too felt that she could manage the child in class.

Polly's third grade teacher, however, sought out the team early in the school year and asked that she be assigned to a child aide because "she is her own worst enemy!" This teacher also saw Polly as bright, but it concerned her deeply that such an intelligent child could be so indifferent to her school work, so self-centered, and so rejected by her peers. The teacher summarized her observations as follows: "She's just obnoxious! Nobody is important to Polly but Polly. She would not hesitate to knock anybody down who gets in her way. Polly simply never gives!"

In the assignment conference, the team presented Polly to both the teacher and the child aide as "a child in search of herself." They explained that she was so involved in this pursuit that she was virtually unaware of others, except when they got in her way. Then, out of desperation rather than aggression, she would strike out. She was also pictured as being more anxious inside than she appeared to be on the surface. Although it seemed, superficially, that she was being spoiled by her mother, the team suggested that such overindulgence might be masking an underlying rejection. For Polly to develop more adaptive behavior, she would need to experience love through discipline and approval following only genuine achievement.

The child aide was instructed to relate to Polly firmly and nonindulgently. It was suggested that the aide could best appear as a strong adult who, although capable of genuine affection, could also express disapproval of inappropriate behaviors. It was also felt that the aide could provide constructive criticism and at the same time give genuine approval when it was earned. In other words, the aide was to try to offer Polly a corrective but nevertheless warm relationship that rested on realism and firmness. The aide's task was to set effective clear limits for the child to help her to become more acceptable socially. This meant, for example, that Polly would have to complete unfinished school work that the teacher sent along with her to the aide before she could engage in other more recreational activities. It also meant that the aide would play down the elaborate toys that Polly typically brought with her to show people for approval, thus indicating to Polly that the aide was more interested in her than her possessions.

So after two years of recognized classroom problems, Polly was finally assigned to an aide, who had 40 contacts (45 minutes each) with her between November and June of her third school year. As expected, Polly brought a new and different toy with her for the first several visits. The aide's strategy was to pay less and less attention to these items on each succeeding visit. At the same time, she sought in many ways to show Polly that she was genuinely interested in her. At first, Polly resisted finishing her class work and used all of her charm and wiles to avoid it. But when she realized that the aide, although kind and gentle, would not allow painting, games, or puppet play until school work had been finished, Polly began to initiate and complete her work more efficiently. By the sixteenth contact, she proudly announced that there was no homework this time; she had finished her assignments in class.

Polly spent much of her playtime with the puppets, pretending that they went to school and had a rough time because they were never ready to recite and the other kids didn't like them. From puppets, Polly moved slowly to role playing, in which she cast the aide as a teacher or mother and herself as a three-year-old nursery school child who played with blocks and finger paints. In this role, Polly often reverted to extremely infantile speech. In time, she "graduated" to kindergarten where she had "lots of trouble with the kids" and a "mean" teacher who ignored her. Around the thirtieth contact, Polly promoted herself to third grade and announced that it was now time "to read and do arithmetic," with which she was still having some difficulty in class. In these enactments, Polly typically cast the aide as a teacher and played the role of several children in her class who were "not doing so well." As her number skills and general academic performance improved, she had less need to pretend that she was someone else and began to ask the aide directly for help.

During several role-playing sessions, Polly pretended that she was a cripple in a wheelchair, at the same time talking about the limitations that the handicap imposed on her. The aide encouraged her to think about things she could do, even with her handicap. Whereas Polly at first saw herself as helpless and doomed to sit in the chair, gradually, with the aide's encouragement, her confidence grew and she discovered that she did indeed have ideas and skills, which she acted out and described to the aide. Significantly, Polly's last problem as a fantasied handicapped person was how she would get home. This she felt she could not do, and the "consequence" was that she would have to stay in school with the aide for the rest of her life. At one session during this period, Polly suddenly announced that she had found a friend who would call for her and take her wherever she had to go. The aide was surprised and pleased since this was the first time in all their many contacts that Polly had verbalized the word friend.

Before the semester ended, Polly took the role of each girl in her class and tried to get the aide to assess the personality and behavior of each child she portrayed. The aide saw this as Polly's attempt to learn what was or was not acceptable, appropriate behavior for a girl of her age.

Although the teacher still found Polly difficult to work with at times, she reported that Polly had started to make friends, some of whom were among the highest achieving, most popular girls in the class. Much of her intrusive classroom behavior had subsided. Polly had become quite reserved and now volunteered relatively little. But on the positive side, she was doing excellent creative writing, which won her the acclaim of the entire class. She was also trying to write stories, with some success, and her art work was excellent. She was being promoted to the advanced reading group. Arithmetic was still something of a problem, but another girl had volunteered to help her, an offer that Polly accepted with notable graciousness. For Mother's Day, Polly made a card with this inscription: "Relax Mother! Take off your girdle." And indeed it seemed that the mother had relaxed. Polly was no longer driven to and from school. Instead, she was walking with other neighborhood children. In her final contact in June, Polly invited her aide to have lunch with her, something that the aide was happy to do.

Polly is a good example of a child who is trying to adjust to the different demands of home and school. The traits, behaviors, and coping styles that had served well at home were completely inappropriate in school. She had to learn how to get along with peers and respond in school to an entirely different environment and set of expectations from those of the home. As a result of her work with the aide, Polly's intelligence, substantial ego strength, and ability to put first things first came to the fore. These assets began increasingly to be reflected in her achievements and behavior. A child who had gotten off to a poor start in school now seemed headed, thanks to the intervention, toward a genuinely rewarding school experience.

LAURA

Laura was referred to PMHP by her first grade teacher, who saw her as a child who craved adult attention and needed much help if she was ever to develop a positive self-concept. Laura was very timid, and she related poorly to her classmates. Some boys "picked on" Laura in class. Others often tried to trip her. Yet Laura never complained about this abuse. In some ways, she seemed retarded, though the teacher doubted this because her reading level approached average.

Laura enjoyed talking with the teacher and always seemed to want to be close to her. When other children were around the teacher's desk, however, Laura withdrew and typically stood alone and detached behind the group. Laura rarely spoke to her peers. For example, when the children were doing art work, Laura would rather tear paper by hand than ask another child to pass her a pair of scissors. The teacher was very concerned about Laura and felt that she needed someone to work with to "open her up." Laura was a truly lonely child who needed to be encouraged to develop relationships with other children and a more positive regard for herself.

During the first grade screening, the psychologist had noted that Laura worked rapidly. Notwithstanding some problems with number concepts, she had an average score on the California Test of Mental Maturity, and she seemed intellectually to be capable of dealing with school demands. The testing, however, indicated significant adjustment problems. For example, her figure drawings pointed to an inability to relate warmly to people. In addition, the psychologist interpreted her test record as reflecting insecurity and feelings of being unwanted and rejected.

The social worker found supporting evidence for this view of Laura during the home visit. The family saw Laura, the youngest of four children, as a cautious child who never tried to do anything unless she was absolutely sure of succeeding. Although she wanted to be helpful, she didn't seem to know how. She set high standards for herself and became frustrated and discouraged when she didn't measure up to them. Her mother has assumed that Laura liked school since the child rarely volunteered information about what went on there and voiced few complaints. Superficially, she got along well with her siblings at home, but further questioning by the social worker established that the latter were in fact regularly involved in their own activities and had little time for her.

Later in the interview, the mother shared with the social worker the fact that she had not been able to get close to Laura physically nor had she been able to show Laura the same amount of affection she had given the other children. The mother also blamed herself for not preparing Laura for school as well as she had prepared the other children. At the end of the contact, the social worker thanked Laura's mother for her cooperation, encouraged her to stay in touch, and invited her to visit the school soon to talk further about her relationship with Laura. Although the mother was willing for Laura to see an aide, she did not respond to the social worker's suggestion to come in for a follow-up visit.

Shortly after being referred to PMHP, Laura was assigned to an aide, whom she continued to see for several school years. Since Laura's coordination was so poor, the aide began by showing her how to use a pencil sharpener. Laura was delighted. Consistently, when the aide picked

Laura up at her classroom, Laura commented in some way about the aide's appearance. Often Laura announced proudly either that she had on a special perfume or hand lotion or that she had just washed herself with some exotic, sweet-smelling soap (though this was always make-believe). Recognizing the child's cathexis to external manifestations of "beauty," the aide brought in some costume jewelry and dress-up clothes for her, which pleased Laura tremendously. She enjoyed parading in front of a mirror, modelling the clothes and bedecking herself with trinkets. Laura also enjoyed playing with a doll's house. Notwithstanding her poor coordination, with some help from the aide she was able to construct small figures representing the people who lived in the house. While working on them, Laura commented sarcastically several times about the "cool mother doll," but she nevertheless continued to work enthusiastically on the project.

About the middle of the second semester, Laura first remarked that she didn't do well in class because the other kids made her "nervous." Later Laura volunteered that she thought the reason why the aide was seeing her was "because first grade is so hard that I need time to play." At the June year-end conference, the aide felt that little progress had been made with Laura. By contrast, the teacher stated that even though Laura still had "a long way to go," there had been definite improvement. The teacher noted that Laura now made more of an effort to do her work and that there had been genuine improvement in her work habits. The teacher added that Laura's mother had said, during a recent meeting, that Laura was much happier at home and much more enthusiastic about coming to school.

Laura was among the first children to be referred by her second grade teacher the following September. Her school work was still poor, but the teacher was even more concerned about her loneliness and inability to relate to other children. Laura seemed to spend a lot of time day-dreaming in class, and she became tense when called upon to speak. The teacher also had some concerns about Laura's health since she often complained about headaches and fatigue and seemed pallid.

Laura was seen 45 times by her aide in the second year. Initially, the aide was quite concerned about her; indeed, at times she seemed even more pathetic than during the previous year. However, on the positive side, Laura had maintained her warm feelings for the aide and was quite open in talking about her home and family life.

Although Laura was more willing now to speak about her own feelings, she required frequent reassurance that the aide really liked and accepted her. For example, she confessed that she had used a bad word when she spilled her paint and looked for the aide's reaction to this. She also reported that she was going to be an "ugly witch" at Halloween because that was what she really was anyway. One day she drew an elephant and called him "Screwy" because he was "all screwed up" just like her. Laura responded well to the aide's verbal and nonverbal reactions to these messages. In each case, the aide tried to assure her that she was good and lovable. Laura continued to talk about cosmetics and how she used lotion to make her face and hands "more beautiful." There was growing evidence of Laura's effort to identify with her teacher and the aide. She proudly exclaimed that she was going to bleach her hair blond (the aide had blond hair) when she became a teen-ager and expressed the wish that the aide were her sister. On occasion, she wished aloud that her teacher were her mother and the aide, her aunt.

By early November, the aide noted that Laura looked much better. One day Laura said that she felt like "the world was a big balloon" and that she finally had her "arms around it." The teacher noticed improvement in her classwork and commented to the aide that Laura looked much happier. Laura was now speaking to the aide about being a "special" teacher (like the aide) when she grew up, rather than the actress she had formerly aspired to be. One day she brought in cupcakes for the aide and proudly announced that she and her mother had made them. This gift was seen by the aide as a nonverbal expression of the mother's appreciation for the aide's efforts with her child.

By January, however, Laura had lost some of her earlier gains both in school work and in personal appearance. Once again she began to complain frequently about aches and pains. During this period she looked preoccupied, depressed, and lethargic. Although the aide was discouraged, she continued to work closely with Laura in hopes of helping the child again to feel better about herself.

In the spring, things did indeed look better. Laura began to concentrate more on school work. During her contacts with the aide, she still enjoyed playing with the doll's house and dressing up. The aide was pleasantly surprised to discover that Laura not only had learned to dance, but that she expressed herself well and had good rhythm and coordination in this modality. This was especially gratifying because Laura's movements initially had been described as "almost spastic." Although her writing and art work were still immature, at least there was some small progress in these areas.

Because Laura's overall growth had been slow and at times erratic, the team decided at the year-end conference that the aide should continue with Laura for another year. The teacher concurred, pointing out that the relationship was the thing that really made school tolerable for the child. The teacher was concerned that Laura might regress socially and educationally if she was unable to work with the aide next year.

Even though Laura's aide had the reputation of being an eternal optimist among her peers, she was discouraged when the third grade teacher referred Laura for "friendlessness, mediocre work, and poor coordination." Her concern grew when Laura "started off in the same old way," playing with the doll house, play-doh, "Silly Sand," and of course the perennial dress-up clothes and jewelry! But this year Laura added a new dimension to her prior make-believe play. She pretended that she was the wicked sister in *Cinderella* or the witch in *Sleeping Beauty.* By late November, she had divested herself of all ornamentation save for earrings and a long chain that her mother had given her.

Early in the second semester, she announced firmly that she was going to be the teacher. She went to the blackboard and pretended to give her class instructions. She continued to do this for weeks, often casting the aide as another teacher to whom she would report her troubles with "those stupid kids." At other times she treated the aide as a child who was doing poor school work and rarely knew her assignments.

Just as Laura was starting to deal openly with her problems rather than fantasizing about them, the teacher angrily told the aide one day that since Laura was not improving very much in class, she thought she should be dropped from the program. The aide tried to explain that Laura was at an important point and needed more time. The aide described how Laura had moved from the fantasy of being a fairy-tale character to play activities in which she took the role of a real teacher instructing a class. Laura, it was explained, was identifying with the teacher, even to the point of wearing a necklace and earrings similar to hers. The teacher was not convinced by this explanation. Indeed she remained angry and attributed Laura's "increased day-dreaming" and poor school work to "fantasy play in the aide's room."

The aide was upset by these developments. She communicated the teacher's concerns and feelings to the team, and the decision was made to have an emergency teacher-team conference. At that meeting, the teacher was encouraged to express her views, and the team tried to clarify the importance of what was happening to the child. Laura's behavior was depicted as a dramatic first step toward moving out of her dream world. She was now emulating her teacher as a positive model. The meeting was effective, and when it was over the teacher was again comfortable about Laura's working with the aide.

Laura continued "being the teacher" for a while longer. Soon after, the teacher noticed her walking to and from school with other children and learned that the mother had allowed Laura to have several friends over to play on the weekends. And a boy in her class even gave her a ring! Toward the end of March, Laura stopped bringing classwork to her meetings with the aide. She reported that she had finished her work in class—a point confirmed by the teacher, who added that the quality of Laura's work had also improved significantly. Near the end of the semester, with her teacher's and aide's permission, Laura brought a classmate along with her to the aide's room. From the start, she was in command of the play situation. She directed all activities for both of them. The aide felt Laura's choice of games and activities expressed how good it felt, at last, to have friends to enjoy. Laura was no longer the "wicked witch;" she was not even the teacher. Instead she had become "the queen mother" and her friend was "the princess." The aide reported that the two played so amiably together that it was as though she were not in the room. The aide had come to feel, for the first time, that Laura could survive in school without her. Reinforcing that perception, Laura arrived alone one day and announced she no longer needed the chain and earrings. In fact, she had given them to one of the other girls in her room. In her own way, Laura was preparing the aide for termination!

When Laura was discussed at the third-year termination conference, the teacher happily reported that her work had improved markedly. She was now well integrated into her peer group and no longer stood back alone. Both from

Laura's own comments and her mother's reports, it appeared that she had developed friends outside of as well as in school. Improvement in her coordination was noticeable and was reflected in better writing and art work. She had had few physical complaints during the year, and her overall physical appearance was of a rosy-cheeked, healthy little girl. In talks with the teacher, which now occurred with greater frequency, Laura's mother expressed great pleasure about her improvement. For the coming school year, Laura was, for the most part, to be on her own. The team agreed to help Laura get started in the fall by speaking with her new teacher about her situation.

Laura is a good example of a child who needed sustained contact with an aide. Family problems, which related to some of Laura's difficulties, could not be directly engaged by the team. Although the mother was concerned about her child, for some reason she was unable at that time to get involved in the helping process directly. Only via messages to the teacher and things like providing baked goods and jewelry did the mother offer tacit, nonverbal approval of the aide's serving Laura in a way in which she could not. Laura's case also illustrates the supervisor's role in supporting and encouraging an aide through many months during which progress was not apparent. In her discussions with the team, the aide could air her disappointment about the episodic nature of the child's gains and be assured that uneven growth is sometimes the way things go before genuine positive change ultimately comes about. Laura's PMHP experience also points up the importance of communication with the teacher about child-aide activities. The teacher cannot be left in the dark about what is happening, nor can it be assumed that she will automatically understand and accept the aide's work with the child. Rather, the teacher must be a part of the total team and be made to feel that her inputs and participation are vital aspects of the child's ultimate response to PMHP.

JOHN, MARY, AND FREDDIE

John, Mary and Freddie were referred by their third grade teacher for academic problems. Specifically, the teacher felt they needed additional help in basic word skills, including phonetics, word attack, initial consonant blends, and vowel recognition. All three children were average to above-average in ability but lacked self-confidence, a problem that the teacher felt could be helped by improving their language skills. The aide found them to be a congenial, cooperative, enthusiastic, and sometimes noisy group. Although they were described as defensive and highly competitive in the classroom, the three children were open, relaxed, and not only willing but eager to help each other when with the aide.

The aide and teacher worked together to develop a strategy for helping the children with their difficulties. According to this mutually devised plan, the aide and the children were to work primarily with flash cards, first learning to identify the sounds of words and then writing them on the blackboard in different-colored chalks. The group made a game out of this "work"; they arranged the flash cards according to sounds and then had contests to see who could find long or short sounds most accurately. They also used the sentence-builder set and played the "Mr. ABC" game—each a favorite activity. Then they discovered chinese checkers. That game was so enjoyable for them that getting to play it became an effective reinforcer for "tending to business" by doing their sound exercises promptly and accurately.

The children differed in personality. Mary was always the little lady. Freddie was somewhat shy but always smiling. And John was a bit of a show off who sometimes used four-letter words. Although the aide typically ignored these Anglo-Saxon invectives, when she reprimanded John once for this, Freddie asked quite seriously: "Why are you in a bad mood today?" The aide and children then had a discussion about good and bad moods, how and why moods change from day to day, and how this applied to everyone —the teacher, the aide, family members, and even children. This helped them to think and talk about how their own moods changed and about the various ways in which moods could be expressed.

This group met for a total of nine 45-minute sessions. The children enjoyed and profited from the experience. Their language and word skills improved noticeably in each case. They offer a good example of the effective use of a short-term group approach with limited initial goals. The three children were well known to their teacher. She knew beforehand that they could interact comfortably, indeed constructively with one another. They were well matched intellectually, shared a common problem, and had the maturity to work at things together. They were all relatively free of serious social or emotional problems and had evidenced adaptive coping mechanisms beforehand.

This group contrasts sharply to the group of four boys described next. Although the latter group was also one in which the members needed to improve academic skills, the different personal statuses and needs of its members were much more difficult to handle with a group approach.

JULIUS, RONALD, SAM, AND DEREK

Early in October, Julius, Ronald, Sam, and Derek were referred to PMHP as a group by their second grade teacher. She felt that they shared similar academic problems and could benefit from extra academic help. The teacher discussed the children at a referral conference, at which time the team agreed that they could indeed potentially profit from PMHP. Although the team doubted that the four boys had comparable adjustment problems and shared their concerns about this with the aide and teacher, a joint decision was nevertheless made to try a group approach with them. The aide saw the boys as a group for eight sessions, during which the five of them worked together on classroom assignments prepared by the teacher. The aide helped the boys to solidify their understanding of basic arithmetic procedures using various number games. When they worked on reading, the aide had them "read" a story by repeating the words that she pronounced. Each child said some of the words, thus making the story a group project. They worked reasonably well together and soon adopted a format of working for 15 minutes, having five minutes off, then working again. After two months with the aide, the teacher reported that all four boys had shown real improvement in their school work.

The aide, however, was less satisfied with their progress. She asked to meet jointly with the team and teacher to discuss her concerns about the boys. Although the aide agreed that the boys had improved academically and was pleased with their progress, she felt that they still had problems that might be more appropriately dealt with individually. She noted, for example, that while doing academic work, Julius manifested a tremendous need to please her and "fell to pieces" when he couldn't do so. Although quite bright, Ronald was very immature, and he required firm regular discipline. Derek, in contrast, was quiet and shy and rarely spoke to the other group members. Sam was the only one who did not seem to need additional help. His class work had improved considerably, and the teacher reported that he was now doing grade-appropriate work. In response to the aide's comments, the team reviewed its original referral notes and discussed options with the teacher and aide. Since none of the boys appeared to have a serious adjustment problem, it was possible to fit them into the existing schedule by having the aide see Julius,

Ronald, and Derek individually once a week for 30 minutes each. Sam was to be prepared for termination the next week, following the last scheduled group session.

When the aide explained what was to happen, Sam indicated that he still wanted to come to the playroom. Indeed, he even wanted a friend to join him. The aide correctly sensed that Sam valued the contacts more because it meant being with friends and away from the classroom than because of a felt personal need for help or adult contact. He had not had a particularly close relationship with her, and essentially she was just another teacher to him. Sam had good socialization skills. Indeed, he was the best liked boy in his class and was always with the other children. He had resented his academic deficiency and had applied himself in a task-oriented way to improve as quickly as possible. Through discussion with the aide, Sam soon came to see he no longer needed to work with her, and an amiable termination was worked out.

The three boys who needed additional individual help were at first uneasy about seeing the aide alone. Whereas Julius had been good-natured, outgoing, and extremely cooperative even when he found the work difficult in the group, he became moody and listless when he began seeing the aide by himself. Being close to her threatened him and made him obviously uneasy. Slowly over time he began to relax with the aide and to join her in play and games. Midway through the second semester, Julius asked if he could play with the puppets. The aide explained that he could spend his time as he chose. Together they set up the puppet stage and worked on readying the puppets. Julius then acted out a touchingly sad story in which the mother asserted indifference for her family and left them, even though the father and the other children begged her to stay. As the story ended, Julius was fighting back tears, and for the first time he allowed the aide to comfort him physically. Later the aide learned that his mother had in fact deserted the family and that the father and the two older girls in the family now managed the household.

From then on, Julius often spoke with the aide about his feelings. He complained of not sleeping well and began to present his dreams through puppet shows. They always centered around the mother's desertion and the associated feeling that she actually had left because she didn't like him. During this period Julius became very attached to the aide. When it was time to go to or from her room, he held her hand as they walked down the hall. He waved to her whenever he saw her and at times dropped by just to say Hi. They had long talks about him, his home, and his family. At one point, he asked if she would be his mother. The aide smiled and explained that she already was another little boy's mother, but she would be proud to be his special friend.

By the end of the school year, Julius's school work had improved considerably. He also became more self-confident and related much better to his peers. Although Julius and the aide agreed to see each other informally during the next year, regular sessions were not scheduled. At their last meeting, Julius gave the aide a handmade card that had a big heart on it and the words "To my special friend. Love, Julius."

Ronald was the brightest group member. In the presence of the others, he was the tough little boy who made a show of his casualness and savoir faire. He was often quite disruptive, failed to stick to his work, and clowned around a lot to make the others laugh. When seen individually, he was initially quite different. He seemed eager to learn and pleased to have the aide's undivided attention. The honeymoon ended, however, when she began to set limits on certain of his behaviors, particularly his use of four-letter words. He resisted these limits and carried on at some length, hoping to get his own way. Gradually, he began to accept limits and to test the aide less frequently. The aide was later able to chuckle when she told her supervisor about Ronald's feigned indignation when he discovered a four-letter word on the walls of the boys' lavatory. Ronald stopped seeing the aide before Easter vacation and showed continuing academic improvement for the rest of the semester.

Derek was a timid, depressed little boy. He was simply overwhelmed by the school's social demands and always seemed frightened and sad. When he began to see the aide alone, he immediately went to the sandbox and played there quietly until the time was up. The aide decided to let him do whatever he wanted to and spent a lot of time just sitting close to him and talking to him while she painted a picture, for example. Derek eventually noticed the paints and asked tentatively if he too could try them. As he began to express himself through his pictures, which really were quite good for a child his age, Derek spoke about himself and his family. His meek facade notwithstanding, considerable anger surfaced when he spoke about fights with his sister or about the lack of toys or opportunities to play at home. From then on, he made good use of his sessions. He told the aide how much he wanted to do good school work. She in turn sensed that he was under considerable pressure to do well. He enjoyed the materials and the games he played with the aide, though it was obvious in the beginning that he had had little previous experience with many of them. Derek learned quickly and happily. Before long his appearance brightened, and he started to take the initiative. He made suggestions for new games. He tried to be helpful to the aide by unlocking the playroom door and turning on the light for her. He even became a prankster, hiding from her, then startling her by appearing suddenly. It meant a good deal to the aide to see this formerly sad boy laugh and enjoy himself.

Early in December, Derek's father was killed in a hunting accident. The aide was alerted to keep a close eye on his reaction. When she saw him, he was surprisingly even more poised and mature than before. He spoke about the accident in an almost adult way. Throughout the subsequent sessions, he maintained a surface air of serenity. He looked and worked better. He was much less apprehensive. He told the aide how much he now enjoyed it when his mother took him and his sister to visit friends out of town. He was pleased with the possibility that the family might return to the mother's home town, where many relatives still lived. As time went on, however, he began to talk more about his father's death in a hushed but otherwise normal voice. He started to draw pictures of open fields, woods, animals, guns, bullets and hunters. He described one picture as portraying the scene in which his father was killed and gave an account of the accident that was very much like the one the aide had read in the newspaper. But basically he continued to be in a good mood. Once he picked up the father puppet and held it up to the aide. When she asked what he was going to do with it, he said, "Hit it," and proceeded to do so. His actions, rather than words, identified feelings he had about his father. Later he spoke more warmly of his father and even cried a little when he said: "I guess I really do miss him."

By June, Derek was much more mature, well stabilized, less angry, and not at all depressed. His attitudes toward school work were far more positive. He seemed less pressured and reported that he now enjoyed his assignments. He was proud of his improvement in arithmetic and writing. His letter and number reversals, evidenced earlier in the year, had disappeared completely. Although Derek still did not always express his feelings directly with words, when the aide took him back to his classroom on the last day, he turned to her and said: "I certainly will never forget *you!*"

The original group meetings gave the aide and team a chance to learn more about the individual needs of these four boys. Their initial academic deficits were in good measure overcome by the early tutorial helping sessions. Later individual meetings with three of the boys dealt less with their academic problems, but focused effectively on specific personal difficulties that had kept them from profiting maximally from the school's educational and social benefits.

PABLO

Six-year-old Pablo was referred by his first grade teacher in February to "get help in becoming acquainted with the English language." He had recently arrived from Cuba. The teacher described him as a likable, happy, somewhat aggressive little boy who in general responded well to correction. The teacher reported that although Pablo could count to ten, that was about all the English he knew. His language deficit interfered prominently, both with learning and with his peer relationships. Accordingly, her initial and strongest request was that the aide concentrate on helping him to pronounce and understand words in the first grade reader.

Neither intellectual nor personality evaluations were available for Pablo because of his language problem and the fact that he had entered school late in the year. The psychologist did, however, observe him in class and saw him as socially well adjusted and motivated to do well in school. The team decided that an interview with the parents might provide some useful data about the family and help to establish contact between the parents and the school.

The father responded promptly to the social worker's invitation. He explained that his wife had just arrived in the country and that she had not come in because she spoke only Spanish. He added that he had been here longer, living with relatives, and during that time he had gained some facility in English. Pablo's father was an intelligent, friendly, well-groomed man with an obvious interest in his children. Pablo was the eldest of five children—the only one of school age. The father indicated enthusiastically that he would welcome any help the school could give his son. He expressed the abstract hope of taking advantage of all of America's "wonderful opportunities." He briefly discussed the problems of his homeland and expressed his wish that his family would benefit from the move.

Pablo was assigned to an aide, who saw him 21 times between March and June. She described him as a delightful, cooperative child who came happily with her each time. At first she and the boy only smiled at each other when she picked him up in class to go to her room. Before long, however, they greeted each other with "Hello," and Pablo responded "Fine" when the aide asked "How are you?" He brought his reader and paper models of people and animals in his classroom stories, sent by the teacher to each session, and quickly learned to say their names. He soon recognized the word pictures that belonged to each character and animal. He learned to match names and pictures, and as the year progressed he was able to match the pictures with names of objects that the aide wrote on the blackboard. The aide used the "Funny Faces" puzzle to teach him facial features. Dominoes helped Pablo to establish number concepts. The aide had Pablo blow bubbles with a pipe as entree to naming colors and counting. Puppets were useful in helping to teach him words such as baby, boy, man, and so forth.

At each session Pablo was helped to "read" a few pages. At first, he simply pronounced words after the aide, but gradually he committed them to memory. Making sure he knew the meaning of these words was not always easy. To facilitate this, the aide encouraged him to draw pictures representing his understanding of the people and objects she named. Abstract concepts were difficult to convey. She taught him the names of colors and asked him to point them out wherever he saw them: in his book, on his clothes, in the room, or even, as noted before, in bubbles. A coloring book also helped. The art exhibit in the hall was a fine resource. The two would stop as they passed it to see which objects and colors Pablo could name. Pablo genuinely enjoyed this activity and was all smiles when he named an object correctly and was praised for it. He was eager to learn, and with the aide's help he was enjoying it. The aide was continually oriented to new ways to help Pablo learn. When she played ball with him, it was an opportunity to teach him ball-playing vocabulary. When he made a paper kite, he learned to name all of its parts as the project progressed. A child's dictionary and the *Golden Encyclopedia* were particularly useful tools in helping the aide to stimulate Pablo's vocabulary.

In mid-May, Pablo spoke to his aide for the first time in short phrases. She suddenly realized that he had not spoken a single word of Spanish during the entire time they had worked together. When he had been unable to say the English word, he had not spoken. Even so, Pablo and the aide had communicated effectively though nonverbally for many weeks and had developed a close relationship.

The teacher was delighted with Pablo's progress during the year. The aide too was impressed by how well he had adapted to a new country with an unknown language, surrounded by people who were essentially strangers to him.

Pablo's experience with PMHP reflects elements of an ideal, uncomplicated helping relationship: an eager happy child, a supportive parent, a cooperative teacher, and a resourceful empathic aide. This example also points to PMHP's preventive potential in that it avoided a situation which could have been frustrating and stressful, and helped this young boy with a total initial language barrier to get off on the right foot in his school adaptation.

JIMMY

Jimmy was a shy, tall, thin boy who was referred to PMHP when he was in kindergarten. He appeared to be of average intelligence, but he was very undersocialized, used baby talk, and refused to work in a group. Other children in the class often made fun of him, particularly about his height and the way he spoke. His one strong point was that he could draw well.

Jimmy had nearly 100 contacts with an aide during the two school years from March of his kindergarten year until June of the first grade year. Initially, the aide found Jimmy to be even more shy, timid, and lacking in self-confidence than she had expected from the teacher's referral. During their first contact, he was totally speechless. When asked what he would like to do, he stood motionless for a long time; then very, very meekly, he pointed to the sandbox. He played there quietly throughout the entire 40 minutes and never uttered a word. The aide sensed that he was extremely frightened and that he might burst into tears at any moment. The next several visits followed the same pattern. Jimmy would stand quietly, waiting for the aide to suggest activities, and would then engage in the nearest one.

During the seventh contact, the aide was pleasantly surprised when Jimmy asked to play a particular game. Although still withdrawn, he was a bit less fearful in the next sessions. About this time, he first asked the aide to read to him. The aide sensed that doing this brought them closer together and gave the boy a feeling of confidence in their relationship. From then on, whenever the aide picked him up, Jimmy greeted her with a friendly smile. As they walked together, he would tell her what he wanted to do when he got to the playroom. Ultimately, Jimmy became sufficiently comfortable to volunteer to teach the aide a card game. He enjoyed this new role and laughed and talked throughout the game.

When the aide felt confident that Jimmy really trusted her, she began to introduce educationally oriented number games, which she and the teacher had jointly designed, into their activities. Jimmy enjoyed these games and played them for many weeks. As he acquired number concepts, he became more self-assured and proudly confided to the aide that he was now able to do the kinds of "problems" that the other kids in his class did.

Late in the second semester of kindergarten, Jimmy began to verbalize feelings about his home and family life and described his own wishes and the things he enjoyed doing. At this time, Jimmy's grandmother died. Jimmy had been very close to her, and both the aide and teacher anticipated some regression as a result. However, he handled the situation surprisingly well and talked openly to the aide about his sad feelings.

At the year-end conference, the aide and teacher agreed that Jimmy had made significant progress in his ability to relate to the teacher, the aide, and his peers. They discussed his remaining difficulties with the team, and it was mutually decided that he should continue in the program for another year, starting just as soon as he and his first grade teacher became acquainted.

During the second year, the aide's focus changed somewhat. She began to work closely with the speech therapist, who was also seeing Jimmy, and at the latter's suggestion, started using word rather than number games. She encouraged Jimmy to talk more freely. In the latter weeks of their contacts, the aide put him into a small group setting with another quiet child, a girl, and a fairly aggressive boy. Jimmy was challenged by the boy. By using his good sense of humor skillfully, he began to compete directly with him and gradually assumed a more masculine age-appropriate role. Jimmy also won the quiet admiration of the little girl. Later, Jimmy impishly confided to the aide his delight in being reprimanded by his teacher for "acting up" in class. He was gaining self-confidence.

Although it was clear to everyone that Jimmy would never be an exceptional student, by the time he finished in PMHP he was well motivated and able to do satisfactory school work. He had become proud of his work, which was a source of genuine recognition and gratification for him. His speech problems had been corrected and he was now quite verbal.

Jimmy's experience further demonstrates how an aide, working closely with the teacher, can help a child with specific classroom problems. It also shows the value of establishing a warm, understanding relationship with the child before involving him in academic achievement and in learning. The aide did not smother this timid child with kindness. She began by expressing acceptance of him and then encouraged him to make choices within the narrow spectrum that he could handle.

KAREN

Six-year-old Karen, a petite, blond first grader in a suburban school, was also very shy, withdrawn, and unable to relate to her classmates. Unlike most children, Karen was referred to PMHP by her mother rather than by her teacher. Early in the school year, the mother asked the school's social worker for an appointment to share her concerns about her daughter. During the meeting, the mother explained that she had always felt inadequate as a child and many of her old fears still haunted her. For example, she confided that she felt anxious about speaking with the social worker and was still afraid of meeting people and dealing with new situations. Karen's behavior greatly concerned the mother because she felt that Karen was developing the same problems that she had had earlier. She expressed the hope that an aide might do what she couldn't do: i.e., free Karen to relate to others and explore new things.

Karen's father was also concerned about his daughter. His wife described him as bright, cheerful, outgoing, and disappointed by his daughter's reticence about exploring or trying new things. The father had little time to spend with her because he was a full-time student and had a part-time job. The family was new to the area and lived in a small apartment not far from Karen's school. Being strangers in the neighborhood, and with the father away so much, Karen and her mother depended on each other for companionship. Unfortunately, there were few neighborhood children with whom Karen could play. She stayed indoors most of the time watching television, coloring, or reading. The mother said that Karen enjoyed school and did well. She was, however, concerned about Karen's many fears: the dark, animals, going outside alone, loud noises, and the like. Karen also cried a lot. She was easy to manage, if only because she never wanted to do anything. Karen's parents had first heard about PMHP at the first PTA meeting of the school year. On the way home, they discussed the program and decided to approach the team about their daughter.

Karen's first grade teacher was surprised when she heard that the mother had referred the child to the program. Although the teacher recalled that Karen had been withdrawn when she started school in the fall, she had become less so when a cousin was placed in the same class. Karen then began speaking up voluntarily during "Show and Tell." When the cousin was moved to another room, however, Karen reverted somewhat to her earlier shyness and alternated between participation and withdrawal. The teacher felt that Karen was bright and conscientious about her school work.

Karen was assigned to a very gentle self-confident aide. The team advised the aide to begin to draw Karen out slowly and to reinforce any moves she made to explore new activities. Ultimately, the plan was to introduce Karen into a group to help her relate better to her peers. At first, Karen wanted to do only class work; she spent all her time reading and completing workbook assignments. But when the aide encouraged her to explore some of the "fun" things in the playroom and assured her that she did not always have to do school work, Karen tentatively picked up some colored chalk and began to draw pictures on the blackboard. In succeeding visits she sculpted faces with play-doh and then moved to finger painting. Karen worked with the aide to make a pair of coveralls to protect her clothes from getting soiled—a fear, the aid learned later, that had kept her from many activities. Although Karen was intrigued with the puppets, she was very guarded in playing with them in front of the aide. She did, however, express personal interest in the aide: for example, in what she wore, why she chose the colors she did, her role, and what she was called. During her last session of the first year, Karen politely thanked the aide for spending time with her, adding that she might not be seeing her again because her family was moving.

At the year-end conference, the aide expressed concern that Karen had progressed so little. She was still fearful and did not play well with peers. Although the teacher felt that Karen was somewhat less moody and depressed, she nevertheless suggested that Karen continue in the program for the next year if she stayed in the school.

Karen was back in school in September, and shortly thereafter her new teacher referred her to the project because of her sporadic crying spells. At that time, Karen's mother again came in to see the social worker. She explained that she and her husband had just bought a small house, and she was thinking about going back to work because the family needed money to pay some of their bills. She hesitated to do so, however, for fear of upsetting Karen. After listening carefully to what the mother had to say, the social worker tried to help her to examine alternatives. The social worker's impression was that Karen's mother really wanted to take the job she had been offered and that she was looking for support. Eventually, the mother decided that she would try it out, pointing out that if Karen became too upset, she could always quit. Realistically, the family needed the money. Equally important, the social worker felt that separating Karen from her mother might help her to overcome her dependency.

The next steps were to arrange a baby-sitter and a lunch plan for Karen. Karen's school had no lunch room and provided no supervision for children who wanted to bring their lunch. Thus all children went home at noon. The aide discussed the problem with Karen's teacher, who arranged for her to go home for lunch with Mary, a quiet friendly little girl who was well liked by her classmates. Karen's mother contacted Mary's mother, who was delighted, not only to have the extra money for looking after Karen at noon and after school until her mother came home, but to have Karen as a playmate for her child. This agreement marked the start of several important friendships for Karen. She started to walk to and from school with Mary and then with several other children. Later, Karen's mother allowed her to visit in other children's homes after school. Karen also began to invite her friends home and even asked if she could have a pajama party for Mary and Alice, her "second best friend." Her mother readily agreed and was delighted to see this change in Karen.

Toward the end of the year, Karen was much happier and less tense. She no longer had crying spells and rarely withdrew in class. During her last contact, Karen confided to the aide with a shy smile that the teacher had made her stand in the corner twice during the year for talking with a friend in class.

This case involved a complicated mother-daughter relationship, which was partly perceived by the mother, who was the referring agent. The child's school adjustment and personal well-being improved considerably through the aide relationship, helped along by the mother's return to work. The parents were seen again by the social worker when aide contacts were terminated at the end of the second year. At that time the father was somewhat terse and more opinionated than he had been in the original meeting and seemed to be rather overwhelmed by his work load. He was, however, very pleased with Karen's new happiness and now had high hopes for her. Even so, the team wondered how he would handle things if Karen didn't meet his expectations later.

The parents announced plans for Karen to visit an aunt, out of state, for a month during the summer, a genuine step toward independence. The mother thanked the team profusely for PMHP's help, indicating that the project had brought about constructive changes in her life as well as in Karen's. She was quite sure that the great improvement she could see in Karen was related, at least in part, to her own improved mental attitude. Although working outside the home and keeping up with housework were full-time jobs for her, she reported that she had gained self-confidence and felt less depressed. The attitude of the entire family had improved and the parents were truly looking forward to having another child.

LARRY

Larry, a seven-year-old boy, was referred by his second grade teacher, who described him as a socially maladjusted child. His academic performance was poor, although psychological testing indicated that he was at least of average intelligence. In class, Larry was overly aggressive, defiant, obstinate, and impulsive. He also lacked self-confidence, often used baby talk, was unable to express feelings, and had no friends. When frustrated, he threw anything that was available: once he had become so angry that he threw a chair at another child. It was more and more difficult to keep Larry's classroom behavior within reasonable limits. The teacher also felt that there was little or no support for education in the home. Larry's mother had said several times that she did not have time to visit the school to discuss his problems; if the teacher did her job, there would be no problem. Larry told his teacher that he did not see his mother very much because she worked from mid-afternoon until late at night and was therefore rarely awake when he left for school in the morning. On weekends, he was often left with baby-sitters or relatives.

At one point, when the teacher felt she could not control Larry for a full school day, the principal decided to send him home at noon, in hopes that he could at least have lunch with his mother and that she could give him some attention. Instead, the mother asked a neighbor to baby-sit with Larry. Shortly thereafter, however, the mother came to the school demanding that the boy be allowed to stay for the full day. At this point, Larry was referred to PMHP.

At first Larry refused to go with the aide. But when Arthur, another Black boy in his class, said, "I'll go! Take me!" Larry decided to accompany him. During the initial contact, after exploring the playroom, both boys decided to paint. When it was time to leave, Arthur asked the aide if he could come all the time. The aide said that the teacher would have to decide that. Larry made no comment either way.

From then until the end of the school year, the aide saw Larry for 82 individual contacts. At the start, when the teacher was extremely upset with Larry, the aide sometimes saw him as often as twice a day, three days a week. During these particularly troubled times, a classmate—first Arthur, then Dennis, then Gerald, then Buster—came along to the playroom with Larry and stayed for the entire period. The teacher was surprised and pleased when Larry selected the latter two, since both were doing very well in school, academically and socially. When the boys came in pairs, the classmate was typically relaxed and engaged in task-oriented activities such as table games, hide-and-seek, painting, using play-doh, or punching the clown. Larry, however, was always restless, moving frequently from activity to activity. Although he seemed relieved to be out of class, he was unable to settle down easily. Being alone with the aide threatened him, and although he rarely played with the classmate, the latter's mere presence seemed to calm him down.

When Larry was alone with the aide, she never knew what to expect of him. At times, he was very moody, and when upset he threw things around the room. He was unable to deal with structure, making it difficult for the aide, in her role of setting limits, to help him improve his social adjustment. Even "teaching" Larry to walk slowly in the halls was a chore. Typically, he raced at full speed, endangering himself and others. Slowly the aide helped Larry to recognize the inappropriateness of his breakneck pace and taught him to slow down. The aide realized that Larry had to trust her and realize that she could not be manipulated if he was to be helped. During the eighth meeting, the aide explained to Larry that he would be coming alone in the future. Although Larry agreed to this, he requested one "last party" for him and his friends that week. The aide agreed, but reaffirmed that from then on, no more friends could accompany him to the sessions unless this was prearranged by mutual agreement for a special occasion.

The party went well. The boys had a good time and thanked the aide. That same afternoon, however, Larry appeared with Dennis for his appointment. The aide knew that the limits were about to be tested sharply. When both boys insisted that Dennis stay, the aide reminded Larry that he knew the new rules. Larry threw a game he was carrying on the floor, and the boys then ran to the lavatory and hid. Two aides carried Dennis down a flight of stairs and back to his classroom. At that point, Dennis, clearly embarrassed, walked into the classroom. Larry somewhat sheepishly followed the aide back to her room. She pointed out firmly that if he left the room again, he could not return that day. When he heard this, Larry quietly entered the room. The aide then told him to pick up the scattered pieces of the game he had thrown down earlier. He did so, sat down at the table, and asked the aide to play the game with him. He was unusually quiet and courteous that day. Apparently, Larry was both frightened and relieved by the aide's firmness. She seemed to care enough to say No. He asked the aide about her family and also looked at her directly for the first time. At the end of the session, he returned quietly to his classroom without protest.

After this incident, Larry showed other signs of misbehavior, but they were always less serious. He kept some of his appointments and missed others. When he showed up, after missing an appointment his speech was often so infantile that the aide had difficulty understanding him. One of his favorite activities was to be pushed around in a book cart that was part of the project's equipment. The end of the session was always a difficult time for him.

Just before Christmas, the aides gave a party for all program children. Larry first said that he wouldn't attend but later changed his mind. He even held the aide's hand on the way to the party. Although he was generally well behaved during the party, he still had some impulsive moments. For example, when he got tired of standing in line for his turn in a game, he ran into the aide's area and took all the pictures off the wall. He also tore down a donkey that was part of the game. The aide held him gently and talked to him, and he calmed down. Then, in a frightened voice, Larry apologized to the other children for spoiling their game. They responded positively to this change in his mood and invited him to join them. It was a good day for Larry! He even made a new friend, Sterling.

Larry's hyperactivity had been noticeable to project personnel from the start, and an early referral for a medical examination was planned. Thus during Christmas vacation, Larry was seen by a neurologist who diagnosed him as hyperkinetic. He was put on medication, which helped him to relax. The teacher noticed the difference and asked that he be seen fewer times a week; he also seemed ready to go to the reading teacher.

During the twenty-first session, Larry asked the aide what she would like to do, and she chose a game. At that time, she explained that it was important for them to reach an understanding about terminating their sessions on time. After much discussion they agreed that if he didn't terminate on time, he could not see her the next day. Although he later questioned this arrangement, the aide explained that it was fair and that he would have to abide by it. With a twinkle in his eye, Larry commented: "I thought so."

In later sessions, the aide noted that Larry was using less baby talk. Even though the reading teacher reported he was giving her trouble, he came willingly to his sessions with the aide, typically still walking ahead of rather than beside her. But, most important, Larry was living up to the agreement. On his hyperactive days, the nurse checked with his mother and consistently found that he had not taken his medication. Careful supervision of his intake of medication by the nurse helped to stabilize his behavior further.

Late in January, Larry put together a little train with a motor. With the aide's permission, he took it to show his class. And at the next session he reported that he had taken it home. The aide asked him to return it but he kept "forgetting." Although the aide knew it was important for Larry to return the train and key, she did not press him for awhile. Several weeks later, he returned the engine at his own initiative, and the week after that, he returned the motor key. The aide told him she was proud of him for doing this. Larry beamed, obviously pleased with her reaction.

At one session in February, Larry arrived in a stormy mood. In his anger he broke a toy. The aide was provoked by his behavior and told him so. The two discussed their feelings about the incident. At the end of their talk, Larry volunteered that he was sorry and would not repeat the outburst. The remainder of the session went well. A week later, Larry broke the earlier termination contract, and the aide reminded him she would not see him the next day. He made no comment other than to shrug his shoulders and say, as before: "I thought so."

In March, Larry began to set his own limits. He played games without cheating. He talked more. He no longer asked to be pushed in the cart. But he continued to be irregular about keeping his appointments. Also, he still tried occasionally to manipulate the aide, but both were aware of this and discussed it openly.

By mid-April, Larry was walking to and from the playroom holding the aide's hand and chatting freely. This became his practice until the end of the year. If he saw something that interested him in the hall showcase or in a poster on the wall, he stopped and asked about it. He was always courteous now. He even said "Bye" when the aide left him at the classroom door. The teacher reported that Larry was now doing very well in the classroom.

In May the neurologist recommended that Larry be placed in a special class for learning disabilities in another school. The parents indicated their intention to follow through on this recommendation. After careful consideration of alternate plans within Larry's school, none of which materialized, the aide began in mid-May to prepare him for termination. It was expected that he would react negatively to this separation and transfer, so the decision was made that the aide should handle this problem. She began by reducing his contacts from three to two times a week and placed a calendar on the wall so he could count the days as they passed. From then on, the teacher noticed a difference in his behavior. He again began to have tantrums in class. He also started wandering around the school, coming down to the aide's area at odd times, accompanied by Sterling. He would remain only a moment or two and then would return to his classroom. The aide felt he was checking to see if she was still there.

Although the sessions, for the most part, went smoothly, the aide noted that twice when Sterling was around and once when a visiting aide sat in on a session, Larry deliberately announced that his aide always lost the games they played and that she cheated. He began to cheat again, for example, by arranging cards so that he would be sure to win the game. He also insisted on staying longer again, but the aide did not permit this. In the next to the last session, Larry and Gerald, who had been invited for the occasion, talked with the aide about what they would be doing during summer vacation. Larry said he was going to play around the school.

For several days during this period, Larry was very difficult in the classroom. He had wide mood swings, varying from quiet and withdrawn, at times, to aggressive, belligerent behavior. When asked by the teacher about his feelings, he was reluctant to discuss them.

The last session, however, went very well. Larry asked to use the typewriter and proceeded to type: "I love you Daddy—Happy Day." This was a birthday card for his father. He signed it "Jr." When the aide asked "How come?" he explained that his father's name was also Larry and added: "My mother says I'm Junior, not Larry!" The two talked about the fact that this was their last session. By this time, it had been arranged to transfer Larry to a "perceptual problems" class in another PMHP school within his home district. The aide told Larry that she would miss him, but there would be a lady like herself in the new school who would be seeing him and from whom she would find out how he was doing. She said that she would also stop by his classroom to say good-bye before school closed.

When the aide arrived at class, Larry was quite withdrawn and wouldn't talk to her. Then he asked her to get the teacher. When the aide found the teacher, she explained that there was to be a birthday party that afternoon for all the children whose birthdays occurred in the summer months. Although Larry was one such child he had refused to come to the party. When the aide got back to Larry, she said she wanted him to help her carry some equipment to her car but wondered if he couldn't like to go to the party first. Larry said he'd go if she would go with him. Later he said he would go by himself after he had helped her. He asked if Gerald could carry some things too. The aide agreed. When she got to the car, she gave each boy a little gift. She wished Larry a Happy Birthday and a good summer. When she said goodbye to the boys, Larry said, "Good-bye, Mrs. B. You have a good summer too." The boys waved to her from the school door until she drove away. As they turned to go into the school, she stopped and watched until the doors closed behind them.

The case just described represents only a few highlights of the 82 contacts the aide had with Larry. His behavior reflected the problems of a child who felt unwanted and appeared to be undisciplined at home. No one in his prior history had been consistent about his need to conform at home or in school. The mother had turned such responsibilities over to baby-sitters and later to teachers. Whatever limits he had previously experienced seemed to have been punitive or arbitrary, imposed more for others' momentary convenience than to help Larry learn the importance of reality. In his struggle for personal satisfaction and independence in school, he set himself aggressively against all authority. Yet his basic yearning for restraint and control was reflected in his response to the aide, who was able to combine discipline with patience, warmth, consistency, and understanding. Fortunately, Larry also had a concerned, forebearing, empathic teacher. The program's emphasis on early detection also led to prompt medical evaluation, which provided a much needed ingredient (medication) in the attempt to achieve an overall resolution of his problems.

The composite-child, case-history approach of this chapter offers a different perspective of PMHP. For teachers, principals, teams, parents, and, above all, aides and children, this is the perspective of their own, direct, immediate, day-to-day experience. The strongly positive "consumer reactions" that come to PMHP, some of which are presented in the next chapter, doubtless result from this—the project's clinical, human side.

10

Participants'
Reactions
to PMHP

Although children are the prime targets of PMHP's efforts, many other project elements—for example, its screening procedures and consultation activities—affect the overall school community. PMHP focuses first on children with school adjustment problems. But in so doing, it hopefully improves the classroom situation for all children. The teacher's time, previously consumed by a few, can be redistributed among the many. Reduction of classroom disciplinary problems can improve the lot of teachers and principals. The project also increases the contacts between teachers and mental health professionals, both through the redefinition of professional roles and through the availability of outside consultants. This helps teachers to acquire new insights about children and to pick up new techniques in classroom management. Ideally, PMHP's effects should spread like ripples on a pond and potentially benefit others in addition to children, including principals, teachers, parents, and even the aides. Our research to date has not systematically assessed the project's indirect consequences. Thus our knowledge about how others react to PMHP is largely restricted to inputs they have shared with us. A series of these reactions, which are essentially unedited impressions about perceptions of and attitudes toward PMHP on the part of principals, teachers, parents, and aides forms the body of this chapter. The following are some reactions to the project in the speakers' own words.

PRINCIPALS

As we have emphasized several times throughout the book, the principal is a central figure in implementing PMHP in a school. His support and encouragement are vital to the program's success. He must "sell" this new approach to serving children to his faculty initially, and he must meet the project's space needs. When we first decided to write this book, we realized that at some point the principal's role and support would have to be clearly described. Accordingly, in the spring of 1973, we asked principals of PMHP schools to comment on the program. They were asked to assess the program's overall effects and to share their views about the reactions of teachers and parents, the role of the aides and senior aides, the value of consultation, and their recommendations for program improvement. The following are excerpts from the principals' letters and interviews:

The project is everything that I feel for children. It is a program that saves kids. The children have a wonderful experience by finding an adult who gives them full attention a couple of times a week and counsels with them. Everybody is talking about the humanistic approach in education these days. In my opinion, Primary Project is a program where that concept is being implemented, not just talked about. It seems such a waste, on the part of government, to be setting

up task forces to explore innovative approaches for introducing "humanism" into the schools when we already have
a tremendously dynamic, tested and proven program right
here. Rather than financing theorists to generate ivory-
tower proposals, the money should be invested in expansion of what we have here—a viable program that·has
evolved from the grass roots.

The principal of a transitional neighborhood school
that has had PMHP for two years said:

Through the project, lots of kids have been helped, but
more than that, the atmosphere of the entire school has
been changed. This is my first year as an administrator in
which I haven't been confronted with a single, really "hard-
core" kid. We have some very disturbed youngsters in this
school, but I haven't had to see any of them, personally, for
acting out, hurting others, or destroying property. I think
the project, with the help of teachers, has brought about
this improved situation. It's really great how teachers and
children now relate to each other. Teachers see kids in
different ways. They look deeper, somehow, behind the
symptoms to the cause. Our psychologist and social worker
—plus, of course, the aides—have fostered that attitude. Of
further interest is the fact that our student body is now 10
percent Black. This is a highly ethnic neighborhood that has
been notorious for antiblack and anti-Puerto Rican attitudes. In spite of this, we've had no racial hassles. As recently as two years ago, if one Black family had moved in,
it would have been a disaster. I attribute the change in
attitude, so far as the school is concerned, to the fact that
both kids and parents have a place, right here, to ventilate
their feelings. It's been my observation that when any of us
can talk directly to someone about what's really bothering
us, we don't have to look for a scapegoat.

Several principals commented specifically about the
overall effects of the project on their schools:

Primary Project creates an atmosphere of understanding in the school. Instead of griping, as teachers do from time to time about "naughty" kids, it's my impression that they are now much more willing to seek ways for helping them. They are initiating face-to-face contacts with project personnel. As a result of working more constructively, and therefore more effectively, with difficult children, the whole atmosphere of the classroom is calmer, quieter.

· · · · ·

I have not only seen changes in children but in teachers. To the extent that teacher attitudes have been positively modified, there is a spin-off in the direction of helping children in their rooms who are not directly involved in Primary Project. It's a chain reaction, if you will. If we can sensitize teachers to an awareness that children have problems which affect their behavior and if we can help teachers to think humanistically about how to deal with such children, they will sort out those children with the biggest problems, who need an aide, and deal on their own with those whose difficulties aren't as monumental. That way, the entire class is helped. You compound the benefits—like compound interest!

In one instance, the principal's remarks focused on how the project's presence had cut down on the school's prior crisis atmosphere:

Since Primary Project was implemented here, we have had less panic-button-pushing by teachers than before, particularly if we judge by the number of referrals that have gone to the assistant principal in charge of discipline. We have the same population and we still have problem kids, but teachers seem to be more understanding and more able to cope with unacceptable behavior. The backup they get from the project is tremendous. We no longer preach to teachers in generalities when the assistant principal and I get involved at crisis points. We no longer spout the old clichés such as "children are individuals" or they "need individual attention." Instead we ask for a conference with the team or talk with the aide for an interpretation of the child's behavior. Then we discuss with the teacher ways of implementing the project personnel's recommendations.

A city principal who had been in his present school for eight years, five with Primary Project, commented:

> There were uptight kids in this school before we had Primary Project, and there still are uptight kids in the primary grades. They are emotionally upset and confronted with a lots of problems. The difference is that the children are being helped, and so are teachers. My teachers have received a lot of direction from the school psychologist and social worker. Teachers' attitudes have changed. They have become better able to cope and more tolerant and understanding of children's behavior than before PMHP was here. Not only are they more comfortable in relating to the individual child, but the skills they've developed with particular children have spilled over into helping others in their classrooms whom they haven't referred, but who may be showing similar symptoms. The project has been like an in-service program for teachers.

In a year-end interview with a staff member, a principal who had been with PMHP for five years said:

> Although I am invited to all conferences, I regret I can't attend them all. But one of the many benefits I see coming out of these meetings in which teacher, aide, psychologist, and social worker discuss a child are the many sides of a child that each adult experiences in his or her relationship with him. An understanding of the many facets that a child reveals provides clues for helping him in the classroom, at home, or through the aide. In these conferences one obtains a total picture of what a child is like. This is what Primary Project brings to the teacher, and it's a tremendous

dimension. I have been so impressed with the value of this aspect of PMHP that I have requested that all teachers have release-time, next year, through substitutes, to sit down with the team and the aides to talk, not just about individual children with special problems, but about their entire classes. I see this as an additional step in continuing staff development in the area of mental health.

Several principals have observed that fewer children are referred to them for disciplinary reasons since PMHP started in their schools and that the bench in the outer office is not as full as it used to be. They believe this is so, not only because aides work with the children who would ordinarily populate the outer office, but also because the teachers can better anticipate and thus prevent school adjustment problems. Teachers are simply better able to deal directly with problems in class.

One principal who has been a state leader in the area of curriculum expressed his concerns about the discrepancy between the insights that teachers develop locally through PMHP and the proposed "objective" criteria for measuring children's achievement used at the state level:

> With traditional services, we tended to refer nonachieving and/or extremely disruptive children on a crisis basis. In Primary Project, while we still work with aggressive, acting-out children, teachers are becoming sensitive to withdrawn and nonachieving children. I would guess that with 90 per cent of those who are not achieving, the cause is emotional rather than cognitive. Here, the project is helping teachers assess the emotional balance that a child needs in order to learn. At the state level, on the other hand, there is more and more emphasis on behavioral, objective, and academic skills along with testing programs that do not take into account the affective factors in a child's learning.

Rare is the school that doesn't have at least several teachers who are reluctant to refer children to any kind of special service, particularly to a mental health program. If the teachers who are reluctant to refer are primary, especially first grade teachers, it deflects PMHP's thrust toward early identification and prevention. Principals have commented that the teachers who resist making referrals the most are the more traditional, structure-oriented ones who feel that if they cannot personally handle all class situations, it reflects negatively on their competence. Some of these teachers justify their behavior by arguing that the child may miss something important when he is with an aide and that this would be educationally detrimental to him.

In handling this problem, one principal explains to such teachers that they are not doing the child a favor by refusing to refer him. He urges them to make the referral, if not to help themselves, then certainly for the child's sake. He reminds them that there are reasons why a child is unable to adjust and that children with such problems should have a chance "to ventilate with an aide—to talk about what troubles them." He points out that "the children need long-range help," even if the teacher can manage to handle them for the moment. "I tell them: 'All you have to say to yourself is, I think these children could use help.'"

Another principal commented on the reactions of several of his teachers who had questioned the value of recreational activities with an aide for a child who is failing academically:

> I remind teachers that even though the child engages in play with an aide, it is not play for play's sake. It is a therapeutic situation geared to a child's needs. Just as we would never think of denying medicine to a child who is physically ill, so we cannot deny a therapeutic experience to a child who is hurting emotionally.

Some principals have observed that as a result of having the project, the need to exclude or suspend children has been greatly reduced. Several felt that this not only improved their image as principals in the school, but gave them more time for program development and for supporting the school's overall educational enterprise. For example:

> As a result of having to assume the role of the disciplinarian less, I am seen much more positively by the children. I am also more free to visit classrooms and observe the educational process. Most important of all, I don't feel I have to be an expert in an area where I am not professionally qualified—mental health.

$$\bullet \quad \bullet \quad \bullet \quad \bullet \quad \bullet$$

> I have noticed a difference in the number of suspensions I have had to make since Primary Project was introduced here. It's three years since I've made one in this school. Before that I made several each year. Some of those children may have been only second, third, or fourth graders, but they were just little terrors.

The principal of an inner-city school reported:

> We have not had to suspend or refer any primary grade children to Central Office this year. One child in PMHP was put on a "modified" school day [See "Larry," Chapter 9], but he did not have to be suspended. Suspension is not a step a principal takes lightly. I repeat, this does not mean we have not had youngsters with problems. But I think the teachers have been able to handle most of them without coming to me or to the assistant principal first. Instead, after the crisis has passed, the teacher usually tells me what happened and how she handled the situation. This is what we are striving for: to help teachers to take care of their own problems. It strengthens the teacher's hand when the children know that she can cope with classroom problems, and it increases the children's feeling of security in the room. Primary Project is giving us a great assist in this direction.

The principal of an inner-city school was very encouraged because more of his parents were now coming in to inquire about having their children referred to PMHP:

> A mother called only yesterday to ask when her child was going to be admitted to the program. Other parents have dropped into my office to thank me for the aide service in the school. I have had nothing but positive comments from those who stop by.

A principal who had received few requests from parents for information about the program attributed this to the annual project-information letter that she sends to all parents, describing the project and explaining that they can contact the school mental health office directly if they have questions or are interested in discussing their children with the team. She has found that this approach relieves her of unnecessary and sometimes inhibiting involvements.

> Also, I see it as better for parents. They know the principal has probably been involved at some point if their child has been having problems. But this way they don't feel that they must share the nitty-gritty, the negative aspects of their family life, etc., with me. Parents share personal information with the team and, there, they know that it will be treated in confidence. Only if there are administrative problems do I have to become involved. Even the child's teacher does not have to know details. All she needs to know is what could be helpful to her in the classroom. Occasionally a parent, out of the blue, will stop by and announce that her child is "doing better" or "I had a good report from the teacher." They know they don't have to come out with chapter and verse. I can interpret what they are saying. This way parents can always put their best foot forward with me.

The two preceding reactions to PMHP illustrate the varied styles that principals develop toward the project. Although both principals were very positively disposed to

PMHP, one encourages and the other shies away from extensive contacts with parents.

A suburban principal whose school (Kindergarten through sixth grade) is located in a large residential tract and whose enrollment numbers about 800 multiracial students wrote:

> For several years before the spring of 1972, an interest was expressed, at budget time, in bringing PMHP to this school. The interest came about as a result of meetings with two other principals who had the project in their buildings at the time and who had seen, through it, various successful experiences for children, parents and staff. The positive attitude projected by these principals made it difficult to understand why the project shouldn't be extended throughout the district, particularly to our school. After preliminary staff discussion, a consensus developed that we make a strong appeal to locate the project in our school during the district's preliminary winter budget hearing, with a target start-up date of September 1972. The presentation was made and accepted. In late spring, information was provided for staff orientation to help advance people's thinking and planning over the summer. I was invited to several orientation meetings with other principals who were new to the program. Good discussions took place and perspectives developed.

At the end of a two-page monthly report, in which he reviews the program's progress for the first year, this principal concludes: "In summary, the project has really sold itself to the children, the parents and the faculty of our school. I am tremendously excited about the amount of good mental health service provided."

Although the project has had across-the-board acclaim, both teachers and principals have offered suggestions for improving and strengthening it. Many have expressed the wish that PMHP should be extended to the intermediate grades. They comment that some of their most difficult children are in that age group and that the majority of these children "transferred in" at fourth grade or above. As one principal put it:

> My main dissatisfaction with the project is that it is not programmed for the intermediate grades. While we follow up by providing service for children who were in the project during the primary grades, many other intermediates need the service.

Some principals have suggested that it would help if each school could have a "crisis room," staffed by project-trained personnel, available to children in the intermediate grades. For example:

> I would like a crisis room for the children who need short-term service. For instance, when father deserts the family, the children are naturally upset for awhile. They need additional support in school. Often the mother needs help at home and can't be of too much help to the kids. Our Primary Project aides could provide such a service if they weren't so tightly scheduled with regular appointments. They have the training and the depth of understanding to handle these situations. This would carry many children over some of the rough spots in their lives.

One veteran PMHP principal found a solution to this problem:

> Aides have been helpful in emergency situations. In our school, if a child is off base and is sent to the office, more likely than not an aide will work him into her schedule, talk with him ten or fifteen minutes until he quiets down, and then send him back to classroom. This is a crisis-room model, I suppose, without calling it that. A custom some aides have developed is to make early morning rounds of the classrooms where they know children may be disruptive

to inquire about how a particular child was when he came to school that day. If the teacher senses trouble, the aide schedules the child to ward off the crisis, even though it isn't his regular day with her.

Another principal spoke of the need for continuing contacts with PMHP "alumni":

> I could cite many instances of older children who were in the program in the primary grades who from time to time seek out their aides when they are troubled about something. One sixth grade girl, who hasn't been worked with for two years but has a particularly rough home situation, came down recently. The aide saw her and has continued to see her for a half-hour a week. No matter how busy they are, these women always manage to see the kids. When they are in the building, they are here to render service. Of course, this doesn't show up in your statistics. This is the human side of the project that could never be measured.

One veteran PMHP principal, who has helped to extend the program to all elementary schools in his district, believes that the entire atmosphere of the elementary wing of his building was markedly improved by the project. He was pleased to find that primary grade teachers seemed so confident and relaxed with the program that the children were calmer. At first he thought these changes might reflect a "Hawthorne Effect." But after five years, he is persuaded that the project stands on its own merits and that properly conducted, it will continue to do so. At the same time, he believes that the program must be monitored and evaluated carefully to insure quality control. Thus he urges (1) annual orientation of teachers and parents, (2) continued in-service training for teachers, aides, and professional mental health workers, (3) maximal involvement of parents, (4) support of aides by the team through close supervision, (5) open communication among individuals in the school and among teacher, aide, and professional groups, and (6) full support of the project by principals. "Standards must be maintained and personnel held accountable. The project is not just a program. It is a spirit—a way of life within the school—that requires constant nurturing."

TEACHERS

Teachers' comments about PMHP have been communicated to us in several ways. In interactions with school mental health teams, child aides, and consultants, teachers have freely verbalized both positive and negative program perceptions. Moreover, some teachers have spontaneously shared their views with us through notes, letters, and comments inserted in the margins or at the bottom of research forms. Since some teacher reactions were reported, or alluded to, among the principals' comments, the present brief section seeks only to provide the reader with several, more direct examples of such reactions.

The following is a letter to the PMHP staff, written during the project's second stage by a teacher-spokesman for the primary grade faculty:

> I hope that you found the evaluation of the Primary Project by the teachers involved this year to be encouraging. I think we are all in agreement with the statement that the program has taken great strides forward this year. The teachers particularly appreciate the tremendous efforts that you have put forth to bring about better communication between the groups involved in the project. I would like to thank all of you personally, not only for your zeal in giving so much of yourselves toward the goal of preventing emotional disturbance in children, but especially for your sensitivity and consideration with regard to the problems and needs of the teacher.

No one can deny that the aims of the Primary Project are to be applauded. As a result of this year's efforts, I feel that your achievements are beyond applause. Nothing is more gratifying for a teacher than to see children very much outside the Society of Childhood suddenly become members of the "insiders" instead of the "outsiders" group. This year I have had the joy of witnessing the growth of five individuals involved in the program. Jamie, who had never been able to function in a classroom situation, is miraculously learning to read. Tom, who didn't lift a pencil for three months, now asks permission to stay after school to finish his work. Leo had no regard for rules or for the people who enforced them. Recently, he began to raise his hand instead of calling out. In addition, he hasn't raced to be first in line for months. Cheryl was working far below her ability and failing in more than one subject. I think that a "C" will be her lowest grade for this last marking period. As for Louis, he never raised his head in the classroom and could not speak above an inaudible mumble, but now lifts up his head and yells, "Oh Boy!" when his aide comes to pick him up.

Needless to say, these kids may never display genius, may never have great missions to fulfill, and, probably, no remarkable feelings to bestow, but they are no longer outsiders. They are beginning to work out their problems. H. G. Wells once said: "If you don't like your life, you can change it." This seemed unrealistically optimistic to me a year ago, but in view of the changes I have seen five children make from the road to oblivion to the road to responsibility, I have revised my opinion. My congratulations to you all.

A veteran teacher in an inner-city school wrote:

If the Primary Project were to favorably affect the mental health of a single child involved in it, it would be worthy of applause. Knowing as I do how very many children are touched and mended, a standing ovation would be a grossly inadequate show of appreciation to you who give so much yourselves.

The Primary Project has helped many children. The children that are selected for the aides need the personal attention which they receive from them. Somehow I sense these boys and girls feel better, just knowing that someone else cares about them and is nice to them.

By having the Primary Project in our school, I have been able to learn much more about each child's background. This is so important in order to be sympathetic with each child. Also of great significance is the free assistance families with problems can receive by consulting with the Primary Project staff.

A teacher in a new PMHP school commented:

The child aide program, as now set up, seems to be working well. The children look forward to going out with the aides. The aides give the children the extra bit of special attention that these children need and cannot get in a large class. All of my children who have been involved in the program have shown some improvement in socialization, behavior, subject matter, or whatever the reason for referral was.

Conferences with the team and aides have also been helpful in giving more insight into the child's problem and how to deal with it. Much more can be accomplished when conferences do not have to be scheduled during the teacher's break time or before and after school.

I feel it would be helpful to have a program such as this in all schools. Much help is gained by the teacher as well as by the student.

Some teachers attributed the "difference" in PMHP service to the quality of the aides. As one teacher said:

The aides could make or break a program like this! Get a group of aggressive, critical women in here with the wrong attitudes towards public schools and the wrong reasons for choosing to be an aide and the results could be disastrous!

The aides I have worked with have been just great human beings. They not only want to help kids, but they have been supportive of me, too. I see them as colleagues.

Another teacher concurred and then commented on how she thought the project might be improved:

Not just any gal with good intentions can work in this program. They have to have some very special aptitudes, and lots of support from all of us, but particularly from the school psychologist and social worker. . . .

For any greater success than is presently being achieved, I believe the answer lies in quantity rather than quality of services. I would like to see:

1. More children reached by more aides.
2. More classroom observation by team members.
3. More communication between team and teachers.
4. More communication among teachers to help in recognition of problems as well as methods of handling problems in a classroom situation.

Following a recent school staff meeting, one PMHP teacher observed:

In college, we teachers do not get enough training in mental health to do a preventive job in the classroom. The Primary Project helps greatly in this respect. In this school, teachers do not have to work through the principal. We have direct access to the school psychologist, the social worker, and the aides, which makes me, at least, feel more involved and potentially competent. We have an opportunity to discuss not only specific children but to talk in general terms about entire classes. We are made to feel that our concerns and observations are important and have validity.

Another teacher, after the same meeting, noted:

I think the most appreciated aspect of Primary Project service from the teacher's point of view is the immediate response we get to referrals. The average teacher continues to feel that unless she can see something tangible being done for a child, making out a referral is worthless. My experience with traditional services was that there was usually very little follow-up after my referral, no doubt because of the workers' heavy case loads. While this is understandable, it is never helpful to teachers. When an aide comes to a teacher's door to pick up a child, and when we consider all of the conferences we have on children, the teacher is assured that someone cares, and that she does not have to deal with the problem alone.

When teachers fill out research forms, they often add spontaneous notes reflecting some specific view of the program. For example, the following note appeared at the bottom of a set of seven-point rating scales measuring children's school adjustment:

I want to take a moment to express my appreciation for the wonderful job which you have been doing and to give my heartfelt thanks to Mrs. M [the school social worker] and to Mrs. Y [an aide], both of whom have helped me so much this year. There is one "change scale" which does not appear on your form, that is "change in teacher effectiveness through the help of the team." There, again, you score a "7." Thanks again.

Other teachers' notes included the following:

I don't know what that aide did with that boy, but whatever it was, it was good. He's a changed child!

• • • • •

I have been teaching in this school for ten years, and this is the first time I feel we've really had mental health services. In the past we had a psychologist and social worker, but they were only able to see the very upset kids who usually ended up being excluded. This year, I am getting help with a wide range of kids. Not only are they evaluated, but I am getting the feedback, and the children are being worked with.

• • • • •

I have had three children in my class this year because of whom I'm afraid I'd have had to resign or ask for a transfer if I hadn't received the project's help. It was a *very* difficult year, but much better than it would have been without project support!

• • • • •

It's good to know that I can talk with people [the team and the aides] who understand how difficult it is to have severe problem children in the classroom. And the project staff helps me carry my burdens.

Another teacher wrote the following letter, addressed to PMHP staff and returned with the research forms:

During the past year, four of my third grade children were involved in PMHP. My impressions of this project grew more and more favorable as the year progressed. Children were involved with aides who could give them needed, undivided attention. By listening to and working with these children, the aides help to make school a positive part of their lives. As a teacher, I also become involved with the aides, chatting with them and discussing specific children, their continuing problems and, oftentimes, their improvement.

I believe that the project is very worthwhile and important. To a large degree I feel that the success of the project is due to the type of aides involved. At our school, we are fortunate to have warm and understanding aides who relate well to children and teachers and, most important of all, are great human beings.

Several themes recur in these teachers' comments: their gratification to see children become positively redirected through the program; their own valuable gains in understanding children—gains that translate into more effective classroom management skills and greater self-confidence as teachers; and the sense of support that they feel from the project—a sense that helps to reduce the pervasive feeling of many teachers, so well captured by Sarason et al. (1966) in the phrase: "Teaching is a lonely profession."

PARENTS

Typically, PMHP parents are not directly involved in the program's efforts to help their children. However, most parents recognize their children's special needs and are pleased that a program is available in their school to help children adjust and learn more effectively. After PMHP has been in a school for a while, parents see the project as an integral part of the school program and tend to take it more for granted. As long as their children are being served and reports of improvement come home, they are rarely heard from. A small proportion of parents, however, has ongoing contact with the team after the initial interview with the social worker. And when PMHP's efforts are less than successful or when additional services are needed, the team becomes more directly involved with parents by helping to make necessary referral arrangements.

One principal spoke of parent involvement in PMHP as follows:

I am pleased when parents come in to speak with me about the difficulties their children are having and I can offer them a helping service which is right in the building. The perception that the project is a good thing is getting around the school community. We have spoken to our PTA about it and, while many of the members responded very positively to the concept, they were hardly to the point of being willing to "lobby" downtown [the school district's central headquarters]. I suppose it's natural that most consumers of this kind of service may be reluctant to acknowledge that they have been helped. Mental health services are not the kind of product that you can sell like candy bars! The parents who are willing to demand an extension of the program are those whose children are in need of service but can't get it because of a waiting list.

In fact, some parents have lobbied effectively for PMHP. They have organized themselves and gone directly to the board of education to argue for PMHP's inclusion in their home schools. On one occasion, parents' vocal reaction prevented PMHP from being phased out of a school that had had the project for several years but was slated to lose it because of a general district-reorganization plan. The correspondence from parents at that time included letters such as the following:

I was called by Mrs. L from our PTA who told me some of the parents of children being seen through Primary Project were going to meet to discuss the project's future in the school. My husband and I both work, but if we can do some telephoning in support of the project when we are not working, we will gladly do it.

Our son Wilbur still talks about the nice lady he worked with in your program. He was always a good student, but the nice part about the time he spent with the lady was that he seemed to become a happier kid. He stopped lying and even his stuttering improved. His father didn't have to punish him as often any more. We became a happier family.

I am not good at writing, but if we can help the program in any way, my husband and I very much want to because we want other kids to feel happy too.

• • • • •

I recently heard that parents were organizing a group from our school to speak out to retain the project. My husband

and I want to be active in the promotion of such services throughout the district, and especially to keep the program in our school.

As you will recall, our daughter, Tanya, was referred to the program in first grade. At that time, were were very concerned with her behavior at home and especially her lack of adjustment to school. She had become extremely withdrawn, very tense and, when called upon by the teacher, would burst out crying. She was assigned an aide in PMHP in January. By June, Tanya had become more verbal in the classroom, volunteered to read assignments, and the relationship with her two brothers and peer groups had improved. My husband and I never expected to see such dramatic changes come about—certainly not so quickly.

It hardly seems sufficient to say we are grateful. We have a whole family that can enjoy each other again and a daughter who is enjoying school. Thanks to you and the project for making it all possible.

Parents have written directly to express their appreciation of PMHP. For example, a mother of a school-phobic child wrote:

I just wanted to drop you a note to let you know how fantastic Tommy is doing. You'd be amazed at the change in him in the morning. He gets up and dresses with no pushing and even walks to school alone. His confidence has increased three times over, and I feel he has returned to his earlier feelings from first grade that "school can be fun." Thanks for all the kindness you've shown Tommy. I can't find words to express how grateful we are to everyone who helped us over this very difficult period.

Another mother wrote at greater length:

The Primary Project did wonders for our son, Dick, in a matter of weeks. My husband and I were amazed that after four half-hour sessions, he showed remarkable improvement. Within two months we felt he was a whole new child. He stayed with the project for the second half of the second grade. We have no more days of morning sickness. He is doing well both academically and socially this year. Obviously, we are pleased that the project was available to Dick.

During a recent parents' meeting, the school psychologist asked me to talk about the parents' role in this. You must understand that what I say about the project is just my personal feelings. I can't be objective since I have only my own experience from which to work. I feel that since the parents do so much to formulate a young child's psychological makeup, it follows that they are responsible, at least in part, for the development of a learning problem which is not physical in origin. If the child is to overcome these problems, he will need the help and understanding of those who had a part in its cause—the parents. After Dick was tested last year, the psychologist had me in for a conference. We discussed what the problems were. He then gave me some positive suggestions on how my husband and I could help Dick. We tried, the project tried, and the results were good.

I was later invited to attend a Monday morning "Mothers Meeting." I include the quotes because, although I have never been in therapy, I have a strong suspicion that these meetings were similar to group therapy sessions. I found them to be helpful but, at the same time, upsetting. At one point I began to question almost every reaction I had to my children. Then gradually, I began to grow in my understanding. Hopefully, I've changed for the better, but what's important is that I'm now confident that I'm doing my best and that my best will be good enough. You have noticed that the preceding paragraph has many "I"s. My husband and I feel that if the project has any weakness, it's in the lack of involvement of the fathers. While I'm sure that most mothers try, as I did, to explain what is happening, it is not the same as direct contact with fathers. We understand the time problem of having both parents in, but we feel there is a need since both parents are necessary to, and responsible for, the child's attitudes. In short, the parents' role is to

learn what the problem is and how to aid the child in over-
coming it. It would be simple if the project personnel could
tell us: "This is the problem and you must do thus and so!"

Even though the school psychologist did give us some
suggestions and direction, there was so much that we had
to discover about ourselves before we could effectively help
Dick. The parents must learn to understand and help their
children. In trying to do so, I would sometimes go into my
bedroom to cry in frustration because it seemed so difficult
to alter my patterns and attitudes. But I firmly believe that
for a child to change, those he loves most must also change.
Your efforts and those of the school professionals and aides
helped us do this. Thank you so very much!

One interesting parental reaction to PMHP came during a meeting with the principal of a suburban project
school. At the time the family was about to move out-of-
state, the mother praised the school and marveled at the
degree to which it had concerned itself and actually worked
with individual children. She said that her child had been
helped through PMHP to mature socially and emotionally
and achieve academically, even beyond her grade level. She
then added:

Without detracting from my own good self-concept as a
mother, I must say that the aide who worked with my girl
helped her in a way I could not have. I suspect I was too
close to see my child as she really was, whereas the aide
could see her more objectively.

Although the mother regretted having to move because her child's project experience had been so good, she
felt that the help she had received from the social worker
would enable her to help her daughter maintain the gains
she had made.

As can be seen, parents, like teachers, express strong
satisfaction with the project when dramatic positive change

takes place in an initially maladapting child. In addition, there is a sense of gratitude in parents' responses to the program's reaching-out and supportive elements and a willingness on the part of some to stand up and be counted when the program is threatened. This is significant because parents' responses are among the most important sources of influence on school boards and school district administrators.

AIDES

Child aides have been a major force in PMHP since the aide program began in 1964. In addition to the effective service they provide to schools and to children, aides speak of their personal growth in the project. We recently invited aides to share their impressions of the project with us. A recurrent theme, illustrated in the following two excerpts, is how aides, through their participation in the project, come to understand and appreciate the teacher's role.

> I had no idea until I came into this program how hard most teachers work, how dedicated they are, and what a challenging, sometimes frustrating, job they have. I just can't imagine myself standing on my feet all day, working with individual children and with groups trying to motivate them to learn! Now that I know how difficult it is to foster learning in one child in a one-to-one relationship in the project, I marvel at how teachers do it with the community cross-section represented by the children in their classes.

• • • • •

> I learned to have a far better understanding of the apprehensions and anxieties that a young teacher feels when coming into her first teaching position and how much she needs to relate to a friend—much in the same way a child does to an aide. My very first experience with a teacher

could be described as a near head-on collision. We both were very positive people and had similar personality traits. Yet, because of the aide-teacher sessions we had, we were able to deal quite openly with our feelings. Because of this openness, we developed a real friendship, an admiration for each other's role and its accompanying frustrations. It was a marvelous period of growth for me in understanding my role as an aide and how I could work with a teacher to help bring about changes in children.

Aides also come to recognize and to deal effectively with new concepts and experiences in the project. One aide shared the following observation with us:

During my first experience in a ghetto school, I had some real apprehensions and anxieties. The team encouraged me to talk about these feelings and helped me to admit some of my unrecognized prejudices. I gradually came to understand that children are children, and all children have similar needs. With supervision, I found that I could relate comfortably to children in all settings, regardless of their location or ethnic background. I learned a great deal about people in each setting I was sent to. I could feel, and begin to empathize with the problems of a mother on a welfare budget whose husband had left her and who was now trying desperately to keep the family together. My experience in PMHP made me the kind of truly open person I had always thought I was.

Another aide, who had been in the project only a year, said:

I had no idea that there were so many children who needed help, nor did I ever realize the depth of their problems. I now find myself involved in situations around children about which I had only read earlier. I have a better understanding of why children sometimes behave as they do and of the importance of early emotional support for all children.

Another commented:

> A year ago I would have described myself as a happily married person with four lovely children. I thought that I was quite content as a mother and homemaker, but I now suspect that I must have been looking for something more because when a friend, who is a teacher in a project school, told me about PMHP's expansion, I was intrigued and immediately applied for a position. Not only have I come to understand better the need for mental health services for children, but I have also come to understand myself better. I was always a somewhat retiring person and have now developed greater self-confidence and am more outgoing. I am convinced this is because I have been able to contribute something to society. Indeed, I am a part of an important new step in mental health.

An aide who has been in the program for three and one-half years spoke about how the experience had widened her personal horizons:

> It has been on a par with four years of undergraduate work. The people I have worked with have become very precious to me, but it is in the area of relating in an empathic and meaningful way to my own family that I have grown the most. My relationship with my aging father has improved, and I now feel better able to understand and respond to the feelings of my own teen-agers. This is a function of having developed a greater awareness of myself, my own needs, and my ability to express and deal with them.

An aide who has been with the project for four years commented:

> My purpose in joining PMHP was not personal gain but to give of myself for the benefit of my very special little friends. However, these children have given me fulfillment, meaningful relationships, and a wonderful feeling that in some ways I have helped them with their problems and to feel better about themselves.

Another aide wrote:

> There have been so many opportunities to learn. The hours
> of discussions and seminars with consultants, supervisors,
> and other aides have been invaluable to me. Some of this
> growth has been painful, but I am still growing! Having
> been born in an era when one asked oneself before acting,
> "What will people think?" I have had much to overcome.
> The "undoing" has taken a long time, and, yet, not so long!
> How *not* to be defensive; how *not* to feel guilty; discovering
> that all my feelings were normal; admitting my angry feel-
> ings; finally, the end of trying to be all things to all people
> all of the time, obtaining a real feeling of confidence, ac-
> cepting myself as me. From the very first session, I have
> always felt that to share a child's world was a privilege. I
> would like to borrow Dr. T's [the psychiatric consultant]
> words and say that I now have a noisy sense of competence
> and I am coping comfortably!

Some aides grow impatient when children progress
slowly. Thus one aide remarked:

> At times I feel frustrated when I can't see that I am making
> headway, but then I realize, as I learned in my training, that
> some children's problems were long in developing and that
> time will be necessary in rectifying them. So I keep on
> trying.

Several aides, as the following comments indicate,
have dealt searchingly with the question of how they have
changed with the project:

> I believe that in a project such as PMHP there is no *status
> quo.* An individual associated with the project either ma-
> tures or eventually falls by the wayside. As I assess my
> thoughts, feelings, and performance during two years with
> the project, I have reached a few conclusions. In the past,
> I have been superficially aware of the problems and frustra-
> tions of others. Dealing with some of these problems on a
> day-to-day basis has been an education in compassion and

understanding. Seeing how these difficulties affect the lives of the children has made me more eager to try to do or say something to help them cope with their present situation. In order to give a child competent help, an aide, herself, needs a great deal of "know-how." I have found that one of the best sources and "on-the-spot" training sessions are the weekly team supervisory meetings. In my first year with PMHP, my supervisor made me aware of many psychological insights into what makes kids with problems tick. He also suggested ways of dealing with them. These suggestions have proven very valuable. I continue to draw upon them. The weekly supervisory meetings are thorough. Each child assigned to me is discussed. His problems, progress, or lack of it, are brought up and reviewed from new perspectives, and the supervisor will then suggest how to handle them from another viewpoint. This too, has broadened my vision and, hopefully, helped me to become a more competent aide.

A senior aide reported the following experience:

At a recent church circle meeting, each of us was asked to answer the question, "What have I done with my hands, my head, and my heart in the past ten years that has been meaningful and helpful to me and to others?" I immediately thought how easy this task was for me because I could answer with five words—"My work in Primary Project." My hands were certainly helpful when I worked with the children as an aide and as a senior aide. As for using my head —certainly, as an aide, I had to be ready to make some instant decisions with the children. As a senior aide I have had to come up with some pretty quick answers when aides and teachers ask questions. There has been a constant learning from our consultants and from reading recommended books and articles. Most important to me, and most difficult to put into words, is to express how my heart has been involved. I guess all I can say is that everything I've done in Primary Project has involved my heart. Perhaps this is why most of us have stayed with the project for so long

and why we're so sure it really "works." I know that I have
changed in the past 8 ½ years. I have a greater understanding of people—both children and adults—which certainly has helped me in my work and in my personal life. I
know I am more sensitive to other people's feelings and
consequently more tolerant than I used to be. I am much
more sure of myself—I am no longer afraid to speak out
when I feel that I have something worthwhile to say.

Another aide reported:

Three years ago mental health was an unfamiliar aspect of
my way of life—a subject rarely discussed openly and, at
times, even avoided—primarily due to a lack of knowledge
and association. After being a so-called "Mother Hen" for
many years—living in my own little world—the opportunity
to become a child aide opened up many doors for me. It was
a reaching out by extending a *hand* to help, lending an *ear*
to hear, and a *heart* to heal the troubled minds of the "little
people." Becoming involved and touching their lives has
been most rewarding. Tremendous satisfaction results from
writing a termination report, due to the goals that are
achieved. The child's emotional development and needs, as
well as my own, have gradually been fulfilled. We all have
a deep desire to be needed. These smiling little faces along
with the affectionate hugs are proof that we are a "friend"
indeed. Maybe somewhere along the way I have prevented
the occurrence of a future traumatic situation. Much credit
is due to the proper guidance, supervision, and consultations by professionals through "team effort." None of us
could perform, or produce, without these functions.
   Yes, I have changed! At times I amaze myself by speaking
out, expressing opinions, asking questions, offering suggestions and even disagreeing. I have learned to see people as
individuals. Believe me, however, I grew the most when
presented with the opportunity—much to my dismay at the
time—of changing to a new school for several months. It
proved to be an enlightening experience and brought into
proper perspective the different family backgrounds and

basic needs which have a powerful effect on the children, along with the crowded conditions and overall structure within the different schools as well as the attitude of teachers and other aides. We aides, also, can fall into a certain pattern and are not immune from becoming short-sighted or concerned just with one particular atmosphere or with a familiar situation. The change proved very significant in broadening my whole concept of the program.

A veteran aide made the following remarks:

Being an aide for PMHP has been a most worthwhile and rewarding experience. It taught me that children feel very deeply and can suffer greatly as a result of these feelings. I only wish that I had been more aware of this as my own children were growing up. Knowing this now, however, has made me more attuned to those I come in contact with. Being a part of this project has given me an opportunity to broaden my knowledge of psychology, a field that I had scarcely scratched in my school years.

I have also been able to complement this knowledge in my daily life. It has been rewarding, also, to think that maybe I may have made life a little better for the few children I come in contact with and, perhaps, have influenced their futures.

A new aide commented:

I have learned a great deal in the past six months. I think I've grown and my hope is that, as time goes by, I will learn more. I enjoy the children just as much as I anticipated, and because of the project I have an even greater desire to help children. It has been a very fulfilling job.

There have been times when I felt a lack of knowledge because I have not been educated in a psychological direction. But even when I have felt that I didn't approach a particular child in a proper manner, I have been very encouraged by the support our team has given us all, as a group and as individuals.

The project has increased my understanding of the problems so many of the children face. I find I enjoy getting out to work each day, enjoy being with my coworkers and, most of all, I enjoy the feeling of satisfaction I receive from dealing with the children.

Finally, another veteran aide commented:

The fulfillment my work as an aide has given me has made me appreciate my home life more and has made me a more sensitive mother, wife, and friend. My awareness of the feelings of the children I work with has heightened my sensitivity to everyone I relate to away from school, and this too has been very gratifying. An outstanding example of this is a hospital visit I recently made to the seven-year-old son of a friend of mine. I walked into the room to find mother and child very tense, and the mother told me that the boy had been very irritable all day and she did not know what to do with him. He argued this point so hotly that she finally walked out of the room in anger. I stayed and began to reflect his anger, and he soon began to share his feelings with me. He was angry and frustrated about his long confinement, but most of all, he was upset about having a roommate put into his room that night when he had had that room all to himself for almost two weeks. For about ten minutes he spoke to me about the various feelings he had about this, and then, suddenly, he asked me to call his mother back in. When she came, he spontaneously apologized to her for having been so irritable and mean. She looked at me as if I had performed a miracle, and I felt pretty wonderful that I had been able to help both of them during this difficult time. I know that my work as a child aide taught me how to handle that situation the way I did.

The comments of aides included in this section well represent the larger sample of aides' reactions. Without question, the experience of being a child aide in PMHP is a gratifying, enriching one. There are the direct observable satisfactions of bringing help to young children who desperately need it. Being an aide also offers continuous opportunities for growth and learning and many other fringe benefits, such as increased understanding of oneself and one's world and more effective interpersonal relations and improved family relations. Beneath these many salutary changes, the aides develop a genuine sense of being involved in a real, very necessary, and socially contributory role that is syntonic with a better-balanced life experience for them and, accordingly, leaves them with the satisfying feeling of having found a valuable niche in life.

11

How
to
Do It

The emphasis of this chapter is practical. It focuses on the question of how actually to go about setting up a PMHP. That question cannot be answered without taking into account a school system's defining realities: i.e., the problems with which it must deal, the personnel it has available to deal with them, and the program resources that can be anticipated. In other words, the question can be answered in almost as many ways as there are systems, though it would be impractical to do so.

At several points earlier in this book, we recognized explicitly the fact that PMHP developed under favorable resource conditions. This happened because of a dual accident: the availability of both outside grant moneys and of a host system with long-established, relatively well-staffed mental health clinical services. It has always been clear to us, however, that few districts elsewhere could realistically be expected to muster comparable resources for a program of this type and that the challenge of translating what we learned for less well-resourced districts would eventually become very important.

Intramurally, a practically oriented "how-to-do-it" document titled "Some Guidelines for Administering the PMHP Method of Delivering School Mental Health Services" has been developed by project staff to fit a relatively well-resourced school situation. The document contains two types of information: (1) descriptions of PMHP's central program elements (e.g., assignment and termination conferences, aide supervision, consultation) and how to develop them most effectively and (2) specification of procedures we have followed to optimize a program's rooting: i.e., procedures that pave the way, whatever a program's resources, for a more smoothly functioning entity.

Much information about key program elements has already been presented, especially in Chapter 6. Accordingly, this chapter starts with a brief resumé of several sections of the "guidelines" document, not yet covered in detail elsewhere, that may be helpful to others faced with the practical job of setting up a PMHP-type program. The style of the write-up is simple and direct. The material is targeted for district administrators or principals who have only a nodding acquaintance with PMHP. The information is general, and it applies best to relatively well-resourced situations. Not all of the content will be relevant to all districts. We prefer, however, to err in the direction of over- rather than underinclusiveness, since it is easier to "tune out" on surplus information than to proceed without essential data.

The chapter's second major section puts core PMHP program elements under a finer microscope in an effort to "prioritize" its components for the many school systems whose resources range from inadequate to virtually none— a difficult but realistic and necessary step.

General Information about Establishing a Program

Basic Descriptive Summary

The project has found it useful to have a brief orienting description available as an initial introduction to the program for school personnel who are interested in but unfamiliar with PMHP. The following statement has been used for that purpose:

> The Primary Mental Health Project (PMHP) is a program for early detection and prevention of emotional, behavioral and learning problems in primary grade children. Its goals are to help children obtain optimal educational levels commensurate with their aptitudes and abilities and to improve their self-concept and socialization skills. In other words, PMHP seeks to identify problems early, to intervene and to remediate them before they become severe or entrenched. The program makes several important assumptions, i.e., that emotional problems can adversely affect learning and *vice versa;* that the influence of the school environment on the child is extremely important; that family relationships and dynamics are important to the child's school adjustment; that early detection of maladaptive school behavior facilitates economic, effective intervention; and that, without effective intervention, early school maladaptation tends to persist through the later school years and to have adverse effects on later life adjustment.

Principal's Role and Space Needs

In setting up a PMHP, care should be given to selection of the site, the principal, the mental health team, and the child aides. Like other school projects, PMHP depends heavily for its effectiveness on the commitment and cooperation of the entire school staff and of parents. The principal is a key figure in promoting PMHP in the school. In the last analysis, the program's success depends largely on his commitment and readiness as well as his ability to sell the program to the faculty and to the larger school community.

An initial, essential project requirement is that adequate housing be arranged by the principal, designating areas of the building in which aides can work comfortably with children. Individual rooms in which aides can "set up shop" and which they can call their own, if available, are preferable. Such facilities obviate the need to carry materials and equipment from place to place, promote the aide's feeling of belonging, and provide the aide and child with the privacy needed to work effectively together. If individual rooms or even nooks are not available, empty classrooms with areas separated by dividers can sometimes be arranged. It may also be possible for an aide to share a room used by "itinerant" staff members, such as music, art, or speech teachers, who are not in the building full-time.

A central conference room where meetings and consultation sessions can take place is also very useful. Such a facility serves as a place for aides to meet to discuss project matters and/or to write reports. It can also be used as a "drop-in" center where teachers and children can meet with aides. Our experience suggests that having a meeting area promotes communication and good group feelings.

Record Keeping

Since records are kept for each PMHP child, a locked file cabinet should be located in an area where folders can be readily available to project personnel. Record information is helpful, not only for the team, but also for project consultants who are not always familiar with the backgrounds of the children being discussed during a particular visit. Records should contain identifying background information about the child, teacher's referral data, the results and interpretation of the psychologist's testing, a summary of the social worker's family contacts, and later project-related documents or measures. The record file also provides a secure place for aides to leave their working notes.

A prime purpose of record keeping is to offer high-quality service to children and families. Records are an important source of information about the behavior of project children and an important index of their growth and development. Well-documented information is often helpful to outside agencies and improves interagency communication. When there are changes in school personnel, either an aide or a professional, the combined child aide/supervisor record provides an important tie with past services.

Project Personnel

Appropriate administrative personnel from the school district should consider carefully the selection of PMHP mental health professional teams. The psychologist and social worker who comprise the team should be sympathetic to the approach and want to be part of the project. They should have some understanding of and sympathy with the concepts of early identification and prevention and should be sufficiently flexible to accommodate to the new modes of functioning that the project requires. They should also have the time and aptitude for supervising aides, be able to respect and work well with teachers, and, above all, be able to work together effectively as a team.

Typically, there are five half-time aides in a medium-to large-sized school; fewer may be needed in smaller ones. The average caseload for an aide working 15 to 20 hours a week is about eight to twelve children. Aides who work with small groups of selected children have heavier caseloads. Brief preliminary training in groups is typically provided for aides before they join their school units. More important is the continuous on-the-job training and supervision as well as support that aides receive from the program psychologist and social worker. Ideally, there should be two hours of individual supervision plus an hour and a half of group supervision monthly. The program's objectives can often be furthered, especially if professional time is scarce, by assigning an experienced senior aide to the program. Senior aides come from the pool of child aides and are selected on the basis of interpersonal and experiential qualities, history of effective performance, and interest in and commitment to the project. Senior aides should have good verbal facility, effective peer relationships, organizational and managerial abilities, and a "presence" or manner that is acceptable, indeed attractive to peers. Senior aides work under the general supervision of the mental health team. Their duties include facilitating the program's overall objectives by working to improve the knowledge and effectiveness of the child aides and by supporting and extending the school activities of the professional mental health teams. The school psychologist, social worker, or senior aide should be available to backstop aides who need help or feedback between supervisory sessions.

Further support to the program, aides, teachers, other school personnel, and the team is provided by regular consultation visits by experienced mental health professionals. These individuals, depending on the host community's profile and resources, may come from nearby universities, clinics, or community mental health centers.

Involvement of Parents

Parents participate in the project in two important ways. First, a general information meeting should be arranged early in the fall for parents of all primary grade children to acquaint them with PMHP's basic concepts, goals, and procedures. Such meetings are facilitated by having as broad a base of participants as possible: for example, team members, aides, teachers, and the principal. The meeting should provide parents with an awareness of the project's presence in their school and some familiarity with its purposes.

Second, parents also become involved in PMHP through the initial contact with the social worker, which usually takes place after testing and teachers' referrals have been completed. This contact permits the social worker to explain the program to the mother in greater detail, obtain her permission for the child to participate, assess her ability and willingness to become involved in the school's efforts to help the child, formulate casework impressions of family dynamics, establish a positive relationship with the mother, and assure her of the school's continuing interest in her child. The more the parent can be involved in the program, the better the results are likely to be with children. Additional parent interviews may be arranged, depending on the particular problem and the parents' readiness to become involved. However, children should not be excluded from the program because of the parents' inability or unwillingness to help. In some situations, all that can be obtained is the parents' permission for the child to be seen. Having such permission is, however, essential. If the social worker does not have sufficient time to interview the mothers of all referred children, every effort should be made to develop alternative provisions for this essential element of the program. If resources permit, it is also helpful, preventively, for the social worker to interview and become better acquainted with mothers of nonreferred children.

Testing and Referral Data

After information meetings for faculty and parents have been held, the psychologist begins testing first grade children. Optimally, this should start around mid-October, by which time the children have become accustomed to desks, pencils, and classroom routine. Around this time, teachers are asked to identify the children about whom they are most concerned, submit behavioral rating data for them, and develop a priority referral list. In selecting children for the program, the team should keep in mind the importance of the teacher's own well-being for an optimal school atmosphere. Although it is theoretically ideal to assign all children referred by teachers, actual practice depends on available resources. Unless a school is well staffed with professionals and aides, it is unlikely that all referred children can be seen by aides immediately. Some youngsters, hopefully those with less urgent problems, can be assigned later. When a program is in full operation, first grade children must compete for time with second and third grade "carryovers," which in some instances creates a waiting list. After a teacher's referral requests have been met, children whom the team or others want to refer may be added. Insofar as possible, parent referrals are given the same priority as those of teachers.

Conferences

Good communication among the team, child aides, teachers, the principal, and other school personnel is important for a well-functioning project. There are three formal PMHP conferences in which teachers, aides, and the professional team should participate: the assignment, progress, and termination conferences. Scheduling teachers well in advance to discuss children at these conferences can be done by the team, the senior aide, or the principal. Substitute teachers should be obtained, whenever feasible, so that teachers can be released from their classrooms to participate. Schools that schedule regular meetings may find it advantageous to use the same substitute teachers for all conference days since this permits the teacher to become acquainted with the substitute and allows the substitute to learn class routine and to observe children over a period of time. Such observations can then be shared with the team. In schools with limited resources, it may not always be possible for both psychologist and social worker to attend all conferences. However, both should be present when assignments are made. One or the other should be present at other conferences, since the team is responsible for making key determinations about optimal programming for the child.

LESS WELL-RESOURCED SITUATIONS

It is the rule rather than the exception in school mental health that resources are insufficient to deal even minimally with the need for help. This is true for the relatively well-resourced Rochester, New York, area and even more so for most school districts around the country. It is thus unrealistic to assume that any district that wished to could develop a well-saturated PMHP. This fact poses the significant challenge of how PMHP's principles and practices can be applied in settings with limited resources.

More concretely, assuming that a well-saturated PMHP requires about one-half time from a school psychologist and a school social worker, which functions should be recommended to schools that have only ten, five, or even one hour a week of a professional's time? This issue can be illustrated by a hypothetical, but not entirely atypical, situation in which a rural school district, 100 miles from the nearest city, with no school mental health services whatsoever, suddenly acquires the services of a mental health professional one-half day per month. What would be the most useful function that professional could perform? Should he see the two most difficult "problem children" in the school for an hour a month each in therapy? Should he do one complex diagnostic battery each month for the child who presents the most pressing problem at the time? Should he divide his limited time between consultation with teachers and training and, later, supervising several nonprofessionals to intervene with problem children? Everything we know about the high incidence of early school maladaptation, its serious potential consequences, and school systems' lack of resources to cope with it says that time allocations that help a system to expand its reach and increase its self-sufficiency are preferable to those that touch only a few children and keep the system dependent on outside experts. Using such a metric, the consultative-training role for the professional who has only half a day to devote to it each month promises greater payoff than do either the therapeutic or diagnostic troubleshooter roles.

The point to be emphasized is that PMHP may be seen either as a literal reified entity to be duplicated like models from a Sears-Roebuck catalogue or as a conceptual framework with key orienting principles that can be implemented in many different ways with differing resources. We consider the latter to be both preferable and more realistic. Indeed, applications of PMHP concepts *must* respect the different realities of the complex world of school resources if they are to generalize.

PMHP Elements and Their Perceived Value

The core of PMHP, in addition to its focus on very young children, includes three elements: (1) systematic, early, mass screening for school maladaptation, (2) the use of nonprofessional child aides as direct helping-agents with the early identified children, and (3) a changing role for school mental health professionals in which traditional clinical service functions such as diagnosis and treatment are in some measure replaced by recruitment, training, supervision of nonprofessionals, and consultation with school personnel.

Although the above effectively describes PMHP's thrust, its form is still too abstract to allow for the differential evaluation of specific project functions or for districts with meager resources to know concretely how to set up a similar program. To get a better idea of the perceived value of various PMHP activities and to develop a preliminary prescriptive taxonomy for districts with limited resources, we recently studied both the perceived benefits values to children and professional time allocations of various PMHP components (Cowen & Lorion, 1975b). Since one of that study's basic aims was to establish how important PMHP professionals considered each project component to be, we first had to develop a descriptive framework that identified these components. Accordingly, PMHP staff members were asked to write brief "activity-defining" statements, the sum of which was to reflect all project elements. These statements were checked for redundancy, edited, and revised several times until a final list of 29 activities, some with several subparts (for a total of 55 items) was developed. (See Appendix 3 for a complete list of these items.)

The 55 items fell into four major groupings:

1. *Conducting PMHP Informational Meetings* (7 items)— e.g., "for parents of first grade children," "for principals and nonteaching school personnel."

2. *Early Detection and Screening Activities* (13 items)— e.g., "intellectual/personality evaluation of referred children," "classroom observation of potential referral children," "social work interviews with mothers of first grade children."

3. *Program-related Activities* (18 items)—e.g., "attend referral assignment conferences," "individual consultation with teachers," "periodic discussion of effectiveness of services to children," "attend termination conferences."

4. *Aide-related Activities* (17 items)—e.g., "individual supervision of aides," "observe aides seeing children," "discussion of evaluation of aide performance."

Two groups of judges, each with extensive PMHP experience, were used in the study. The first group consisted of 16 mental health professionals directly involved in the day-to-day conduct of the school programs; the second included central PMHP staff, consultants, and recent postgraduate trainees, each of whom had spent one or more years with the program. Two sets of judgments, "benefits" estimates and "time allocation" estimates, were obtained. For the benefits estimate, judges were asked to rate the extent to which each of PMHP's 55 defining activities contributed, directly or indirectly, to the child's well-being and development. For this judgment, five-point rating scales were used, with point five representing "extremely beneficial" and point one representing "of no benefit whatsoever."

Only the 16 school-based professionals were able to complete time-allocation estimates. To do these it was necessary first to determine how much time per week professionals spent in PMHP-related, as opposed to other nonproject activities. This turned out, on the average, to be 11 hours per week, with a range from five to fifteen hours. Then professionals estimated for the full year how much time they devoted to each of the 55 activities. These sums were converted back to percentage allocations of time per activity to control for differences in the total amount of time spent by professionals in different schools.

Several useful, informative findings about judged benefits emerged from the study. For example, overall, PMHP staff judged *all* activities to be more beneficial to children than did the school professionals. It was not that one group did and the other did not see project activities as beneficial. Rather, both groups rated project activities, overall, as highly beneficial, and the two sets of ratings correlated well. But the absolute benefit values rated by project staff were higher than those of the field professionals. This fact is informative for school systems that are considering related projects because it suggests that a program's founders and defenders have a greater stake and vested interest in it than do the "worker-bees," who must carry it out on a day-to-day basis.

This overall difference in perceived benefits between policy-makers (PMHP staff) and executors (line school psychologists and social workers) was mirrored in specific activities. Thus staff valued the use of intellectual and personality screening measures as well as aides' summary and termination forms significantly more than did line professionals. Conversely, although both groups considered teacher contacts to be very important, line personnel saw them as even more vital than did core staff. Such findings are useful in several ways. Not only do they establish the actual perceived benefits values of project functions, but in pinpointing differential values of leaders and implementers, they also identify areas of potential conflict between those who plan and those who carry out a program. If a harassed professional does not have enough time to do everything listed in his hypothetical job description, he may understandably drop the functions that he believes contribute least to the child's welfare. Aside from such islands of disagreement however, this part of the study showed a reasonable consensus across groups about which PMHP functions were judged to be either quite beneficial or unimportant.

Using an average overall benefits score of 4.25 (based on the five-point scale) to identify extremely useful activities, the following were judged to best serve project children. (1) social work interviews with parents of all PMHP referred children, 4.57, (2) individual consultation with teachers, 4.51, (3) participation in the referral-assignment conference, 4.51, (4) individual supervision of aides, 4.49,

(5) participation in the selection and training of aides, 4.38, (6) participation in the progress-evaluation conference, 4.37, (7) participation in the end-of-year termination conference, 4.34, (8) individual conferences with parents of PMHP children, 4.29, and (9 and 10) conducting fall informational meetings about PMHP for primary and first grade teachers, 4.26 each.

It is equally important, especially for less well-resourced districts, to consider which PMHP functions were given low (an average of 3.0 or less) benefits values. These included (1) conducting fall PMHP information meetings for parents of upper-grade children, 1.80, (2, 3, and 4) intellectual appraisal of all primary grade children, 2.05; all first grade children, 2.47; and all PMHP referred children, 2.59, (5) conducting fall PMHP informational meetings for upper-grade teachers, 2.31, (6) personality appraisal of *all* primary graders, 2.58, (7) monitoring completion of the aides' prose summaries, 2.74, (8) individual interviews by professionals with PMHP children, 2.80, (9) social work interviews with mothers of all, not just referred first grade children, 2.91, (10) submitting evaluations of aides' performance, 3.00, and (11) individual intellectual or personality evaluations of PMHP children, 3.00. These are the PMHP components judged to have the fewest benefits values for children and thus, inferentially, were considered to be the most dispensable under less opulent resource conditions.

A second pertinent body of information comes from the reports of how PMHP professionals actually allocated their time. First, there was a substantial positive correlation (.56) between professional time allocations and the judged benefits values of PMHP activities. This says that professionals do, in the main, allocate their time in ways that correspond to how they perceive program values.

Professionals, in submitting utilization data, were instructed to omit activities that took up less than two hours per year of their time. Accordingly, certain functions (e.g., conducting informational meetings for parents of children in the upper grades, and individual personality assessments) ended up with zero scores. It turned out that a limited number of activity clusters accounted for nearly 75 per cent of the professionals' time, according to the following frequency pattern:

Aide supervision, 21.62 per cent—including 9.62 per cent and 4.87 per cent in regular, formally scheduled individual and group supervision, respectively; 4.13 per cent in informal ad hoc supervision; and 3.00 per cent in aide selection and training.

Attending formal "gut" PMHP conferences, 12.06 per cent —approximately equally distributed across assignment, progress-evaluation, and termination conferences.

Participation in consultative contacts, 16.50 per cent—including 8.50 per cent in individual contacts with teachers and other school personnel and 8.00 per cent in group consultation meetings with teachers, aides, principals, and sometimes outside consultants.

Social work interviews with parents, 11.19 per cent—including 8.19 per cent in initial screening and interview meetings and 3.00 per cent in follow-up contacts.

Intrateam conferences including the senior aide, 11.97 per cent—dealing with such matters as the effectiveness of children's services, aide performance, and program-related concerns.

As a point of contrast, the entire cluster of seven PMHP informational meetings collectively accounted for less than 2 per cent of all professional time.

This resumé of PMHP professionals' use of their time can be viewed in two ways: (1) how it defines differences in function between the PMHP professional and the traditional school-based mental health professional and (2) its implications for districts wishing to start similar programs. Concerning the first point, virtually none of the PMHP professional's time is devoted to the traditional, time-honored clinical roles of rendering direct, individual, diagnostic, or remedial services to children. He is truly a mental health "quarterback" (Cowen, 1967), heading a team that collectively provides augmented services to many young maladapting school children in need. The essence of his function is found in a cluster of relatively new activities, not including direct child services. He spends about 20 per cent of his time with nonprofessionals—who are the backbone of the expanded service delivery system—in selection and training and in both formal and informal individual and group supervision. He directs and participates actively in a network of conferences, beginning with assignment and ending with termination, that frame the program's clinical services. His most active technique is consultation with teachers, aides, and other school personnel. He thus gives an appreciable fraction of his time to upgrading the knowledge and skills of people who have everyday contacts with children by supporting them, strengthening their hand, and bridging the gap between the activities of the classroom and those of the aide intervention so that children's needs are better served. He establishes and maintains family contacts and integrates these as best he can into an overall effort to improve the child's school experience. And, with other members of the team, he gives time to those administrative, program-review, evaluative, and problem-solving activities that are an important, but not always apparent part of the cement that holds the program pieces together.

The PMHP professional's role is thus definable, and it appears at first blush to be distinguishable from that of the traditional school mental health professional. A recent interesting survey of the actual job activities of 905 school psychologists in New York State (Sivers, 1974) bears directly on this point. Sivers' data provide a composite picture of professional functions for a large sample of school psychologists who may be assumed, collectively, to reflect a traditional definition of their role. The responses of this group with regard to time allocation indicated that four major classes of professional activity were by far the most important role-definers: (1) administering individual psychological examinations, (2) recommending developmental, remedial, and corrective learning programs, (3) conferring with concerned parties about individual cases, and (4) providing psychological counseling.

Differences in the profiles of the foregoing data and the PMHP survey are obvious and striking. Illustratively, whereas 45.6 per cent of Sivers' sample indicated that 25 to 50 per cent of the professional's time was spent in psychological examination of individual children, PMHP professionals spent an average of only 1.5 per cent of their time in this activity. Similarly, 43.5 per cent of Sivers' group checked 25 to 50 per cent as the frequency category for "time devoted to direct individual pupil contact" in contrast with an average figure of 1 per cent for the PMHP professionals.

Thus there is clear evidence that the PMHP professional's role and job functions differ materially from those of the typical school mental health professional. In other words, the PMHP role model offers a clear alternative for practice. The merit of this alternative must be considered in the light of data already cited about PMHP's reach and effectiveness. In any case, the time-allocation data help to pin down the PMHP professional's role and indicate how this role differs from traditional roles.

A second important area to consider concerns the implications that can be drawn from the combined benefits and time-allocation data for establishing programs in settings with limited resources. Some of PMHP's components, as we have seen, are viewed as more beneficial to some children than others, and PMHP professionals allocate a high proportion of their time to a relatively limited group of activities. These two bits of information are helpful in developing "do" and "don't" recommendations for minimally resourced settings.

Applications

In the section to follow, we consider several hypothetical, but nevertheless concrete "lesser"-resource saturations and suggest for each what seem to us to be the most useful PMHP elements to consider. Two structural types of resource problems can be imagined: the simple obvious case in which little professional or aide time is available, and a more specific deficit situation in which a core PMHP ingredient (e.g., the psychologist or social worker) is not available. In the latter instance, the resulting program would lack elements that are uniquely linked to the missing role (e.g., without a social worker, the screening and interviewing of parents would be seriously short-changed). Although this would be regrettable and would undoubtedly mean the loss of real program benefits, it is certainly something that could happen. If it should, two prime options would be available: to get as much as possible from the program model with that component lacking or to develop makeshift alternatives which, though less satisfying than the "real McCoy," nevertheless try to "recover" the missing functions.

A more typical resource situation would be one in which a district's base-rate service patterns allow only "x" hours per school per week (two, four, nine, or whatever) of the professional's time and/or there is no budget for aides. This type of deficit is possible and may occur in multiple degrees and combinations. Several different examples of serious personnel shortages are chosen to illustrate how various program applications might be developed under those specific circumstances.

A significantly less than ideal saturation is one with only eight to ten hours a week of a school professional's services. This saturation, though reduced, still allows for a program entity that substantially resembles the basic PMHP model. At present, PMHP consultation schools average no more (indeed sometimes less) than that amount of professional time. With school assignments of eight to ten hours a week for professionals, about 325 to 350 hours per professional, or 650 to 700 hours per team, are available during a school year. Although there are important seasonal variations in the PMHP professionals' activities (e.g., informational meetings come up early in the year, whereas aide supervision doesn't peak until much later, after the aides have acquired a substantial caseload), an optimal overall time-allocation profile for this saturation can be depicted.

Thus, on the average, professionals might most profitably spend their time as follows: (1) about two to three hours per week working with aides, including training and both formal and informal supervision, (2) about two to three hours per week for individual and group consultation with school personnel and intrateam administrative, planning, or evaluation contacts, (3) about two hours per week for the project's basic clinical conferences—i.e., assignment, progress, and termination of services to children; these time obligations are, however, uneven because assignment conferences peak in the second and third program months, progress conferences peak at mid-year, and termination conferences peak in the final month of the school year, (4) about one to two hours per week in parent contacts, though these too are uneven "pressures" because they pile up early in the year and are typically part of the social worker's rather than the psychologist's role. Thus an overall average of one and one-half hours per week may in fact consist of two and one-half hours per week for the social worker and half an hour per week for the psychologist. The limited time remaining would be devoted to other project functions.

Inevitably, a staffing pattern of eight to ten hours of professional time would curtail or eliminate some functions associated with a "pure" PMHP. For example, there would be fewer informational meetings, and they would have to be directed to persons with the closest relationship to the project. Individual and some group screening activities would suffer, and the program would have to depend more on teachers' screening data for that purpose. Less time would be available for activities such as agency contacts in the community, classroom observation, some aspects of report writing and record keeping and detailed individual evaluation of children. Nevertheless, the reduced program could still bring effective services to many children, a key fact that should not be ignored.

A "harsher" and probably more typical resource situation is one in which only half a day or so a week of professional time is available. In many districts around the country, a school mental health professional must provide services to ten, fifteen, or even more schools at any one time. Under these circumstances, a likely consequence is that schools would stockpile lists of troublesome children, and the professional's job would become one of working incessantly against a neverending list to assess children diagnostically and to eke out from such tests recommendations that can ease the school's burdens stemming from the children's failure to adapt. Again, in this circumstance, the issue raised by the PMHP experience is practical: Is there a more socially utilitarian alternative to typical usage of professional time that does not tamper with the reality of how much time is available?

With professional time so drastically limited, many key PMHP functions will fail to survive or will at best be carried out only superficially. Assuming that seeing children would remain the backbone element of the project, the system's resources would not permit a full aide complement. Quite likely, the program could absorb no more than two or three aides. Some professional time would still be needed for training and supervising aides—perhaps as much as an hour a week. Since the program would serve fewer children, it would require fewer in-service conferences. But, on the average, this function too would be likely to require an hour a week of the professional's time. The function that would perhaps take on the greatest importance under such austere staffing conditions is consultation with school personnel, especially teachers. In situations where staffing shortages are likely to be permanent, the importance of strengthening the hand of those people with day-to-day line contacts is heavily underscored. Many key project functions, including group assessment procedures and parent contacts, would suffer seriously since, in effect, all other functions would have to be combined or dealt with on a catch-as-catch-can basis in the extremely limited amount of residual time. Indeed, one important thrust in the use of such residual time would be to train people "in and around" the system—undoubtedly atypical persons for such roles—to discharge PMHP-related functions that would otherwise disappear. The choice, if viable program elements are to continue under sharply constrained conditions, is between preserving paper fictions about traditional professional roles or developing pragmatic means for getting those essential functions carried out. Harsh reality thus forces reexamination of whether various helping roles are inextricably tied to professional as opposed to human attributes. To what extent can teachers be trained to do screening functions? Can lay persons be trained to do parent interviews and other social work functions effectively? As difficult and threatening as such questions are, they must be examined in the cold light of finite professional resources.

The hypothetical, limited saturation described above is certainly removed from even the weakest concept of "ideal" PMHP conditions. But it *is* an effort to cope that does not begin by giving up. It adjusts as well as possible to practical constraints and, through optimal use of scarce professional time, articulates a minisystem that can bring effective help to perhaps 20 to 25 of a school's neediest primary graders. Such an approach, though far from ideal, may enable some of these children to turn the extremely difficult corner toward effective school adaptation.

From this same perspective, we can now reconsider the instance with which this section started: the district with zero mental health resources that has just acquired the services, one half-day per month, of a single mental health professional from a community mental health center 100 miles away. Our experience with PMHP suggests that the most socially utilitarian use of such a person's time would be for him to spend a good portion of it in mental health consultation with teachers and perhaps to train several people within the system with appropriate personal and stylistic qualities, *whatever their backgrounds,* in techniques of early identification and in the training and supervision of a limited number of nonprofessionals to work with children.

We have not yet considered an important resource question having to do with aides. In PMHP, aide time has been available from several sources. In the RCSD—a typical urban school district with limited, indeed shrinking resources—money for aides has never been available from district budgets. The money has come from outside sources, either agency or voluntary donations obtained primarily through the efforts of PMHP Inc. In contrast, PMHP county schools have been largely self-sustaining with respect to aide support. These districts, through their affiliation with a regional, federated, BOCES organization, are rebated by state agencies for portions of the aide program. These rebates vary somewhat from district to district in a manner that is complexly related to tax structures. Overall, however, about two-thirds of the county's aide salaries come from state moneys and the remaining third, from local tax moneys.

For some districts wishing to establish PMHP-type programs, there may be funding possibilities similar to those described above. For example, one semirural district with very limited resources that has succeeded in implementing an admirable PMHP-related model has aggressively and effectively tapped local industries for program support. Depending on the district's modus operandi and the surrounding community profile, other potential sources of support for an aide program (e.g., community mental health centers) can also be developed. If such good fortune exists, there will be no problem in having an aide program. It is quite likely, however, that some interested districts will be unable to identify immediate funding sources and even after serious searching will not find such moneys. Although many theoretically sound arguments can be mustered to document the ultimate economic and human savings that accrue from effective intervention, those are not the terms under which districts must operate. A school district's problems are rarely if ever defined in terms of how things will or should look 20 years hence. They are structured in a world of immediate needs and pressures. Necessarily, districts must respond to today's most urgent problems and to highly vocal constituencies, each voicing active support for its own special program. More often than not, a district must try to satisfy everyone with pared down, compromise budgets that many irate taxpayers continue to view as excessive or frill-laden. Realistically, the argument that small increases in program costs, as with PMHP, yield immediate dividends or dramatically reduce later costs associated with such social blights as delinquency or addiction has far less weight for the politician or taxpayer than does the immediate fact that the program will add yet another $5,000 to $10,000 to a projected $4.5 million budget deficit. It is thus a grim reality that many school districts, especially urban ones, may be financially unable to support even the most modest aide program.

Our purpose in this chapter is not to deny such immutable facts but to pose the question: Given reality, what alternatives are there and what are the consequences of each? If, for example, moneys are not available for any kind of aide program, the most immediate and obvious reflex is to throw up one's hands in despair and say that nothing can be done. And indeed it is quite clear that the aide problem cannot be solved, *as PMHP has solved it,* without budget. When PMHP's aide program started in 1964, we considered several alternatives and decided to use paid aides, working on regular schedules approximately half-time each week. One reason for this was that we wanted committed women upon whom we and, more importantly, the children could depend. Since the intervention was built around a committed human relationship, we wanted to maximize the likelihood of such a relationship by having aides available at predictable times during the school year. Moreover, since much time and effort was to be invested in aide training and program development, we hoped to protect our investment by being as certain as possible that aides would stay with the program. This meant two things: careful evaluation of a candidate's motivation and commitment and reimbursement. Actually, our first aide group was paid only a token sum—$25 a week for five half-days. At the time, that sum, combined with strong motivation and interest, was sufficient to "bind" an aide's commitment. Since then, PMHP has become considerably more complex and today has nearly 100 aides. All of them are employed by the school district to which they are assigned and all are paid according to the specific district's reimbursement schedules for such workers.

Thus the practice of having paid, part-time child aides was one that fit PMHP's early needs, aims, and profile. Given our situation, we have not had reason to question that decision. We have been able, although only with considerable investment of time and effort, particularly by the corporation, to continue to finance such programming. But that was our solution. Without question, in many other districts the only aide program that could be developed would be a volunteer program. Although volunteer programs doubtless present major disadvantages, surely some children in need could benefit from them. A committed human relationship cannot be created through reimbursement; it can only be supported by it. Thus faced with the choice between a volunteer program and no program, the decision seems easy: use volunteers and provide whatever services you can to those in need.

This in no sense implies that volunteer programs will be trouble free. There have been countless such programs in the human services, and some of their obvious difficulties have been well documented (Ewalt, 1967; Schindler-Rainman & Lippitt, 1971). For example, volunteers often wish to preserve more personal freedom and flexibility in terms of time than do paid employees. That being the case, they may have less moment-to-moment task commitment, and their sense of responsibility to the program may be less urgent than the paid employee's. Accordingly, in a project such as PMHP it is less likely that the volunteer will be with the child for any specific, preplanned session. Furthermore, because volunteers would be in a school less often, they would be likely to have fewer contacts with a child or group of children over the school year. Vacations may also be more disruptive in a volunteer program than in one with paid employees. This is a matter of concern in a program such as PMHP, which is predicated on stable, predictable relationships. Also, when a program rests on the help-agent's personal and human characteristics, as in PMHP, volunteer programs increase the danger of having people with less than optimal helping attributes since they require more people to do the same amount of work. A volunteer program may also present substantial logistical problems because with many people having limited, perhaps idiosyncratic schedules, conferences, and supervision would be difficult to arrange. Finally, volunteer programs usually have more turnover of personnel than those with paid employees. Since PMHP aides require training before they start to work with children, turnover would add to the burdens on professionals' time, both in recruitment and training.

It is not wise to ignore such problems. Some will surely occur in volunteer programs. Even so, if the latter is the only available approach, it should be considered seriously by districts that are concerned about the large, oft-neglected groups of young maladapting children. The best strategy under such circumstances is to anticipate as many problems as possible beforehand and to develop a program that holds the most promise for circumventing them. Careful prior screening of volunteers is one such adaptation. Selection factors that may contribute to a smooth effective volunteer program include heavy weighting of (1) human and experiential attributes that bespeak effective helping roles with children, (2) seriousness of commitment and assurances that a volunteer will be available for contracted times during the *entire* school year, and (3) willingness to give time in addition to actual contacts with children for training, conferences, and supervision. Prior screening to assure the presence of such attributes will surely increase the professional's initial time investment. But, hopefully, a heavier initial investment would produce a program that is both effective and reduces wasted motion later for professionals. Wasted motion would surely occur if poorly qualified, ill-motivated volunteers fail to "cut it"—an outcome that would require even more time-consuming, repetitive cycles of recruitment and training.

Indeed, several districts with limited resources have already established PMHP-related programs based almost entirely on volunteer services. In one case, interested parties "bootstrapped" professional time for training and supervision of aides by bringing a plan, with the school district's approval and support, to a nearby community mental health center. In that program, each prospective volunteer was asked at the time of screening to make a commitment to see three children during the school year. With 20 committed volunteers, it was possible to bring helping services to 60 maladapting primary graders.

Following this lead, it seems reasonable, when setting up volunteer programs, for commitments to be made in terms of children rather than hours. Thus volunteers might agree to see three children, rather than simply agree to be available Tuesday morning, for example. Such a contractual arrangement establishes the volunteer's personal responsibility for specific children and at the same time allows her the flexibility of working at a time that she herself defines as convenient. If, among a group of carefully selected and flexibly contracted volunteers, some common time for training, conferences, and supervision can be developed, the makings of a modestly effective program, even in an extremely limited resource situation, can be envisioned.

This chapter has attempted to provide a concrete framework for program implementation. First, some broad general guidelines that may be useful in starting up PMHP-type programs have been suggested. Less well-resourced situations were also considered, and, for each, we have used our experience in PMHP to identify the seemingly most important and appropriate project components. Although we have not argued that better, or even equally good programs can be developed with fewer resources, we have continually tried to let reality prevail over fantasy. At any resource level, alternative utilizations must be considered, and the pattern that promises the greatest payoff for the most children must be chosen. If PMHP is to have more general value, it must transcend its own literal operations as these happened to evolve at a certain time in a single community. Others must be able to draw broad orienting principles from our experience that will help them to generate conceptually related but concretely individualistic programs to fit their needs, problems, operating styles, and resources.

12

An
Epilogue

A SUMMARY OF PMHP's EVOLUTION

Founders and long-time purveyors of deeply invested so-cial programs, like parents, are among the least qualified to evaluate their products objectively. That fact notwithstand-ing, the present chapter backs away from PMHP's "nitty-gritty" to review what has been accomplished, what it suggests for the future, and how our experience sheds light on several critical mental health issues considered in the first chapter of this book.

PMHP grew out of observational-clinical soil. In our community, as elsewhere, many youngsters were failing in diverse ways to adapt satisfactorily in school. Such poorly laid foundations often led eventually to seriously adverse personal and educational outcomes. School failure thus breeds great human and social waste. Despite that reality, however, traditional helping services for children, even in our relatively well resourced, enlightened, progressive sys-tem, were not nearly sufficient to bring help to the many who needed it. From the start, we recognized that some aspects of reality must remain reality. For that reason, we never defined our mission as that of waving a magic wand to bring about the impossible—i.e., increase available pro-

346 NEW WAYS IN SCHOOL MENTAL HEALTH

fessional resources suddenly or dramatically. Rather, our concerns pushed us to consider alternative program definitions and personnel utilizations and, from among the feasible alternatives, to select the one that seemed to have the greatest social potential.

This way of defining the issue established an orienting set that has governed 17 years of subsequent program development and exploration—namely, to invest whatever limited resources were available in the earliest possible identification and prevention of school dysfunction for the many, in contrast with past dominant efforts to neutralize or repair gross dysfunction in the few. Although we chose to work in the primary grades of the school and our key objective was to promote effective school adaptation, we have learned over time that effective early detection and prevention, as approaches, have important implications for other unfortunate personal and social outcomes in addition to the failure to "cut it" in school.

Our way, from the beginning, has been slow, additive, and backed by empirical study. Even when viewed retrospectively, the PMHP experience does not smack of dramatic breakthrough or sudden awarenesses of key connections; rather, we have cumulated building blocks steadily and, guided by the above conceptual view, have followed a logical path toward fuller definition and application of the program.

At the start, we redefined the school mental health delivery system of a single school to concentrate its full resources in the primary grades. This necessitated relinquishing other traditional, time-honored professional roles, such as direct services to older children. But that step was taken wittingly in the light of our orientation and objectives. The major accomplishments of our first five years were, first, evolving a technology for identifying vulnerable school children accurately and quickly; second, studying the development of such youngsters, unattended, over time; and, third, exploring a small, skeletal preventive program and assessing its effectiveness. Professional roles and time allocations were redefined to further these objectives.

Our main early findings were that school-dysfunctional children could indeed be detected early and that if they were not helped, they were far behind their peers in most ways by the end of the third school year. We also found that even a gross, primitive, preventive program helped children to have a more effective, productive school experience. Although this early work was important in establishing a "hunting license," it largely confirmed a prior hunch that there were indeed many youngsters with serious school adaptation problems, which, if not resolved, would soon have important negative consequences.

The practical question of what to do about this situation flushed out a harsh reminder of the then-current, serious shortages of professional manpower. This forced us to reconsider a gut issue for school mental health services, indeed for all human-service helping areas: What is it that allows one person to help another person in distress? In the past, that question has been answered, operationally, in terms of attributes such as advanced degrees, IQ, educational background, and formal clinical training—a set of highly selective, costly, time-consuming inputs which are so demanding socially that even our relatively affluent society cannot produce enough people to get the job done. This limitation forced us to consider alternatives. One alternative was that human and personal factors, experiential interest, and life-style might, perhaps, be as or more important than characteristics traditionally assumed to determine whether one person could significantly help another, particularly a maladapting school child.

This concept led to PMHP's second five-year effort, in which housewives, selected for their personal-experiential backgrounds, were trained as nonprofessional child aides to work with primary graders who were maladapted in school. This "solution" was born initially of fiscal and resource constraints, rather than wholehearted positive conviction. We provided a small pilot group of carefully selected child aides with focused, time-limited training to help young, maladapting school children under close professional supervision. Developing the child aide program forced important changes in the school mental health professional's role. Direct assessment and treatment functions were in good measure supplanted by training, supervision, and consultative activities—a set of functions elsewhere (Cowen, 1967) subsumed under the rubric mental health "quarterback." Behind these changes was the goal of expanding, geometrically, the reach of the helping arm to many children who needed immediate assistance. Subsequent data suggest that PMHP has met this latter objective well.

Both clinical and empirical evidence indicated that the new system worked. Not only did aides bring effective help to individual children in need, but the total system dramatically augmented the reach of school mental health services. During this second phase of the project, new things were learned and new instrumental roles, such as that of senior aide, were developed. Whereas initially we had viewed the aide role as an expedient born of necessity, we came more and more to see it as viable in its own right. The role is both natural, because as a mother, an aide brings important, highly relevant, experiential background to it, and challenging because the task of helping children in real difficulty is alive, different, and palpable for her. She views it as vitally important. The aide role, the program environment, and their gestalt encourage personal growth, continuous challenge, and opportunities for aides to see important payoffs from their efforts. Unlike professionals, who become disenchanted in repetitive service activities with low observable payoff (e.g., in state hospitals), PMHP aides do not "burn out." They remain excited and challenged by the job, and, although not always free of problems, they retain a basic sense of achievement and job gratification. The efficiency and effectiveness of the new delivery system was further enhanced through developing the new senior (consulting) aide role, which capitalized on the know-how and experience of women who had grown in and with the system.

The overriding conclusion of PMHP's second stage was that the child aide role was meaningful and viable and an important way of bringing augmented, effective, helping services to many young school children. It is thus a reality-anchored approach that effectively addresses a heretofore thorny, unresolved problem—the inability of many children to profit from the school experience.

The project's first two stages (11 years) took place under relatively sheltered, encapsulated conditions in a single pilot-demonstration school. The key issue raised by that experience was how to apply more broadly what had been learned. If, under laboratory conditions, we had indeed succeeded in "building a better mousetrap," how could this demonstration be generalized under real-life conditions? This led to the third, most recently completed, and considerably less antiseptic stage, which also lasted nearly five years. The problems of this third phase were qualitatively and quantitatively different from earlier ones, touching as they did on complex matters ranging from how to define the project under very different resource conditions to the political and economic headaches of getting started in diverse school districts. Perhaps the most important constructive factor in advancing this dissemination was the serious involvement and support of a dedicated citizen's group, which engineered the climate and budget required for the expanded project to root.

Thus, following a long period of planning and dialogue characterized by many hassles, in 1969 PMHP ceased to be a pilot-demonstration program in the favored soil of a single school "greenhouse" and was transplanted under multiple circumstances to 11 schools in four districts. At the start of the 1973-74 school year, that expansion had advanced to 17 schools. This major change in PMHP's character could not have occurred without several important implementing steps. Thus selected school mental health professionals were given training in PMHP's ways of operating, including metatraining to train nonprofessionals. Child aides were recruited and trained to staff the new program. Schools were prepared (e.g., necessary space and materials were developed and referral systems were established) to receive the new program. And after a three-month "debugging" period, the expanded program moved into high gear and ran for three full years.

Although the expansion was in many ways rewarding, it was not without major frustrations. Gratification came from the marked increase in services to needy children and the awareness that although the program worked differently under different circumstances, it nevertheless worked and was generalizable. An important negative feature was the fact that program expansion led to poorer communication and thus less informed, less committed participants in some settings. Resource shortages caused program dilution, cutting of corners, and either the omission or underplay of heretofore key program elements (e.g., aide supervision and group screening). These painful realizations generated concern on our part that the "real" program would be lost. Moreover, program dilution became a source of conflict. Thus the essential message from project staff to professionals was: "You're not doing all of your job the way you're supposed to!" The professionals replied, in effect: "How can we do all those things when we don't have the time to do half of them?" Out of such conflict has grown accommodation and the realization that although PMHP provides a useful orienting set for choosing among alternative service modalities, a given school's version of the program must reflect its own problems, resources, priorities, and realities.

The PMHP experience can be assessed from three main perspectives: rational, clinical, and empirical. Rational assessment is framed by the question: Does the approach make sense? Given current data on the extent of early school adjustment problems and the rampant scarcities of helping resources, without question the approaches that bring effective helping services to early vulnerable school children, help them to right their course, and allow them to profit from the educational experience are sorely needed. We considered it probable that this was so before PMHP ever started, and everything we have since learned strongly reinforces the belief. Although PMHP is a system with evident imperfections and is doubtless not the only conceivable way of increasing the scope of helping services to maladapting school children, it is a sensible approach and seems intuitively to improve on traditional school mental health delivery systems.

PMHP's clinical evaluation rests on impressions and reactions gleaned over the years from project staff and teachers, parents, aides, principals, other school personnel, and children. The content and flavor of such impressions, exemplified in Chapter 10, are fallible, to be sure, because they are subject to the frailties of ego-involved observers. Thus, although they do not tell the whole story, they do tell one important part of it. Clinical evaluation is a necessary but insufficient hurdle for a service project to surmount. If persons associated with PMHP failed to see good in the project or did not view it as a sensible meaningful delivery system, that alone would be sufficient reason to doubt the program's worth.

In fact, however, PMHP has fared well in clinical-intuitive evaluations. That it has made sufficient good sense for PMHP staff to develop, continue, and expand the program is an evident fact of our history. Although that alone might only reflect our own investment and/or rigidity, school districts, even in troubled fiscal times, have also struggled valiantly to maintain and expand PMHP. This could not have happened unless they were convinced that the program was useful and effective. Indeed, in one district the project is now located in all nine elementary schools. The strong support of an active citizens' group, which has been so important to the project's growth and development during the past five years, also mirrors positive feedback from school personnel.

Principals have been pleased to have PMHP as the backbone of their school mental health programs. This too is reflected in several ways. For example, at key points in PMHP's history (e.g., in 1969, when it became an 11-school project, and again in 1973, when it became a CORE/consultation school entity in 17 buildings), principals were actively jockeying for position to have PMHP located in their schools. Also, PMHP principals have sometimes displayed (a not always entirely advantageous) elitism toward their peers about having the project in their buildings. This has led to some expressed resentment by non-PMHP principals and several not-so-veiled threats by principals of control schools involved in PMHP research that they would discontinue that role unless they too could have their own PMHPs soon.

Parents too have been extremely supportive and appreciative of PMHP and have viewed the project as a strong asset in a school's overall program. Indeed, there are instances in which parents have decided to move *into* a particular neighborhood because they knew that PMHP was located in the neighborhood school and believed that the program could help their child. PMHP has also accumulated an array of testimonials from PMHP parents. And several times, when the project's existence has been threatened by impending budgetary or administrative disasters, parent groups have organized and become vocal lobbyists in support of its continuation in their schools—typically with good results. Parents are often crucial in determining the destiny of school programs, and "satisfied," vocal parents have been an important factor in the project's survival. By definition, teachers are key, first-line PMHP consumers. Because the program touches many hundreds of teachers, there can be no simple summary of their reactions to it. The latter are complexly determined, both by obvious factors such as what the program is all about and by subtle ones such as the teacher's orientation to mental health, her attitudes about and interpersonal relations with program personnel, or perhaps even the extent to which she feels that the program encroaches on her turf. So, understandably, there are many teacher reactions to PMHP, ranging from divine worship, through disinterest, to dissatisfaction. Despite this broad range of reactions, teachers in the main have had positive, welcoming feelings about the project (Dorr & Cowen, 1972), both because it provides services for children in obvious need of help and because, through consultation, it provides knowledge and information that can be translated into more effective classroom management.

The most enthusiastic project approbation comes from child aides (Dorr & Cowen, 1973a). This group is unanimous in its conviction that PMHP brings appreciable help to many children in need. Although less than objective, aides' reactions are understandable. They see children's distress firsthand and are often the closest people to a helping process that yields happier, more effectively functioning youngsters. Few people have trouble understanding when a child needs help. To see a malfunctioning child's fate reversed and to be part of an active process that brings about this desirable end is a clinically persuasive experience. Thus, notwithstanding the acknowledged shortcomings of clinical evidence, those who have been closest to PMHP have viewed it in consistently positive ways. Such reactions lend further credence to the view that the project is effective.

Empirical assessment has been part of PMHP from the start. By now, more than a dozen studies evaluating the project's effectiveness have been reported. These investigations are based on diverse measures of children's educational and personal status and behavior, objective test scores, and the judgments of teachers and aides. The studies range from the tightly controlled to the considerably less rigorous. As the project moved from a limited, fairly precise laboratory-demonstration program to a broadly based federation of like-minded programs under real conditions with looser project and research controls, weaker communications networks, less homogeneous criteria and so forth, the purity and power of its research evaluations suffered. Thus there has been some variability in findings on outcome from study to study, from year to year, from phase to phase, and from one set of evaluative criteria to another. Since school mental health services in general are rarely evaluated, an adequate metric for comparing PMHP with them is not typically available. Viewed in the aggregate, however, the sum of PMHP's findings on outcome over its 17-year history suggest that the system works. Such evidence, along with supporting rational and clinical-impressionistic data, indicate that the approach has much to offer in bringing needed help to large numbers of maladapting primary graders.

Thus PMHP's 17-year panorama establishes the approach as a meritorious alternative in school mental health services—one that warrants careful consideration by school districts that take seriously their mandate to optimize children's educational and personal development. It is this view that strongly shapes PMHP's current form—a form that features elements which have grown logically from our natural evolution thus far. Thus, in the local geographic area where PMHP is most firmly rooted, we are shifting from roles as innovators and program leaders to those of interested advisers. If there is intrinsic merit to the PMHP approach, we must assume that it transcends the special wisdom, interest, or even charisma of a special group of devoted founders. This means that the program's ultimate locus and responsibility for its leadership and direction must come increasingly to rest with the school districts themselves. Training district leaders, transmitting knowledge and technology we have acquired, and planning for an orderly transfer of program leadership are among our most important current objectives.

Equally important is the goal of transmitting our knowledge and experience on a broader national scale. If indeed a more utilitarian delivery model has evolved, how can school districts around the country best harvest our experience? In a small way, this book is a step in that direction. In addition, we have developed a systematic program of dissemination that begins with intensive PMHP workshops for interested district representatives and later includes on-site, facilitating, follow-up visits by PMHP staff as well as local internship experiences for school mental health professionals from implementing districts. It is still too early to know the effects of this plan. Given present-day resource limitations and broad-gauged retrenchments in educational spending, problems are to be expected in rooting new programs. Nonetheless, we believe that the PMHP approach is sufficiently different and promising to merit an investment of effort in helping other districts to get started. Rooting of only a small number of effective programs around the country could eventually permit regional training centers to develop—a step that would markedly facilitate the spread of information and additional new programs in many more districts nationwide. Such an outcome would indeed bring help to a significant percentage of young maladapting school children whose talents and potential would otherwise remain stagnant and under-developed.

PMHP: ITS CORE AND PERIPHERY

The vague descriptive terms that frame PMHP's coat of arms are early detection and prevention. Virtually all of the project's specific activities serve those masters. But to actually implement a program of this type calls for the inclusion, in some way, of three specific sets of components that are at its core: mass screening and early detection of school dysfunction, the use of nonprofessionals as help-agents with maladapting primary graders, and significant modifications in the school mental health professional's role.

Many of PMHP's key steps in the model's "pure" form have to do with early detection. The use of the word early in that phrase is genuinely intended. It mirrors several of the project's key assumptions: one, many early school adjustment problems, left alone, will exact steadily increasing tolls over the years and, two, the young child is pliable and accordingly can change more readily and easily than an older person. In other words, a fixed amount of help, equally skillfully given, is more likely to be helpful to a six-year-old than to a 12-year-old or, certainly, to a 50-year-old.

Early detection is the process by which the vulnerable young school child is identified. Although the procedures we have developed are less than precise and can surely profit from greater refinement, they are reasonably accurate and efficacious. Early detection, even if less than 100 per cent accurate, is essential since the social and human risks of not helping young children who would otherwise fail are far greater than those of providing additional help to children who don't really need it (i.e., those who might spontaneously "outgrow" their problems). To intervene effectively with maladapting children, we must first know who requires help. For that reason, mass early screening is a vital cornerstone of a preventively oriented program. The practical issue for a new program is not whether early detection is needed; rather, it is how extensive and systematic this process can be, given the setting's resources. The critical questions are whether a system should use one, two, or five different approaches to early detection, how formal should these be, and which specific approaches should be used. Although, in principle, as many components should be used as add to the sensitivity of screening, practical decisions about these and other matters must be based on the school's needs and resources. The PMHP experience tells us, primarily, that systematic early detection is a key element of an effective school mental health delivery system.

No matter how valuable effective early detection may be, it is limited by the system's ability to follow through on what has been learned: i.e., to help the many maladapting children known to need help. This bald fact, plus an awareness of realistic limits in professional resources, led to the development of PMHP's second critical component—the use of nonprofessional child aides as prime, direct help-agents with young maladapting school children. This step encouraged geometric expansion of helping services because it was a realistic way to bring needed assistance to those youngsters otherwise fated for, at best, lackluster and, at worst, disastrous school experiences. Carefully selected, well-trained, supervised child aides are very effective help-agents with young school children. Their experience, life-style, and personality makeup are as important as lengthy, formal educational experiences and advanced degrees in bringing immediate help to young children. Although one can, as we have tried to do, consider specific program issues, such as how many aides for how many children, optimal time schedules, pay levels, and so on, the form of an aide program must, in the last analysis, respect the school's profile, needs, and resources. Thus using nonprofessionals as help-agents is a helpful orienting set, but precisely how this can best be done must be determined by individual school districts and schools.

A school mental health approach that rests on widespread early detection of dysfunction and the use of nonprofessional help-agents necessarily implies new professional roles. The PMHP professional's activities differ notably from those of more traditional school mental health delivery systems. About three-fourths of his time goes into five major clusters of activity: training and supervising aides, consultation with school personnel, program liaison and coordination, work with parents, and clinical conferences for planning and evaluating service programs for referred children. These activities exemplify the concept of mental health "quarterbacking" (Cowen, 1967). The professional thus reduces his direct service contacts with children and uses his energies and know-how to weld a unit that harnesses the resources of talented but less well-trained, day-to-day-contact people to promote better school experiences for a geometrically larger group of early maladapting children. Although the characteristics of the PMHP professional's role are clear in principle, in reality specific program objectives and resources must again determine the best allocations of time among these functions.

PMHP's cornerstones thus include systematic early detection, the use of nonprofessionals as help-agents, and a sharply changed professional role. Those are the ingredients that make this approach a bonafide alternative to traditional delivery systems. And in a real sense, these are the program messages that should come through for school districts, even those with limited resources, that wish to develop helping programs to reach the many youngsters who show early signs of failing to "cut it." Were a single overarching recommendation to emerge from our effort, it would not be that schools must do, literally and exactly, what we have done, but rather that they should apply, as befits their needs and resources, PMHP's guiding directional concepts as described previously. School districts, like people, are highly individual. Each has its own special pond ecology, and surrounding flora and fauna will thrive only to the extent that the characteristics of that ecology are taken seriously into account. Mass prescriptions that literally say "Do this" or "Do that," oblivious of the reality of circumstances, are likely to fail.

Long-term rewarding association with PMHP makes it easy to overlook the importance of serendipitous historical and environmental factors in the project's success. Among such historical considerations is the fact that PMHP began in a school district whose mental health services had always been forward-looking and innovative. Moreover, the project was nurtured by a diligent committed staff that has stayed together as a closely knit team for many years. Equally influential have been the environmental facts of relatively well-resourced school systems and the availability of generous outside sustaining support from several sources. Thus the particular program evolution that made sense and developed naturally in Rochester, New York, is not assumed to apply equally well to the rest of the world. Nevertheless, we believe that PMHP's main conceptual anchor points suggest workable, socially utilitarian program derivatives that promise, whatever a district's resources, to bring more help to more children.

We are, of course, suggesting the potential for many different types of PMHP implementations. Early mass screening is unquestionably a crucial PMHP thrust. But it can be done in many ways. We have described how we have approached this area and why, and we can transmit our experience for whatever it is worth to others. But we cannot say that our way of early detection is the best or only way. In the end, we come back to the harsh reality that a full-time mental health professional can do a lot more than one who can spend only one half-day a week in a school. Similar statements can be made, both about the use of nonprofessionals and exactly how the professional's role should be defined. With respect to program specifics, as opposed to program orientation, a "Maoist line" is both unreal and inadvisable. New PMHP developments must take form in the spirit of "different strokes for different folks."

COST CONSIDERATIONS

Cost is a critical aspect of any implementation plan. Indeed, in many instances it is the first matter considered (Sarason, 1974). This too is a simple fact of life. Costs can be reckoned either in direct, immediate terms (e.g., How many dollars are needed in this year's school district budget to run a project of this type in school X?) or in impersonal, social, abstract, futuristic terms (Given X expenditures for this program over the next five years, what benefits or savings can be anticipated 20 years hence?). Schools necessarily use the first rather than the second metric. Each year, schools must make decisions about many seemingly worthy but, in the last analysis, competing programs in different areas. They must face parents whose children have diverse here-and-now problems. They must face the irate citizen's onslaughts about rising taxes often supported by political pressures on duly vested, budget-determining community agents. Hopefully, social planners are less vulnerable to such concrete day-to-day pressures, and their decision-making can be guided more by facts and informed judgments about social good.

But the budgetary needs of would-be implementers are almost always in the here-and-now. Mental health programs in general are rarely defined as having a high priority among the full range of a school's needs. They are not typically perceived as a central aspect of the school's mandate. Moreover, interconnections between emotional problems and learning difficulties are only dimly perceived by many parents, who do not, in the main, define their children's school difficulties in psychological terms. Reading problems, hot lunches, interscholastic athletic programs, driver education are all far more immediate, palpable, and "grabbing" to parents. These are issues that concern many, attract vocal constituencies, and build political pressures— far more so than do mental health projects such as PMHP.

In actual fact, the costs of running a project of this type, even a relatively well-resourced one, are low. Since PMHP accepts professional resources as they are, rather than tampers with them, the program does not add to the budget at that level. The key issue for the professional is not how much time he devotes to the project, but how he uses the time he has. The main additional cost of PMHP-type projects is for child aides. In an average-sized school, five half-time aides can provide a fairly well-resourced program. Because of the normal scurrying and frenzy during the first few weeks of the school year, aides do not typically start before October 1. Given school recesses and vacation periods, an aide's year, on the average, is about 32 weeks, 15 hours a week. Assuming an hourly reimbursement of $2.50 (the current figure in our county districts) the total cost of a five-aide school program is around $6,000. In many suburban school districts, not urban ones, fiscal rebates are available for such helping services. Currently, in county districts, this rebate factor is about two-thirds. In other words, the annual net cost to the district of a five-aide, half-time program in a single school is around $2,000. Such a program "buys" intensive services for about 50 primary graders who, up to that point, have not adapted well to the school.

Out of these simple facts grows what, to school districts, has been the single most persuasive argument favoring adoption of PMHP—an economic argument. Many schools, especially in federated suburban districts, have communal special-education facilities. In this geographic region, placement in such a setting costs nearly $4,000 a year per child, or roughly twice the net cost per school year for a five-aide program. Since schools do understand the possibility that aides can help children, the point can be made that if an aide program in a school of 600 succeeds only in preventing the placement of one child in a special education facility, the entire cost of the program will be repaid. That argument not only can be grasped, but districts can place it in an immediate (i.e., this year) cost-accounting framework. This concrete cost-reckoning argument has been far more powerful in advancing acceptance of the program by district administrators than PMHP's myriad hypothetical virtues, its research findings, or its potential long-term benefits for the many. Thus practicality, economically defined, rather than merit or potential value for children is—perhaps sadly, yet realistically—the ground on which decisions to implement programs are most likely to be made.

Less germane to issues of immediate acceptance of a program, but quite pertinent to social planners in education and mental health, are considerations of PMHP's long-term potentials. At this level, powerful arguments in its favor have been mustered. Dorr (1972), for example, evaluated PMHP costs and compared them to tax-dollar costs for maintenance and care of children who end up in various social care settings because their early dysfunctions can neither be contained nor reversed. Residential treatment facilities, highly specialized and individualized, now cost from $25,000 to $30,000 on the average for one child per year. Treatment in state hospitals costs the taxpayer more than $10,000 per child per year. Societal burdens caused by later, profound social problems of youth—for example, delinquency, and addiction—are heavy. Moreover, putting the issue, as we have, primarily in economic terms does not take into account factors such as human suffering, ineffective functioning, and wasted talent. The likelihood of long-term preventive benefits of PMHP dictates that tomorrow's social planners, if not today's harried, overburdened school districts, reapportion their priorities to permit small immediate investments to reduce long-term, socially and humanly debilitating outcomes.

It has been estimated in PMHP that the roughly 40 per cent increase in immediate outlay purchases as much as a 1,000 per cent increase in direct helping services to children. If only a portion of that percentage represents effective service, the long-term gain to individuals and to society can be enormous. Thus Dorr (1972, p. 27) states that *"unchecked emotional disturbance eventually eats up great sums of tax money,"* and "the soundest possible investment of tax monies in mental health lies in early, clinically effective, socially impactful programs concentrating on the prevention of later costly . . . problems."

BROADER IMPLICATIONS

This book began in a way that some might describe as "curiously far afield." On the surface, the first chapter had little if any direct connection with PMHP. Rather, it overviewed today's major unresolved mental health issues and problems to provide a context for better assimilating the project's aims and activities. Since PMHP in some measure first came into being in the light of these problems, it seemed appropriate to cast the book's introduction into the larger mold from which the project had evolved.

It would be grandiose to think that a fallible social experiment of limited scope, such as PMHP, has widespread implications for society's many, chronic, unresolved mental health problems. But it would be just as wrong to ignore several clear inputs to such problems that emerge from the experience. One such bridge has to do with the chronic imbalance between the need and supply in mental health. The PMHP model offers a viable, effective way of extending helping services to many more people in need, who happen, in this case, to be young maladapting school children. The broader message is that nonprofessional help-agents are fully capable of bringing effective services to people with problems, doubtless including some who were previously thought to fall exclusively within the professionals' zealously guarded domain. The basic point extends beyond child aides, children who maladapt in school, and schools. What our experience suggests is that the personal-experiential qualities rather than the formal training and degrees of a help-agent are vital in determining whether people in need are in fact helped. This notion is testable and can be extended to many other situations involving relief of human distress through interpersonal interaction. Systematic use of nonprofessional help-agents requires further development of a professional role model in which some socially less parsimonious, direct service time is replaced by training, consultative, and supervisory roles that help the newly expanded cadre of helpers to function most effectively.

Another of PMHP's key implications has to do with the optimal timing of helping interventions. Among the most serious indictments of the mental health fields considered in Chapter 1 was the argument that they had classically defined their helping mandate and had oriented their ameliorative efforts toward end-states—i.e., well-articulated, entrenched conditions of human dysfunction. Too often, it was argued, we began our interventions when the battle had already been lost. Thus too much of mental health's past effort has been directed precisely to those conditions with the poorest prognoses. As a result, the resources and muscle needed for socially more promising activities have been preempted. The PMHP model redresses this imbalance in a small way. Its focus is on very young children in the natural social environment of their maladaptation. Although this approach, to be sure, still deals with problems, it does so much earlier, when they are less rooted and debilitating and before they have exacted an extensive toll. Not only does this approach increase the likelihood of better, immediate educational adaptations, but in arresting or reversing early dysfunctional nodes and in establishing *bonafide* bases of competence, it reduces the probability of later, socially disastrous consequences. Hence, PMHP implicitly offers an alternative social strategy for short-circuiting those end-states that have been the historical essence of abnormal psychology. Rather than deal with rooted, flagrant conditions, PMHP, through systematic early detection and effective early intervention, seeks to cut down the flow of diverse disorders.

There is an interesting structural parallel between the child-aide interaction and psychotherapy. Both pivot around a dyad consisting of a help-agent and a person who is experiencing problems. An important difference between the two, however, is that PMHP's targets are all very young, and their difficulties are presumably less rooted and profound. Moreover, the problems of PMHP children have some communality of focus and definition in that they all relate to school behavior and performance. These factors may make for easier (i.e., less complex and prognostically more positive) interventions in PMHP than in adult psychotherapy. The relatively narrow initial pool of referral problems in PMHP also means that specific problem-types are easier to identify, and the effects of different interventions for different types can be assessed more readily. Compared with psychotherapy, it may thus be easier for PMHP to evaluate the effects of specific helping interventions for different people with different problems. Although not all of PMHP's findings generalize automatically to other dyadic helping situations, they contribute to our understanding of such interactions. Given PMHP's narrower focus and tighter control over inputs, the approach can help to generate important leads to be evaluated in the context of other, more traditional helping dyads.

Because PMHP is located in the school, the approach can potentially reach social groups that have been shortchanged with respect to helping services in the past. PMHP's applications are thus equipotent in diverse groups. The usual problems of delivering meaningful services to low-income groups, for example, can be avoided in several ways. First, a school system can make the decision to allocate its helping resources in terms of need rather than money or social status. Moreover, "technology" gaps in reaching low-income groups, so evident at the adult level, are less likely to be present or can more easily be circumvented with the very young. Exploring a range of helping approaches in an effort to identify ones that are effective with young disadvantaged children in need is feasible and less complicated than doing the same thing for adults.

In speculating about PMHP's potential applications for disadvantaged school children, our intent is not to sweep under the rug the more serious challenges of how to engineer schools and articulate educational programs for such youngsters. Rather, it is to recognize that such primary preventive steps will at best be painfully slow. If we take things as they are, PMHP offers a way of making the educational experience of disadvantaged children more effective and rewarding. Assuming that effective school adaptation is indeed a critical stepping stone to important adaptations in later life (Jason, 1975), establishing PMHP-type programs for disadvantaged children may help them to acquire the tools needed to negotiate later hurdles—an important, socially contributory step.

Although PMHP is admittedly a finite effort in a specific sphere of mental health, its paradigmatic "solution" has orienting value for engaging other pressing mental health problems. Certainly in relation to its potential for bringing about short- and long-term gain, PMHP costs are low.

PMHP AND BEYOND

An objective reader could well have assumed at several points in this book that PMHP was being advanced as a "final" ideal solution for school mental health problems. Such an assumption would be seriously off base. In clarifying this point, it may help to separate the obvious issue, How good is PMHP? into two components: (1) Is PMHP preferable to traditional school mental health approaches? and (2) Is the PMHP delivery model a conceptual ideal in approaching school mental health problems?

The first question can be answered affirmatively. But just as clearly, and perhaps more importantly, the second question must be answered with a flat No! These conflicting answers bear further explanation, hopefully to clarify further what PMHP is and is not. All schools face the important challenge of optimizing, as best they can, children's educational and personal development. These two developmental strands are complexly interwoven, so that personal factors often determine how well the child learns and vice versa. Indeed, it is the recognition of exactly such an interface that justifies having mental health services in the schools. School mental health units are set up in a way that reflects prevailing concepts of mental health and views of its mandates. Since, historically, the latter have been defined as repairing dysfunction and because mental health resources for schools, overall, are scarce, school mental health services have typically been defined in crisis-oriented, troubleshooting terms. Thus, when a child's school adjustment problems reach extreme, sometimes unbearable proportions, a mental health expert is called in to do his magic as best he can. Necessarily, only a few of the most dysfunctional children are reached using this approach. Because these children have severe, deeply rooted problems, which have often spread to many areas of their functioning, they have relatively poor prognoses and/or require much time and effort in working toward amelioration. There is thus little or no time available for children whose problems, although significant, are not "boat-rocking." Accordingly, most school mental health systems, by default, guarantee a perpetual pipeline of problems and permit long, festering periods during which initially minor troubles become extended and disruptive.

PMHP's great virtue is that it breaks into this vicious circle by identifying problems early and bringing immediate service to the child in need. Early correction hopefully short-circuits later problems before they reach disabling proportions and require extensive services, typically unavailable, to reduce symptomatology and to help the child reach a plateau of minimally effective functioning (i.e., to establish a momentary truce that can, at any moment, erupt again into open difficulties). This way of perceiving the issue lies behind the answer to the question: Is PMHP preferable to traditional school mental health approaches? In other words, PMHP seems conceptually preferable to traditional school mental health delivery systems.

On the other hand, no matter how impeccable PMHP's underlying rationale and no matter how much more sensible its timing or the extent to which it expands and improves traditional delivery systems, it remains basically a *secondary* preventive (i.e., restorative) approach and as such is insufficient. It is helpful to ask the hypothetical question: If there were no such thing as school mental health services, how could one best approach, from scratch, the issues of school effectiveness that typically fall within the mental health fiefdom? Conceptually, the most logical attractive alternative, in the spirit of primary prevention, is to create school environments that maximize the adaptation of *all* children in the first place (Cowen, 1967; Cowen, 1973; Moos, 1973; Sarason, 1971; Zax & Cowen, 1972). Influential social systems in general and schools in particular have key defining attributes (some planned, most neither planned nor even perceived), such as warmth-coldness, rigidity-flexibility, organization disorganization, that necessarily affect in important ways the children who live in them. This is particularly true for the primary grade classroom, which houses malleable young children for long periods during their formative, impressionable years (Bardon, 1968).

The initial broad wave of research-framing questions raised by this orientation includes: What are the salient dimensions of the school's impact and how can these be measured? What effects do variations on these dimensions have on young children's educational and personal development? In what ways can classroom environments be modified to optimize the development of the many? These are heavy, complex questions and very difficult to study. For one thing, mental health professionals, because of the ways in which their disciplines have evolved and have been defined, neither perceive issues in social-system terms nor see how this approach is relevant to their job mandates. For another, we lack the tools and methodologies needed to explore such questions. And perhaps most important of all, schools overwhelmingly see their headaches as related to failures in the performance of individual children, rather than define their potential in terms of the positive impact that the classroom environment can have on children's development. In other words, given schools' definition of their problems and needs, a social system approach is abstract, futuristic, and impalpable. This is so, notwithstanding the availability of important but seldom-cited data indicating that school environments significantly influence the behaviors of children who inhabit them (Barker, 1968, 1969; Barker & Gump, 1964; Barker & Schoggen, 1973; Gump, 1969).

The argument can be made that we must, no matter how difficult it is to do so, back away from the all-too-evident need to undo damage and allocate more of our skills, energies, and resources to the challenge of articulating school environments that permit children to grow and develop optimally in all respects from the very start. This challenge goes beyond the need to study the effects of school environments on behavior since what has been learned from lower organisms, and occasionally from human beings, suggests that the issue is more complicated than determining the main effects of environments. There is the need to interpose *people* somewhere along the line, as Kelly and his associates have done (Insel, & Moos, 1974; Kelly, 1969a; Kelly, 1969b; Kelly, 1971; Moos, 1973; Moos & Insel, 1974; Trickett, Kelly & Todd, 1972; Trickett & Moos, 1973, 1974) and to spotlight the problem of "ecological match"—i.e., the consequences on outcome of pairing particular individuals and particular environmental properties. This is an approach with practical as well as theoretical value because it holds promise of providing data that can optimize children's class assignments by taking into account whatever is known about the child, the teacher, and the characteristics of the classroom. An example of this approach is found in a study by Allinsmith and Grimes (1961), who showed that anxious compulsive children did better in structured, as opposed to unstructured school environments.

Thus, without demeaning our own effort, we end up with the Avis-like conclusion that PMHP, conceptually, is only second best. Though the approach is realistic, responsive to present realities, and preferable to established, rutted, school mental health practices, it does not come to grips with the heart of the problem. Although it establishes a utilitarian new role for school mental health professionals (the mental health "quarterback"), that takes an important preventive stride, the role nevertheless maintains a major repair component. Nor does this new role begin seriously to explore the important, sorely needed functions of the social system analyst and modifier required as core elements in an ideal, future, school mental health role.

But PMHP does indeed offer a meritorious viable alternative to traditional school mental health delivery systems. We hope that school districts, in their future thinking about and concrete planning for school mental health services, seriously consider the potential for implementing elements of this approach. Schools will, and must pay heed to today's problems. But we also hope that this need is not so overwhelmingly indulged that it blocks progress toward establishing school environments that promote healthy development, rich in learning, for all children and thus obviate the future need for restoration.

Bibliography

Albee, G. W. *Mental health manpower trends.* New York: Basic Books, 1959.

Albee, G. W. The relation of conceptual models to manpower needs. In E. L. Cowen, E. A. Gardner & M. Zax (Eds.), *Emergent approaches to mental health problems.* New York: Appleton-Century-Crofts, 1967.

Allinsmith, W., & Grimes, J. W. Compulsivity, anxiety, and school achievement. *Merrill-Palmer Quarterly,* 1961, **7,** 247–271.

Arnhoff, F. N., Rubenstein, E. A., & Speisman, J. C. (Eds.) *Manpower for mental health.* Chicago: Aldine, 1969.

Bardon, J. I. School psychology and school psychologists. *American Psychologist,* 1968, **23,** 187–194.

Barker, R. G. *Ecological psychology.* Stanford, Calif.: Stanford University Press, 1968.

Barker, R. G. Wanted: An eco-behavioral science. In E. P. Willems & H. L. Raush (Eds.), *Naturalistic viewpoints in psychological research.* New York: Holt, Rinehart & Winston, 1969.

Barker, R. G., & Gump, P. V. *Big school, small school.* Stanford, Calif.: Stanford University Press, 1964.

Barker, R. G., & Schoggen, P. *Qualities of community life.* San Francisco: Jossey-Bass, 1973.

Beach, D. R., Cowen, E. L., Zax, M., Laird, J. D., Trost, M. A., & Izzo, L. D. Objectification of a screening procedure for early detection of emotional disorder. *Child Development,* 1968, **39,** 1177–1188.

Bergin, A. E. The evaluation of therapeutic outcomes. In A. E. Bergin & S. L. Garfield (Eds.), *Handbook of psychotherapy and behavior change: An empirical analysis.* New York: Wiley, 1971.

Bloom, B. L. The "medical model," miasma theory, and community mental health. *Community Mental Health Journal,* 1965, **1,** 33–38.

Bower, E. M. *Early identification of emotionally handicapped children.* Springfield, Ill.: Charles C Thomas, 1960.

Caplan, G. *Support systems and community mental health.* New York: Behavioral Publications, 1974.

Castaneda, A., McCandless, B. R., & Palermo, D. S. The children's form of the manifest anxiety scale. *Child Development,* 1956, **27,** 317–326.

Clarfield, S. P. An analysis of referral problems and their relation to intervention goals in a school based preventive mental health program. Unpublished doctoral dissertation, University of Rochester, 1972.

Clarfield, S. P. The development of a teacher referral form for identifying early school maladaptation. *American Journal of Community Psychology,* 1974, **2,** 199–210.

Clarfield, S. P., & McMillan, R. C. High school students in a human service practicum. *American Journal of Community Psychology,* 1973, **1,** 212–218.

Cowen, E. L. Emergent approaches to mental health problems: An overview and directions for future work. In E. L. Cowen, E. A. Gardner & M. Zax (Eds.), *Emergent approaches to mental health problems.* New York: Appleton-Century-Crofts, 1967.

Cowen, E. L. The effectiveness of secondary prevention programs using nonprofessionals in the school setting. *Proceedings, 76th Annual Convention, APA,* 1968, **2,** 705–706. (a)

Cowen, E. L. The utilization of nonprofessionals in mental health roles. *Proceedings of the 16th Inter-American Congress,* Mexico City: 1968. (b)

Cowen, E. L. Combined graduate-undergraduate training in community mental health. *Professional Psychology,* 1969, **1,** 72–73. (a)

Cowen, E. L. Mothers in the classroom. *Psychology Today,* 1969, **2,** 36–40. (b)

Cowen, E. L. Training clinical psychologists for community mental health functions: Description of a practicum experience. In I. Iscoe & C. D. Spielberger (Eds.), *Community psychology: Perspectives in training and research.* New York: Appleton-Century-Crofts, 1970.

Cowen, E. L. On broadening community mental health practicum training for clinical psychologists. *Professional Psychology,* 1971, **2,** 159–168. (a)

Cowen, E. L. Coping with school adaptation problems. *Psychology in the Schools,* 1971, **8,** 322–329. (b)

Cowen, E. L. Emergent directions in school mental health: The development and evaluation of a program for early detection and prevention of ineffective school behavior. *American Scientist,* 1971, **59,** 723–733. (c)

Cowen, E. L. Primary Mental Health Project. In R. Quinn & L. M. Wegener (Eds.), *Mental health and learning.* Washington, D.C.: U.S. Dept. of H.E.W., Public. No. (HSM) 72–9146, 1972.

Cowen, E. L. Social and community interventions. In P. Mussen & M. Rosenzweig (Eds.) *Annual Review of Psychology,* 1973, **24,** 423–472.

Cowen, E. L., Carlisle, R. L., & Kaufman, G. Evaluation of a college student volunteer program with primary graders experiencing school adjustment problems. *Psychology in the Schools,* 1969, **6,** 371–375.

Cowen, E. L., Chinsky, J. M., & Rappaport, J. An undergraduate practicum in community mental health. *Community Mental Health Journal,* 1970, **6,** 91–100.

Cowen, E. L., Dorr, D., Clarfield, S. P., Kreling, B., McWilliams, S. A., Pokracki, F., Pratt, D. M., Terrell, D. L., & Wilson, A. B. The AML: A quick screening device for early detection of school maladaptation. *American Journal of Community Psychology,* 1973, **1,** 12–35. (a)

Cowen, E. L., Dorr, D., Izzo, L. D., Madonia, A., & Trost, M. A. The Primary Mental Health Project: A new way of conceptualizing and delivering school mental health services. *Psychology in the Schools,* 1971, **8,** 216–225.

Cowen, E. L., Dorr, D., & Orgel, A. R. Interrelations among screening measures for early detection of school dysfunction. *Psychology in the Schools,* 1971, **5,** 135–139.

Cowen, E. L., Dorr, D., & Pokracki, F. Selection of nonprofessional child-aides for a school mental health project. *Community Mental Health Journal,* 1972, **8,** 220–226. (b)

Cowen, E. L., Dorr, D., Sandler, I. N., & McWilliams, S. A. Utilization of a nonprofessional child-aide, school mental health program. *Journal of School Psychology,* 1971, **9,** 131–136. (a)

Cowen, E. L., Dorr, D., Trost, M. A., & Izzo, L. D. A follow-up study of maladapting school children seen by nonprofessionals. *Journal of Consulting and Clinical Psychology,* 1972, **36,** 235–238. (a)

Cowen, E. L., Gardner, E. A., & Zax, M. (Eds.) *Emergent approaches to mental health problems.* New York: Appleton-Century-Crofts, 1967.

Cowen, E. L., Huser, J., Beach, D. R., & Rappaport, J. Parental perceptions of young children and their relation to indices of adjustment. *Journal of Consulting and Clinical Psychology,* 1970, **34,** 97–103. (b)

Cowen, E. L., Izzo, L. D., Miles, H., Telschow, E. F., Trost, M. A., & Zax, M. A mental health program in the school setting: Description and evaluation. *Journal of Psychology,* 1963, **56,** 307–356.

Cowen, E. L., Izzo, L. D., Trost, M. A., & Monjan, S. V. The Secret Stories Test: A projective approach for young children. *Journal of Clinical Psychology*, 1964, **20**, 184–486.

Cowen, E. L., Leibowitz, E., & Leibowitz, G. The utilization of retired people as mental health aides in the schools. *American Journal of Orthopsychiatry*, 1968, **38**, 900–909.

Cowen, E. L., & Lorion, R. P. Which kids are helped? *Journal of Special Education*, 1974, **8**, 187–192.

Cowen, E. L., & Lorion, R. P. Changing approaches in school mental health: Basic issues and a specific program. In H. H. Barten & L. Bellak (Eds.), *Progress in community mental health*, Vol. 3. New York: Grune & Stratton, 1975, in press, (a)

Cowen, E. L., & Lorion, R. P. Multiple views of a school mental health project: A needed focus in community programs. *Community Mental Health Journal*, 1975. **11**, in press. (b)

Cowen, E. L., Lorion, R. P., & Dorr, D. A. Research in the community cauldron: A case report. *Canadian Psychologist*, 1974, **15**, 313–325.

Cowen, E. L., Lorion, R. P., Dorr, D. A., Clarfield, S. P., & Wilson, A. B. Evaluation of a preventively oriented, school based mental health program. *Psychology in the Schools*, 1975, **12**, in press.

Cowen, E. L., Lorion, R. P., Kraus, R. M., & Dorr, D. Geometric expansion of helping services. *Journal of School Psychology*, 1974, **12**, 288–295.

Cowen, E. L., Pederson, A., Babigian, H., Izzo, L. D., & Trost, M. A. Long-term follow-up of early detected vulnerable children. *Journal of Consulting and Clinical Psychology*, 1973, **41**, 438–446. (c)

Cowen, E. L., & Schochet, B. V. A comparison of the referral and outcome status of terminated and nonterminated children seen by nonprofessionals in a school mental health project. *American Journal of Community Psychology*, 1973, **1**, 103–112.

Cowen, E. L., Trost, M. A., & Izzo, L. D. Nonprofessional human service personnel in consulting roles. *Community Mental Health Journal*, 1973, **9**, 335–341. (b)

Cowen, E. L., & Zax, M. The mental health fields today: Issues and problems. In E. L. Cowen, E. A. Gardner & M. Zax (Eds.), *Emergent approaches to mental health problems*. New York: Appleton-Century-Crofts, 1967.

Cowen, E. L., & Zax M. Early detection and prevention of emotional disorders: Conceptualizations and programming. In J. W. Carter (Ed.), *Research contributions from psychology to community mental health*. New York: Behavioral Publications, 1969.

Cowen, E. L., Zax, M., Klein, R., Izzo, L. D., & Trost, M. A. The relation of anxiety in school children to school record, achievement and behavioral measures. *Child Development,* 1965, **36,** 685–695.

Cowen, E. L., Zax, M., Izzo, L. D., & Trost, M. A. The prevention of emotional disorders in the school setting: A further investigation. *Journal of Consulting Psychology,* 1966, **30,** 381–387. (a)

Cowen, E. L., Zax, M., & Laird, J. D. A college student volunteer program in the elementary school setting. *Community Mental Health Journal,* 1966, **2,** 319–328. (b)

Donahue, G. T. A school district program for schizophrenic, organic and seriously disturbed children. In E. L. Cowen, E. A. Gardner & M. Zax (Eds.), *Emergent approaches to mental health problems.* New York: Appleton-Century-Crofts, 1967.

Donahue, G. T., & Nichtern, S. *Teaching the troubled child.* New York: Free Press, 1965.

Dorr, D. An ounce of prevention. *Mental Hygiene,* 1972, **56,** 25–27.

Dorr, D., & Cowen, E. L. Teachers' perceptions of a school mental health project. *Journal of School Psychology,* 1972, **10,** 76–78.

Dorr, D., & Cowen, E. L. Nonprofessional mental health workers' judgments of change in children. *Journal of Community Psychology,* 1973, **1,** 23–26.

Dorr, D., Cowen, E. L., & Kraus, R. M. Mental health professionals view nonprofessional mental health workers. *American Journal of Community Psychology,* 1973, **1,** 258–265. (c)

Dorr, D., Cowen, E. L., & Sandler, I. N. Changes in nonprofessional mental health workers' response preferences and attitudes as a function of training and supervised field experience. *Journal of School Psychology,* 1973, **11,** 118–122. (b)

Dorr, D., Cowen, E. L., Sandler, I. N., & Pratt, D. M. The dimensionality of a test battery for nonprofessional mental health workers. *Journal of Consulting and Clinical Psychology,* 1973, **41,** 181–185. (a)

Eisenberg, L. Possibilities for a preventive psychiatry. *Pediatrics,* 1962, **30,** 815–828.

Ewalt, P. L. (Ed.) *Mental health volunteers.* Springfield, Ill.: Charles C Thomas, 1967.

Eysenck, H. J. The effects of psychotherapy: An evaluation. *Journal of Consulting Psychology,* 1952, **16,** 319–324.

Eysenck, H. J. The effects of psychotherapy. In H. J. Eysenck (Ed.), *Handbook of abnormal psychology.* New York: Basic Books, 1961.

Eysenck, H. J. *The effects of psychotherapy.* New York: International Science Press, 1966.

Faris, R. E. L., & Dunham, H. W. *Mental disorders in urban areas.* Chicago: University of Chicago Press, 1939.

Felner, R. D., Stolberg, A. L., & Cowen, E. L. Crisis events and school mental health referral patterns of young children. *Journal of Consulting and Clinical Psychology,* 1975, **44,** in press.

Garfield, S. L. Research on client variables in psychotherapy. In A. E. Bergin & S. L. Garfield (Eds.), *Handbook of psychotherapy and behavior change: An empirical analysis.* New York: Wiley, 1971.

Gartner, A. *Paraprofessionals and their performance.* New York: Praeger, 1971.

Gesten, E. A Health Resources Inventory: The development of a measure of the personal and social competence of elementary school aged children. Unpublished doctoral dissertation, University of Rochester, 1974.

Glidewell, J. C., & Swallow, C. S. *The prevalence of maladjustment in elementary schools: A report prepared for the Joint Commission on the Mental Health of Children.* Chicago: University of Chicago Press, 1969.

Golann, S. E., & Eisdorfer, C. Mental health and the community: The development of issues. In S. E. Golann & C. Eisdorfer (Eds.), *Handbook of Community Mental Health.* New York: Appleton-Century-Crofts, 1972.

Gump, P. V. Intro-setting analysis: The third grade classroom as a special but instructive case. In E. P. Willems & H. L. Raush (Eds.), *Naturalistic viewpoints in psychological research.* New York: Holt, Rinehart & Winston, 1969.

Gurin, G., Veroff, J., & Feld, S. *Americans view their mental health: A nationwide survey.* New York: Basic Books, 1960.

Hobbs, N. Helping disturbed children: Psychological and ecological strategies. *American Psychologist,* 1966, **21,** 1105–1115.

Hobbs, N. The reeducation of emotionally disturbed children. In E. M. Bower & W. G. Hollister (Eds.), *Behavior science frontiers in education.* New York: Wiley, 1967.

Hobbs, N. Re-education, reality, and community responsibility. In J. W. Carter (Ed.), *Research contributions from psychology to community mental health.* New York: Behavioral Publications, 1969.

Hollingshead, B. B., & Redlich, F. C. *Social class and mental illness: A community study.* New York: Wiley, 1958.

Holzberg, J. D. The significance of the companionship experience for the college student. In *College student companion program: Contribution to the social rehabilitation of the mentally ill.* Hartford, Conn.: Conn. State Dept. of Mental Health, 1962.

Holzberg, J. D. The companion program: Implementing the manpower recommendations of the Joint Commission on Mental Illness and Health. *American Psychologist,* 1963, **18,** 224–226.

Holzberg, J. D., Gewirtz, H., & Ebner, E. Changes in moral judgment and self-acceptance in college students as a function of companionship with hospitalized mental patients. *Journal of Consulting Psychology,* 1964, **28,** 299–303.

Holzberg, J. D., Knapp, R. H., & Turner, J. L. College students as companions to the mentally ill. In E. L. Cowen, E. A. Gardner, & M. Zax (Eds.), *Emergent approaches to mental health problems.* New York: Appleton-Century-Crofts, 1967.

Insel, P. M., & Moos, R. H. Psychological environments: Expanding the scope of human ecology. *American Psychologist,* 1974, **29,** 179–188.

Izzo, L. D. The Rochester City School District Primary Mental Health Project. In *Protection and promotion of positive mental health in the schools.* Des Moines: Pupil Personnel Services Branch, State of Iowa Department of Public Instruction, 1968.

Izzo, L. D., & Trost, M. A. Learning difficulties: Early detection and prevention. *Today and Tomorrow in Education,* 1968, **2,** 3–8.

Jason, L. Early secondary prevention with disadvantaged preschool children. *American Journal of Community Psychology,* 1975, **3,** in press.

Jason, L., Clarfield, S. P., & Cowen, E. L. Preventive intervention with young disadvantaged children. *American Journal of Community Psychology,* 1973, **1,** 50–61.

Jason, L., & Kimbrough, C. A preventive educational program for young economically disadvantaged children. *Journal of Community Psychology,* 1974, **2,** 134–139.

Joint Commission on Mental Illness and Health. *Action for mental health.* New York: Basic Books, 1961.

Joint Commission on Mental Health of Children. *Crisis in child mental health: Challenge for the 1970's.* New York: Harper & Row, 1969.

Kelly, J. G. Towards an ecological conception of preventive intervention. In J. W. Carter (Ed.), *Research contributions from psychology to community mental health.* New York: Behavioral Publications, 1969. (a)

Kelly, J. G. Naturalistic observations in contrasting social environments. In E. P. Willems & H. L. Raush (Eds.), *Naturalistic viewpoints in psychological research.* New York: Holt, Rinehart & Winston, 1969. (b)

Kelly, J. G., Edwards, D. W., Fatke, R., Gordon, T. A., McClintock, S. K., McGee, D. P., Newman, B. M., Rice, R. R., Roistacher, R. C., & Todd, D. M. The coping process in varied high school environments. In M. J. Feldman (Ed.), *Studies in psychotherapy and behavior change, No. 2: Theory and research in community mental health.* Buffalo: State University of New York, 1971.

Knapp, R. H., & Holzberg, J. D. Characteristics of college students volunteering for service to mental patients. *Journal of Consulting Psychology*, 1964, **28**, 82–85.

Levine, M., & Graziano, A. M. Intervention programs in elementary schools. In S. E. Golann & C. Eisdorfer (Eds.), *Handbook of community mental health.* New York: Appleton-Century-Crofts, 1972.

Levitt, E. E. The results of psychotherapy with children: An evaluation. *Journal of Consulting Psychology*, 1957, **21**, 189–196.

Levitt, E. E. Psychotherapy with children: A further evaluation. *Behavior Research and Therapy*, 1963, **1**, 45–51.

Levitt, E. E. Research on psychotherapy with children. In A. E. Bergin & S. L. Garfield (Eds.), *Handbook of psychotherapy and behavior change: An empirical analysis.* New York: Wiley, 1971.

Lewis, W. W. Project Re-Ed: Educational intervention in discordant child rearing systems. In E. L. Cowen, E. A. Gardner & M. Zax (Eds.), *Emergent approaches to mental health problems.* New York: Appleton-Century-Crofts, 1967.

Liem, G. R., Yellott, A. W., Cowen, E. L., Trost, M. A., & Izzo, L. D. Some correlates of early detected emotional dysfunction in the schools. *American Journal of Orthopsychiatry*, 1969, **39**, 619–626.

Lorion, R. P. Socioeconomic status and traditional treatment approaches reconsidered. *Psychological Bulletin*, 1973, **79**, 263–270.

Lorion, R. P. Patient and therapist variables in the treatment of low-income patients. *Psychological Bulletin*, 1974, **81**, 344–354.

Lorion, R. P., Caldwell, R. A. & Cowen, E. L. Effects of a school mental health project: A one year follow-up. *Journal of School Psychology*, 1975, **13**, in press.

Lorion, R. P., & Cowen, E. L. Comparison of two outcome groups in a school based mental health project. *American Journal of Community Psychology*, 1975, **3**, in press.

Lorion, R. P., Cowen, E. L., & Caldwell, R. A. Problem types of children referred to a school based mental health program. *Journal of Consulting and Clinical Psychology*, 1974, **42**, 491–496. (b)

Lorion, R. P., Cowen, E. L. & Caldwell, R. A. Normative and parametric analysis of school maladjustment. *American Journal of Community Psychology* 1975, **3**, in press.

Lorion, R. P., Cowen, E. L., & Kraus, R. M. Some hidden regularities in a school based mental health project. *Journal of Consulting and Clinical Psychology*, 1974, **42**, 346–352. (a)

Lorion, R. P., Cowen, E. L., Kraus, R. M., & Milling, L. S. Familial correlates of school adjustment problems. In preparation.

McMillan, R. C. Attitudinal and behavior changes in tuned out high school students as a function of participation in a human service program as mental health aides in an elementary school. Unpublished doctoral dissertation, University of Rochester, 1973.

McWilliams, S. A. A process analysis of a school-based mental health program. Unpublished doctoral dissertation, University of Rochester, 1971.

McWilliams, S. A. A process analysis of nonprofessional intervention with children. *Journal of School Psychology*, 1972, **10**, 367–377.

McWilliams, S. A., & Finkel, N. J. High school students as mental health aides in the elementary school setting. *Journal of Consulting and Clinical Psychology*, 1973, **40**, 39–42.

Magoon, T. M., Golann, S. E., & Freeman, R. W. *Mental health counselors at work.* New York: Pergamon, 1969.

Miller, S. M., & Riessman, F. *Social class and social policy.* New York: Basic Books, 1968.

Moos, R. F. Conceptualizations of human environments. *American Psychologist*, 1973, **28**, 652–665.

Moos, R. F., & Insel, P. M. (Eds.) *Issues in social ecology: Human milieus.* Palo Alto, Calif.: National Press Books, 1974.

Myers, J. K., & Bean, L. L. *A decade later: A follow-up of social class and mental illness.* New York: Wiley, 1968.

Myers, J. K., & Roberts, B. H. *Family and class dynamics in mental illness.* New York: Wiley, 1959.

Osgood, C. E., Suci, G. J., & Tannenbaum, P. H. *The measurement of meaning.* Urbana, Ill.: University of Illinois Press, 1957.

Primary Mental Health Project. *Manual for the training of nonprofessionals as child-aides.* Unpublished manuscript, University of Rochester, 1970.

Poser, E. G. The effect of therapist training on group therapeutic outcome. *Journal of Consulting Psychology*, 1966, **30**, 283–289.

Rappaport, J., Chinsky, J. M., & Cowen, E. L. *Innovations in helping chronic patients: College students in a mental hospital.* New York: Academic Press, 1971.

Reiff, R. Mental health manpower and institutional change. In E. L. Cowen, E. A. Gardner, & M. Zax (Eds.), *Emergent approaches to mental health problems.* New York: Appleton-Century-Crofts, 1967.

Reiff, R., & Riessman, F. *The indigenous nonprofessional.* New York: Behavioral Publications, Community Mental Health Journal Monograph No. 1, 1965.

Riessman, F. The "helper" therapy principle. *Social Work*, 1965, **10**, 27–32.

Riessman, F. A neighborhood-based mental health approach. In E. L. Cowen, E. A. Gardner, & M. Zax (Eds.), *Emergent approaches to mental health problems.* New York: Appleton-Century-Crofts, 1967.

Riessman, F., Cohen, J., & Pearl, A. (Eds.) *Mental health of the poor.* New York: Free Press, 1964.

Rioch, M. J. Pilot projects in training mental health counselors. In E. L. Cowen, E. A. Gardner, & M. Zax (Eds.), *Emergent approaches to mental health problems.* New York: Appleton-Century-Crofts, 1967.

Rioch, M. J., Elkes, C., & Flint, A. A. *National Institute of Mental Health pilot project in training mental health counselors.* Washington, D.C.: U.S. Dept. of Health, Education & Welfare, Public Health Service Publication No. 1254, 1965.

Rioch, M. J., Elkes, C., Flint, A. A., Usdansky, B. S., Newman, R. G., & Silber, E. National Institute of Mental Health pilot study in training of mental health counselors. *American Journal of Orthopsychiatry,* 1963, **33,** 678–689.

Rotter, J. B. The future of clinical psychology. *Journal of Consulting and Clinical Psychology,* 1973, **40,** 313–321.

Sanders, R. New manpower for mental health service. In E. L. Cowen, E. A. Gardner, & M. Zax (Eds.), *Emergent approaches to mental health problems.* New York: Appleton-Century-Crofts, 1967.

Sanders, R., Smith, R. S., & Weinman, B. S. *Chronic psychosis and recovery.* San Francisco: Jossey-Bass, 1967.

Sandler, I. N. Characteristics of women working as child-aides in a school based preventive mental health program. *Journal of Consulting and Clinical Psychology,* 1972, **39,** 56–61.

Sandler, I. N., Duricko, A., & Grande, L. Effectiveness of an early secondary prevention program in an inner-city elementary school. *American Journal of Community Psychology,* 1975, **3,** in press.

Sanua, V. D. Sociocultural aspects of psychotherapy and treatment: A review of the literature. In L. E. Abt & L. Bellak (Eds.), *Progress in clinical psychology, Vol. 8.* New York: Grune & Stratton, 1966.

Sarason, S. B. *The culture of the school and the problem of change.* Boston: Allyn-Bacon, 1971.

Sarason, S. B. *The psychological sense of community: Prospects for a community psychology.* San Francisco: Jossey-Bass, 1974.

Sarason, S. B., Levine, M., Goldenberg, I. I., Cherlin, D. L., & Bennett, E. M. *Psychology in community settings.* New York: Wiley, 1966.

Scheff, T. J. *Being mentally ill: A sociological theory.* Chicago: Aldine, 1966.

Schindler-Rainman, E., & Lippitt, R. *The volunteer community: Creative use of human resources.* Washington, D.C.: NTL Learning Resources, 1971.

Schofield, W. *Psychotherapy: The purchase of friendship.* Englewood Cliffs, N.J.: Prentice-Hall, 1964.

Shore, M. F. The federal scene. *Professional Psychology,* 1972, **3**, 383–384.

Sivers, W. A. *Report of 1972–73 survey of school psychologists.* Albany: New York State Education Department, 1974.

Sobey, F. *The nonprofessional revolution in mental health.* New York: Columbia University Press, 1970.

Specter, G. A., & Cowen, E. L. A pilot study in stimulation of culturally deprived infants. *Child Psychiatry and Human Development,* 1971, **1**, 168–177.

Strupp, H. H., & Bergin, A. E. Some empirical and conceptual bases for coordinated research in psychotherapy: A critical review of issues, trends, and evidence. *International Journal of Psychiatry,* 1969, **7**, 18–90.

Terrell, D. L., McWilliams, S. A., & Cowen, E. L. Description and evaluation of group-work training for nonprofessional child-aides in a school mental health program. *Psychology in the Schools,* 1972, **9**, 70–75.

Trickett, E. J., Kelly, J. G., & Todd, D. M. The social environment of the high school: Guidelines for individual change and organizational redevelopment. In S. E. Golann & C. Eisdorfer (Eds.), *Handbook of Community Mental Health.* New York: Appleton-Century-Crofts, 1972.

Trickett, E. J., & Moos, R. H. The social environment of junior high and high school classrooms. *Journal of Educational Psychology,* 1973, **64**, 93–102.

Trickett, E. J., & Moos, R. H. Personal correlates of contrasting environments: Student satisfactions in high school classrooms. *American Journal of Community Psychology,* 1974, **2**, 1–12.

Trost, M. A. The preventive role of the social worker in the school setting. *Child Welfare,* 1968, **17**, 397–404. (a)

Trost, M. A. The child-aide program. In *Protection and promotion of positive mental health in the schools.* Des Moines: Pupil Personnel Services Branch, State of Iowa Department of Public Instruction, 1968. (b)

Trost, M. A. The child-aide mental health program. *Mental Health in the Classroom,* 1968, **7**(4), 1–7. (c)

Umbarger, C. C., Dalsimer, J. S., Morrison, A. P., & Breggin, P. R. *College students in mental hospitals.* New York: Grune & Stratton, 1962.

Van Vleet, P., & Kannegieter, R. *Investments in prevention: The prevention of learning and behavior problems in young children.* San Francisco: PACE ID Center, 1969.

Weinstein, L. Project Re-Ed schools for emotionally disturbed children: Effectiveness as viewed by referring agencies, parents and teachers. *Exceptional Children,* 1969, **35**, 703–711.

Yellott, A. W., Liem, G. R., & Cowen, E. L. Relationships among measures of adjustment, sociometric status and achievement in third graders. *Psychology in the Schools,* 1969, **6,** 315–321.

Zax, M., & Cowen, E. L. Early identification and prevention of emotional disturbance in a public school. In E. L. Cowen, E. A. Gardner, & M. Zax (Eds.), *Emergent approaches to mental health problems.* New York: Appleton-Century-Crofts, 1967.

Zax, M., & Cowen, E. L. Research on early detection and prevention of emotional dysfunction in young school children. In C. D. Spielberger (Ed.), *Current topics in clinical and community psychology.* New York: Academic Press, 1969.

Zax, M., & Cowen, E. L. *Abnormal psychology: Changing conceptions.* New York: Holt, Rinehart & Winston, 1972.

Zax, M., Cowen, E. L., Beach, D. R., & Rappaport, J. Longitudinal relations among aptitude, achievement, and adjustment measures of school children. *Journal of Genetic Psychology,* 1972, **121,** 145–154.

Zax, M., Cowen, E. L., Izzo, L. D., & Trost, M. A. Identifying emotional disturbance in the school setting. *American Journal of Orthopsychiatry,* 1964, **34,** 447–454.

Zax, M., Cowen, E. L., Izzo, L. D., Madonia, A. J., Merenda, J., & Trost, M. A. A teacher-aide program for preventing emotional disturbance in primary grade school children. *Mental Hygiene,* 1966, **50,** 406–414.

Zax, M., Cowen, E. L., Rappaport, J., Beach, D. R., & Laird, J. D. Followup study of children identified early as emotionally disturbed. *Journal of Consulting and Clinical Psycholgoy,* 1968, **32,** 369–374.

APPENDIX 1

Guidelines for the AML

The scale calls for you to indicate how often you have observed certain behaviors in the classroom. To help you interpret the five rating points, brief descriptions are provided for each.

(1) *Never*—You have literally never observed this behavior in this child.

(2) *Seldom*—You have observed this behavior once or twice in the past three months.

(3) *Moderate frequency*—You have seen this behavior more often than once a month but less often than once a week.

(4) *Often*—You have seen the behavior more often than once a week but less often than daily.

(5) *Most or all of the time*—You have seen the behavior with great frequency, averaging once a day or more often.

Two things should be kept in mind while completing the AML: (a) Work rapidly and don't fret too much about making fine discriminations, (b) It is extremely important that your ratings realistically reflect problems in misbehavior that children evidence. Teachers sometimes tend to be reluctant to note on paper when a child is evidencing problems. These scales will be used for research purposes; therefore, no one will be hurt by a bad score. Please make your ratings reflect problems as you have perceived them. Thank you for your attention.

Pupil _____ Date _____ Teacher's Name _____

Sex   M   F   School _____

This is pupil's 1st 2nd time in this grade.
(teacher: please circle one)

AML BEHAVIOR RATING SCALE

PLEASE RATE THIS PUPIL'S BEHAVIOR AS YOU
HAVE OBSERVED AND EXPERIENCED IT:

This Pupil —

		Never (1)	Seldom (2)	Moderately Often (3)	Often (4)	Most or all of the time (5)
1.	Gets into fights or quarrels with other students	( )	( )	( )	( )	( )
2.	Has to be coaxed or forced to work or play with other pupils	( )	( )	( )	( )	( )
3.	Is restless	( )	( )	( )	( )	( )
4.	Is unhappy or depressed	( )	( )	( )	( )	( )
5.	Disrupts class discipline	( )	( )	( )	( )	( )
6.	Becomes sick when faced with a difficult school problem or situation	( )	( )	( )	( )	( )
7.	Is obstinate	( )	( )	( )	( )	( )
8.	Feels hurt when criticized	( )	( )	( )	( )	( )
9.	Is impulsive	( )	( )	( )	( )	( )
10.	Is moody	( )	( )	( )	( )	( )
11.	Has difficulty learning	( )	( )	( )	( )	( )

APPENDIX 2

Guidelines for the Teacher Referral Form

We are interested in learning about *your* reasons for referring this child. On the next page, we have listed specific behavior and adaptation problems which may appear to you as interferring with the child's ability to profit from his school experience. For each child referred, please rate *every* item in Section I on the following scale of problem severity:

1 = not a problem

2 = very mild problem

3 = moderate problem

4 = serious problem

5 = very serious problem

Specific instructions are provided for Sections II and III.

TEACHER REFERRAL FORM

Child's Name _____ Birth Date _____

School _____ Teacher _____ Referral Date _____

Section I. Please rate *every* item on the following scale:

1 = not a problem   3 = moderate problem   5 = very serious problem
2 = very mild problem   4 = serious problem

Child's Classroom Behavior:
__ disruptive in class
__ fidgety, hyperactive, can't
     stay in seat
__ talks out of turn, disturbs
     others while they are working
__ constantly seeks attention,
     "clowns around"
__ overly aggressive to peers,
     (fights, is overbearing,
     belligerent)
__ defiant, obstinate, stubborn
__ impulsive, is unable to delay
__ withdrawn
__ shy, timid
__ does not make friends
__ over conforms to rules
__ daydreams, is preoccupied,
     "off in another world"
__ unable to express feelings
__ anxious
__ worried, frightened, tense
__ depressed
__ cries easily, pouts, sulks
__ does not trust others
__ shows other signs of "nervous-
     ness"
     specify: _____
__ specific fears
     specify: _____

Other Behaviors:
__ lacks self-confidence
__ overly sensitive to criticism
__ reacts poorly to disappoint-
     ment
__ depends too much on others
__ pretends to be ill
__ other, specify: _____
__ poor grooming or personal
     hygiene

Child's Academic Performance:
__ underachieving (not working
     up to potential)
__ poorly motivated to achieve
__ poor work habits
__ difficulty following directions
__ poor concentration, limited
     attention span
__ motor coordination problem
__ other, specify: _____

*Child has specific academic
problems in:*
__ reading __ math __ numbers
__ writing __ colors __ concepts
__ language skills problems,
     specify: _____
     _____

Section II. From your experiences with this child, please check (√)
any of the following which you believe relate to the problems you have
reported:

___ separation or divorce of
parents
___ illness or death of a family
member
___ lack of educational stimulation in the home

___ economic difficulties
___ under family pressure to
succeed
___ family difficulties

Section III. From your experiences with this child, please check (√)
where he would lie on the following dimensions taking into account the
direction of each item:

Know child well   Barely know child
1_____2_____3__ ____4_____5_____6_____7

Child seems easy to like   Child seems difficult to like
1_____2_____3_____4_____5_____6_____7

Child has significant   Child has no school
school adjustment problems   adjustment problems
1_____2_____3_____4_____5_____6_____7

APPENDIX 3

List of 55 PMHP-Defining Activities

Informational Meetings

1. Conduct informational meetings about PMHP in the fall for:
   _____ a) parents of first grade children
   _____ b) parents of primary grade children
   _____ c) parents of upper grade children
2. Conduct informational meetings about PMHP in the fall for:
   _____ a) first grade teachers
   _____ b) primary grade teachers
   _____ c) upper grade teachers
   _____ d) principals and other non-teaching school personnel

Screening

_____ 3. Observe children during the administration of group testing.
4a. Use intelligence and achievement tests for screening:
   _____ a) PMHP referred children
   _____ b) all first grade children
   _____ c) all primary grade children
4b. Use personality tests for screening:
   _____ a) PMHP referred children
   _____ b) all first grade children
   _____ c) all primary grade children
_____ 5. Classroom observation of PMHP referred and potentially referred children.
_____ 6. Consideration of kindergarten teacher comments and evaluations on all current first grade children.

7. Social work interviews with parents for background information of:
   _____a) all PMHP referred children
   _____b) all first grade children
_____ 8. Conferences between PMHP team members around screening findings.
_____ 9. Conferences between Mental Health team, teachers, principals, and appropriate school personnel around screening findings.

Program

_____ 10. Monitor completion of Teacher Referral Forms.
_____ 11. Review PMHP records and screening data for identification of potentially referred children.
12. Attend the following formal conferences with teachers, aides, and principals:
   _____a) referral-assignment conferences
   _____b) progress evaluation conferences during the year
   _____c) termination-disposition (end-of-year) conferences
13. Individual conferences during the school year concerning PMHP children with:
   _____a) parents
   _____b) teachers
   _____c) appropriate other school personnel
_____ 14. Individual intellectual or personality evaluations for PMHP children.
_____ 15. Individual interviews with PMHP children during the school year.
_____ 16. Within-school conferences to obtain additional school services for PMHP children.
_____ 17. Exchanging information (including referral) with outside service agencies about PMHP children.
18. Conferences between team members around issues of:
   _____a) service to children
   _____b) aide performance
   _____c) program related concerns
_____ 19. Arrange and participate in psychiatric, psychological, social work, and educational consultations with PMHP staff, aides, teachers, and other appropriate school personnel.
_____ 20. Attend regular bi-monthly PMHP professional meetings at the Center for Community Study.
_____ 21. Establish a Primary Mental Health Project file for information on project children and all screening data.

Aides

_____ 22. Participate in selection and training of aides.

23. Regular conferences between team members and senior aides around issues of:

_____a) service to children

_____b) aide performance

_____c) program related concerns

_____ 24. Insure that adequate working space and materials are provided for the aides.

25. Meet regularly with child-aides for:

_____a) individual supervision

_____b) group supervision

_____c) PMHP program conferences

_____ 26. Provide non-scheduled supervision for aides, "as needed" (i.e., "P.R.N").

_____ 27. Actually observe aides while they are seeing children.

28. Participate in periodic evaluation of aides through:

_____a) submission of evaluation forms

_____b) discussion of evaluative impressions with aides

_____c) discussions with PMHP staff

29. Monitor completion of forms:

_____a) Aide Goals Form

_____b) Aide Prose Summary

_____c) Initial Professional Report

_____d) Year-end Professional Summary

INDEX

aide-child interaction, 53, 169, 182, 186, 226, 229, 332, 340, 364, 365
process analysis, 175, 182, 215
Aide Status Evaluation Form (ASEF), 222
Albee, G. W., 21, 72
Allinsmith, W., 370
AML, 44, 146-47, 206-9, 222, 238
Arnhoff, F. N., 21

Babigian, H., 218
Bardon, J. I., 32, 369
Barker, R. G., 370
Beach, D. R., 10, 206, 218, 227
Bean, L. L., 25
Beers, Clifford, 126
Bennett, E. M., 108, 303
Bergin, A. E., 25
Bloom, B. L., 19
Board of Cooperative Educational Services, 113, 183, 189, 338
Bower, E. M., 67, 146, 206, 226
Breggin, P. R., 73

Caldwell, R. A., 11, 151, 186, 208, 225
Caplan, G., 71
Carlisle, R. L., 203
Castaneda, A., 67
Cherlin, D. L., 108, 303
child aides, 10, 11, 39, 41, 43, 45-49, 51-54, 77-101, 103, 113, 116-17, 120-35, 139-55, 159-64, 167-69, 172, 175-78, 180, 185, 193-94, 203, 211-16, 220-24, 240-44, 248-302, 307-16, 319-26, 332-42, 347-58, 361-62, 365
interview, screening, 81, 82, 121, 185-86, 211
meetings, 88-89, 168, 180
recruitment, 79, 117, 119, 135, 326, 342
selection, 53, 84, 117, 151, 185-86, 332
selection study, 122, 175
senior, 10, 11, 111, 168, 170, 171, 181, 195, 215, 312, 322, 325, 348
supervision, 119, 134-36, 142, 145, 155, 159, 161-63, 168-69, 180,

182, 186, 193-95, 214, 296, 309, 311-12, 318, 322, 327-28, 335, 337-38, 348, 358, 364
test characteristics, 123-25, 175, 186, 212, 216, 229
training, 78, 82-84, 90, 95, 117-19, 125-35, 139, 151, 155, 161, 169, 185-88, 213, 321-22, 326, 332, 335-38, 340, 342, 348, 358, 364
Chinsky, J. M., 202, 203
Clarfield, S. P., 10, 203-4, 207, 221-22
Cohen, J., 25, 74
community mental health centers, 28
conferences
assignment, 45, 46, 49, 91, 148-52, 154, 180, 186, 193, 194, 248, 261, 318, 325, 327, 335
progress, 48, 49, 92, 131, 152-54, 186, 193, 318, 325, 335
team, 162-64, 166-68
termination, 49, 92, 154, 186, 193, 254, 258, 271, 274, 313, 318, 325, 327, 335
consultant, 10, 47-49, 51, 63, 65, 85, 88, 127, 139, 149, 156-58, 160, 168-70, 172, 173, 175, 211, 285, 297, 311, 320
meetings, 172, 173
psychiatrist, 63, 83, 86, 111, 311
school mental health, 42, 62, 195, 322
consultation, 30, 47, 52, 62, 119, 131, 141, 155-60, 163-64, 168-69, 186, 188, 193-94, 285, 318-20, 327, 332, 335-38, 348, 358, 364
Cowen, E. L., 11, 19, 23, 28-30, 68, 99, 122, 125, 134, 151, 154-55, 169-70, 180, 186, 202-13, 217-30, 327, 332, 348, 353, 358, 369
Cumulative Psychiatric Register, 218, 219

Dalsimer, J. S., 73
Donahue, G. T., 74
Dorr, D., 11, 99, 110, 122, 125, 134, 202, 206-7, 210-13, 220-21, 223-24, 230, 353, 362-63
Dunham, W., 26
Duricko, A., 198

early detection/identification, 8, 16-17, 28, 30, 38, 39, 41, 43, 45, 54, 58-59, 62, 64, 66, 71, 80, 101, 103, 118, 127, 139, 142, 148, 175-76, 205-6, 284, 291, 319, 338, 346, 356-58, 360, 365, 368
screening, 36, 41-46, 52-54, 61, 80-81, 119, 139-43, 146-49, 152, 182, 186, 206, 209, 229, 232, 252, 285, 326, 334-37, 356-57
Ebner, E., 73
Eisdorfer, C., 19
Eisenberg, L., 27
Elkes, C., 74
Ewalt, P. L., 341
evaluation, 52-53, 59, 92, 189, 206, 221
project, 98, 206, 230-31, 235, 237-38, 242
test battery, 59, 66-67, 68, 141-42
Eysenck, H. J., 24

Faris, R. E. L., 26
Fatke, R., 370
Feld, S., 21, 156
Felner, R. D., 213, 214
Finkel, N.J., 203
Flint, A. A., 74
Freeman, R. W., 74

Gardner, E. A., 203
Garfield, S. L., 25, 166
Gartner, A., 21
Gesten, E. A., 10, 210
Gewirtz, H., 73
Glidewell, J. C., 33, 51, 224
Golann, S. E., 19, 74
Goldenberg, I. I., 108, 303
Gordon, T. A., 370
Grande, L., 198
Graziano, A. M., 34
Grimes, J. W., 370
guidelines for establishing programs, 318
Gump, P. V., 370
Gurin, G., 21, 156

Health Resources Inventory (HRI), 210
helping services, geometric expansion, 30, 46, 51, 54, 71, 75, 102, 135, 139, 156, 175, 176, 203, 348, 357
Hobbs, N., 75
Hollingshead, B. B., 25, 27
Holzberg, J. D., 73
Huser, J., 227

identified children, 89, 90, 149, 218
Insel, P. M., 370

internship, P.M.H.P., 180, 198, 355
intervention, 36, 38, 41, 45, 52, 57, 69, 77, 83, 87, 91, 99, 100, 132, 139-42, 148-52, 159, 166, 204, 205, 210, 222, 232, 234, 242
early, 29
crisis, 119
Izzo. L. D., 11, 68, 99, 170, 202, 206, 217, 218, 220, 226, 227

Jason, L., 204, 366
Joint Commission on Mental Illness and Health, 21, 23, 72
Joint Commission on Mental Health of Children, 33

Kannegieter, R., 206
Kaufman, G., 203
Kelly, J. G., 370
Kimbrough, C. A., 10, 204
Klein, R., 226
Knapp, R. H., 73
Kraus, R. M., 11, 154, 155, 180, 186, 223, 225, 228
Kreling, B., 11, 207

Laird, J. D., 10, 203, 206, 218
Leibowitz, E., 203
Leibowitz, G., 203
Levine, M., 34, 108, 303
Levitt, E. E., 24
Lewis, W. W., 74
Liem, G. R., 227
limited program resources, 325, 326, 334-38, 339, 340-43
Lippitt, R., 341
Lorion, R. P., 11, 25-27, 151, 154, 155, 180, 186, 202, 208, 221, 223, 225-27, 230, 327

McCandless, B. R., 67
McClintock, S. K., 370
McGee, D. P., 370
McMillan, R. C., 203
McWilliams, S. A., 10, 134, 169, 202, 203, 207, 215, 216, 223
Madonia, A., 10, 202
Magoon, T. M., 74
maladaptation, 44, 45, 129, 135, 147, 155, 218, 225, 238, 343, 347, 348, 351, 356, 357, 364
maladapted child, 36, 47, 56, 78, 85, 99, 101, 125, 139, 204, 206, 213, 242